CISI

CHARTERED INSTITUTE FOR SECURITIES & INVESTMENT

FSA Financial Regulation

The Official Learning and Reference Manual

18th Edition, September 2012

This workbook relates to syllabus version 18.0 and will cover examinations from 21 November 2012 until 31 March 2013

PROFESSIONALISM | INTEGRITY | EXCELLENCE

CISI
CHARTERED INSTITUTE FOR SECURITIES & INVESTMENT

FSA Financial Regulation

Welcome to the Chartered Institute for Securities & Investment's *FSA Financial Regulation* study material. This workbook has been written to prepare you for the Chartered Institute for Securities & Investment's *FSA Financial Regulation* examination.

PUBLISHED BY:

Chartered Institute for Securities & Investment

8 Eastcheap
London
EC3M 1AE
Tel: +44 20 7645 0600
Fax: +44 20 7645 0601

WRITTEN BY:
Catherine Lumb

TECHNICAL REVIEW:
Phil Read

SENIOR REVIEW:
Stephen Holt

A Learning Map, which contains the full syllabus, appears at the end of this workbook. The syllabus can also be viewed on the Institute's website at www.cisi.org and is also available by contacting Client Services on +44 20 7645 0680. Please note that the exam is based upon the syllabus. Candidates are reminded to check the Candidate Update area of the Institute's website (cisi.org/candidateupdate) on a regular basis for updates that could affect their examination as a result of industry change.

The questions contained in this manual are designed as an aid to revision of different areas of the syllabus and to help you consolidate your learning chapter by chapter. They should not be seen as a 'mock' examination or necessarily indicative of the level of the questions in the corresponding examination.

Learning manual version: 18.2 (September 2012)

Foreword

Learning and Professional Development with the CISI

The Chartered Institute for Securities & Investment evolved from the London Stock Exchange and was initially known as the Securities Institute. We currently have around 40,000 members, who benefit from a programme of professional and social events, with continuing professional development (CPD) and the promotion of integrity very much at the heart of everything
we do.

This learning manual (or 'workbook' as it is often known in the industry) provides not only a thorough preparation for the CISI examination it refers to, but is a valuable desktop reference for practitioners. It can also be used as a learning tool for readers interested in knowing more, but not necessarily entering an examination.

The CISI official learning manuals ensure that candidates gain a comprehensive understanding of examination content. Our material is written and updated by industry specialists and reviewed by experienced, senior figures in the financial services industry. Quality is assured through a rigorous editorial system of practitioner panels and boards. CISI examinations are used extensively by firms to meet the requirements of government regulators. The CISI works closely with a number of international regulators that recognise our examinations and the manuals supporting them, as well as the UK regulator, the Financial Services Authority (FSA).

CISI learning manuals are normally revised annually. It is important that candidates check they purchase the correct version for the period when they wish to take their examination. Between versions, candidates should keep abreast of the latest industry developments through the Candidate Update area of the CISI website, cisi.org/candidateupdate. (The CISI also accredits the manuals of certain Accredited Training Providers.)

The CISI produces a range of elearning revision tools such as Revision Express Interactive that can be used in conjunction with our learning and reference manuals. For further details, please visit cisi.org. The CISI is committed to using the latest technology to introduce interactivity in its revision tools, and, over time, the Revision Express Interactive will be expanded for each examination.

The questions in the manuals are selected to be at the same standard as the questions in the examination itself, but they are not the same questions as in the examination. During 2012, mock examination papers will be made available on our website, as an additional revision tool.

As a Professional Body, around 40,000 CISI members subscribe to the CISI Code of Conduct and the CISI has a significant voice in the industry, standing for professionalism, excellence and the promotion of trust and integrity. Continuing professional development is at the heart of the Institute's values. Our CPD scheme is available free of charge to members, and this includes an online record-keeping system as well as regular seminars, conferences and professional networks in specialist subject areas, all of which cover a range of current industry topics. Reading this manual and taking a CISI examination is credited as professional development with the CISI CPD scheme. To learn more about CISI membership, visit cisi.org/membership.

We hope that you will find this manual useful and interesting. Once you have completed it, you will find helpful suggestions on qualifications and membership progression with the CISI at the end of this book. We are also always pleased to receive comments and feedback; please see cisi.org/feedback.

With best wishes for your studies.

Ruth Martin
Managing Director

Contents

It is estimated that this workbook will require approximately **70 hours** of study time.

1

The Regulatory Environment

This syllabus area will provide approximately 5 of the 50 examination questions

CISI
CHARTERED INSTITUTE FOR SECURITIES & INVESTMENT

The Regulatory Environment

1. The Regulatory Infrastructure

Learning Objective 1.2.1

Know the regulatory infrastructure generated by the FSMA 2000 and the status of and relationship between the Treasury, the OFT, the Financial Skills Partnership and the FSA and also the relationship between FSA and the RIEs, ROIEs, DIEs, RCHs, MTFs and DPBs

1.1 Financial Services and Markets Act (FSMA 2000)

The Financial Services and Markets Act came into effect on midnight on 30 November 2001. It introduced a new structure for the regulation of the financial services industry in the United Kingdom (UK). The purpose of the FSMA was to provide for stronger protection for consumers of financial services than had been the case under the previous regulatory framework. The FSMA established:

- a single regulator – the Financial Services Authority (FSA) – that replaced all the existing self-regulatory organisations (SROs);
- a single ombudsman service (the Financial Ombudsman Service (FOS)) to provide for resolution of consumer disputes;
- a single compensation scheme (the Financial Services Compensation Scheme (FSCS)) to provide a fund for consumer compensation if failed firms are unable to meet their liabilities;
- penalties for the new crime of market abuse;
- the UK listings regime, which replaced the London Stock Exchange (LSE) powers.

The FSMA is defining legislation; it applies to all persons within the UK and sets out the scope for the conduct of regulated activity. 'Persons' in this context – and throughout this workbook – means natural persons and all other types of legal person, such as incorporated bodies, partnerships, trusts and other types of unincorporated associations. It is a criminal offence to conduct regulated activity by way of business in the UK unless a person is either authorised to do so, or is an exempt person. This is known as the **General Prohibition** and it is set out in Section 19 of FSMA.

Contravention of the General Prohibition is punishable by a maximum sentence of two years' imprisonment and/or an unlimited fine. Agreements entered into are likely to be unenforceable. It is a defence to show that a person has taken all reasonable precautions and exercised all due diligence to avoid committing the offence. The FSMA provides for attaining authorised status or for conducting regulated activity under exemption.

Authorised persons are:

- those who have been given permission to conduct regulated activity by the FSA (Part IV FSMA);
- certain overseas firms that qualify for authorisation under special provisions (European Economic Area (EEA), treaty firms and Undertakings for Collective Investment in Transferable Securities (UCITS) qualifiers);
- investment companies with variable capital (ICVCs) established under open-ended investment company (OEIC) Regulations 2001;
- the Society of Lloyd's (s.315 FSMA).

Part IV of the FSMA enables businesses to apply directly to the FSA for permission to conduct regulated activity in the UK. When the FSA grants this permission, the business becomes an authorised person under the FSMA and has a **Part IV permission** to conduct regulated activities. The firm has entered into a legally binding relationship with the FSA. We shall look at the process for applying for Part IV permission in Chapter 2.

Exempt persons attain this status by way of specific sections within the FSMA and/or by way of **exemption orders** made by the Treasury. The Treasury can create orders to make certain persons fully exempt for all regulated activity, or to make the activity exempt when it is conducted in a certain way. This distinction is significant because the way in which a firm has attained exempt status determines the way in which legal provisions will apply.

Examples of exempt persons are:

- appointed representatives of authorised persons (s.39 FSMA and the FSMA (Appointed Representatives) Regulations 2001);
- recognised investment exchanges (RIEs) and recognised clearing houses (RCHs) (s.285 FSMA);
- the Bank of England other central banks (FSMA Exemption Order 2001);
- operators of multilateral trading systems exercising certain rights (s.312A FSMA).

A person cannot be both authorised and exempt at the same time. For example, a firm cannot conduct some regulated activities as an authorised person and others in the capacity of an appointed representative of another firm. We shall look further at exemptions in Chapter 2.

Since it was enacted, the FSMA has been amended and expanded a number of times in order to accommodate changes in the regulatory landscape and, increasingly, to give effect to European Community (EC) directives in the UK.

1.2 The Financial Services Authority (FSA)

The Financial Services Authority (FSA) was established by the FSMA. The FSA is a private company, but it has been given a special dispensation that allows it not to use the word **limited** as part of its name. The FSMA gives the FSA certain duties and objectives in relation to its role as financial services regulator and establishes the legal powers to enable the FSA to fulfil its role.

These regulatory powers are over firms carrying on regulated activities, the exchanges that are used by many of those firms, and individuals carrying out particular functions for firms. In some cases, they also extend to those not currently authorised, for example, formerly authorised firms, or firms which ought to have had authorisation but which have been doing business without it.

The FSA is funded entirely from fees paid by the firms it regulates.

The FSA is accountable to the government on how it carries out its functions, via HM Treasury; we will look at the mechanism for this accountability next.

1.3 HM Treasury

The FSA is accountable to Her Majesty's (HM) Treasury through a variety of mechanisms.

First, the Treasury has the power to appoint or dismiss the FSA's board and chairman.

Secondly, the FSA is required to submit a report to the Treasury at least once a year – covering matters such as the way in which it has discharged its functions, the extent to which its objectives have been met and any other matters the Treasury may direct. This report is accompanied by a report from the FSA's non-executive directors and is laid before Parliament.

Thirdly, the Treasury has the power to commission reviews and inquiries into aspects of the FSA's operations. Reviews are conducted by someone the Treasury feels is independent of the FSA, and are restricted to considering the economy, efficiency and effectiveness with which the FSA has used its resources in discharging its functions. Such inquiries may relate to specific, exceptional events occurring within the FSA's range of regulatory responsibilities.

1.4 Recognised Investment Exchanges (RIEs) and Recognised Overseas Investment Exchanges (ROIEs)

Since a large proportion of trades in financial instruments are carried out via established stock exchanges, the FSA has also been given the responsibility of recognising and supervising them.

Any body corporate or unincorporated association may apply to the FSA for an order declaring it to be a **recognised investment exchange (RIE)**. The FSA will look to establish whether the applicant is **fit and proper** to operate as an exchange – including whether it has sufficient financial resources to carry out its activities properly. The applicant must be willing and able to share information with the FSA, and to promote and maintain high standards of integrity and fair dealing, including laying down rules for activities on the exchange. It must record, monitor and enforce compliance with these rules.

Once recognised, these exchanges are subject to supervision and oversight by the FSA. Being granted **recognised** status relieves the organisation of the requirement to be an authorised person to conduct financial services business.

RIEs can be UK- or overseas-based. Overseas-based exchanges are known as **recognised overseas investment exchanges (ROIEs)**.

The UK-based RIEs are:

1. **The London Stock Exchange (LSE) plc** – this is the largest formal market for securities in the UK. It facilitates deals in shares, bonds and some derivatives (for example, those that take the form of covered warrants).
2. **LIFFE Administration and Management** – this is the largest derivatives exchange in the UK, trading a wide range of instruments including equity futures and options and some commodity products.
3. **The London Metal Exchange (LME) Ltd** – this exchange provides trading in a variety of futures and options on base metals and some plastics.
4. **PLUS Stock Exchange plc** – this market offers trading and listing facilities for small and mid-capitalisation companies.

ROIEs are based outside the UK, but carry on regulated activities within the UK (eg, by offering electronic trading facilities to members in this country) and because of this they are regulated and supervised by the FSA. The ROIEs are:

- Australian Securities Exchange (ASX);
- Chicago Board of Trade (CBOT);
- EUREX (Zurich);
- ICE Futures US Inc;
- National Association of Securities Dealers Automated Quotations (NASDAQ);
- New York Mercantile Exchange (NYMEX);
- NYSE Liffe US;
- SIX Swiss Exchange AG;
- Chicago Mercantile Exchange (CME).

1.5 Designated Investment Exchanges (DIEs)

DIEs are, like ROIEs, overseas-based, but unlike ROIEs they do not conduct regulated activities in the UK. For this reason, they do not have to be regulated by the FSA, but they can choose to apply to the FSA for designated status. In considering the application, the FSA assesses whether the investment exchange offers an appropriate degree of consumer protection.

The designated status allows firms to treat transactions conducted on a DIE in the same way as they would treat transactions conducted on an RIE. There are too many DIEs to list but they include international exchanges such as the NYSE, the Channel Islands Stock Exchange (CISX) and Hong Kong Exchanges and Clearing Limited (HKEx) Ltd.

1.6 Recognised Clearing Houses (RCHs)

Clearing houses facilitate the clearing and also, sometimes, the settlement of trades. As with recognition as an RIE, recognition as an RCH means that the clearing house does not need to become an authorised person in order to conduct financial services business in the UK.

The UK clearing houses are:

1. **LCH.Clearnet Ltd** – a leading clearing house, serving the major international exchanges and platforms.
2. **Euroclear UK & Ireland Ltd** – this firm offers the CREST system, whereby trades are settled in dematerialised form. It is mainly known for UK and Irish equity clearing, and also provides clearing and settlement for a variety of other equities, bonds and funds.
3. **European Central Counterparty Ltd (EuroCCP)** – a wholly-owned subsidiary of The Depository Trust & Clearing Corporation (DTCC). It provides clearing services for a number of trading platforms.
4. **ICE Clear Europe Ltd** – a clearing house for energy and emissions markets.
5. **CME Clearing Europe Ltd** – a London-based clearing house for derivatives.

1.7 Designated Professional Bodies (DPBs)

There is a special section of the FSMA – Part XX (20) – that enables professional firms (such as law firms and accountancy practices) to conduct some types of regulated activity in certain circumstances without contravening the General Prohibition.

This special regime is available because professional firms are already subject to high standards of supervision by their professional body, and so an additional layer of regulation is unnecessary.

Broadly, the activity must be conducted in connection with the firm's professional service, and it must be governed by rules made by the relevant **designated professional body (DPB)**. For example, a firm of accountants legitimately advising its client on how to optimise his tax affairs might advise that he divest himself of certain investments on which he has accumulated a certain level of gains. While the advice might be given with the aim of minimising the client's tax bill, the ancillary effect is to advise him to undertake a specific investment deal. This advice constitutes regulated activity.

The accountant must apply to its DPB to obtain a licence to conduct this activity, and must abide by the DPB's rules. Although the DPB makes these rules, they have to be approved by the FSA.

The Part XX regime is available for five professions: solicitors, accountants, actuaries, chartered surveyors and licensed conveyancers. The professional bodies for each of these professions – namely, the Law Society, the Institute of Chartered Accountants in England and Wales (ICAEW) and the Association of Chartered Certified Accountants (ACCA), the Institute of Actuaries, the Royal Institution of Chartered Surveyors (RICS) and the Council for Licensed Conveyancers – all have the status of DPB. DPB status is granted by the Treasury under s.326 of the FSMA, and the DPB pays fees to the FSA each year to maintain its status.

Professional firms using the Part XX regime are known as **exempt professional firms**.

A professional firm that wishes to conduct regulated activity over and above what is allowed by the Part XX regime can apply to the FSA for Part IV permission and so become an **authorised professional firm**.

1.8 Multilateral Trading Facilities (MTFs)

One example of how the FSMA has been amended is to give effect to the impact of the **Markets in Financial Instruments Directive (MiFID)** – a European directive which came into force 1 November 2007 to harmonise investment services throughout Europe. MiFID provisions had to be incorporated within the UK regulatory framework. Under MiFID a new activity became regulated – that of operating a **multilateral trading facility (MTF)**, and this activity had to be incorporated within the UK regulatory framework.

An MTF is any system that brings together multiple third-party buying and selling transactions in financial instruments (eg, shares, units in collective investment schemes, derivatives). Retail investors and other investment firms can all trade together via the MTF. MTFs purport to be faster and more cost effective than the traditional exchanges and they have had some impact on trading practices. One example of an MTF that has had a significant impact is Chi-X Europe. A less successful example was Turquoise, established in 2008 by nine investment banks to challenge the LSE's dominance. It did gain a 7% share of the trading market but accumulated losses and in 2009 it was purchased by the LSE. However, it still trades as Turquoise and offers MTF services for members ranging from large global banks to local brokers.

An important distinction between exchanges and MTFs is that the latter don't have the power to list a security to enable the security to be traded on a regulated market.

2. The FSA and its Statutory Objectives

Learning Objective 1.1.1

Know the FSA's statutory objectives and rule-making powers in respect of authorisation, supervision, enforcement, sanctions and disciplinary action [FSMA]

Learning Objective 1.1.7

Know the FSA's supervisory approach to more 'outcomes-focused and more intrusive' regulation (FSA Discussion Paper DP 09/2 pp 183–196 and Turner Review pp.86–104

2.1 The FSA's Statutory Objectives and Principles of Good Regulation

The FSA has four **objectives**, established under FSMA 2000 and, latterly, under the Financial Services Act 2010. These are:

1. **Market confidence** – maintain confidence in the financial system. This means the financial system operating in and from the UK, including all of the firms involved in regulated financial services, as well as the related financial markets and exchanges.
2. **The protection of consumers** – secure the appropriate degree of protection for consumers. This does not necessarily mean preventing all risk of loss to consumers. In considering what is the appropriate degree of protection, the FSA should have regard to the different degrees of risk involved in different kinds of investment, the differing levels of experience and expertise of consumers, the needs of the consumers for advice and accurate information and the general principle that consumers should take responsibility for their decisions.
3. **The reduction of financial crime** – reduce the extent to which it is possible for firms within the financial system to be used for purposes connected with financial crime.
4. **Financial stability** – contribute to the protection and enhancement of the UK financial system; the FSA must have regard to: the economic and fiscal consequences for the UK; the effects (if any) on the growth of the economy; and the impact (if any) of the domestic or international economic climate on the stability of the UK financial system.

The FSA's objectives also provide for a degree of accountability:

- **Annual report** – the FSA's annual report to Treasury (as mentioned in Section 1.3) contains an assessment of how well or otherwise the FSA has met its statutory objectives. The report is scrutinised by various Parliamentary committees.
- **Rules** – the FSA has to show how the rules it makes relate to the statutory objectives.
- **Judicial review** – if the FSA fails to consider the objectives, or incorrectly interprets the objectives, they can be challenged in the courts.

The FSA previously had the objective of promoting public awareness of the financial system. However, this responsibility was transferred to the **Consumer Financial Education Body (CFEB)**, which was established by the FSA for this particular role. The CFEB trades as the **Money Advice Service** and provides a wide range of free information for consumers (its website address is moneyadviceservice.org.uk).

In carrying out its duties, the FSA must have regard to the **Principles of Good Regulation**. There are seven principles of good regulation as follows:

1. **Efficiency and economy** – the need for the FSA to use its resources in the most efficient and economic way.
2. **Role of management** – this principle is designed to secure an adequate but proportionate level of regulatory intervention, by holding senior management responsible for risk management and controls within firms.

3. **Proportionality** – the restrictions that the FSA imposes on the industry must be proportionate to the benefits that are expected to result from those restrictions.
4. **Innovation** – the desirability of facilitating innovation in connection with regulated activities. This involves not placing undue restrictions on market participants launching new financial products and services.
5. **International character** – including the desirability of maintaining the competitive position of the UK. The FSA takes into account the international aspects of much financial business and the competitive position of the UK. This involves co-operating with overseas regulators, both to agree international standards and to monitor global firms and markets effectively.
6. **Competition** – the need to minimise the adverse effects on competition that may arise from the FSA's activities and the desirability of facilitating competition between the firms it regulates.
7. **Public awareness** – the desirability of enhancing public understanding of the UK financial system.

The FSA's role in the failure of the financial markets has been the subject of a number of reviews. Consequently, a new regulatory structure is evolving, scheduled to take effect during 2013 – see Section 2.3 below.

2.2 Rule-Making Powers

Part X (10) of the FSMA empowers the FSA to make rules that are legally binding on authorised firms concerning regulated activity and also activity that is not regulated.

The FSMA confers general rule-making powers, and also specific powers in the following areas:

- price stabilising;
- financial promotion;
- money laundering;
- control of information.

Rules are made by way of statutory instruments. The FSA is required to consult with a wide range of parties when making or changing rules, and must prepare a cost-benefit analysis regarding the proposals. Rules become legally binding when the proposed changes are made (confirmed) by the FSA's board and are incorporated within the FSA's Handbook. Firms can apply to have a rule varied or modified in specific circumstances.

In addition to rule-making powers, the FSMA empowers the FSA to:

- grant authorisation to persons applying for Part IV permission, vary a firm's permission and cancel authorisation;
- supervise authorised persons on an ongoing basis to ensure that they continue to meet the FSA's authorisation requirements and that they comply with the Handbook rules and other regulatory obligations;
- employ a range of disciplinary measures and sanctions, to punish or limit the activities of firms that fail to comply;
- enforce the regulatory framework – the FSA's approach is one of credible deterrence, using enforcement strategy as a tool to change behaviour in the industry.

2.3 A New Regulatory Framework

The current government intends to transfer operational responsibility for prudential regulation from the FSA to a new subsidiary of the Bank of England. The **Prudential Regulation Authority (PRA)** will be responsible for prudential regulation of all deposit-taking institutions, insurers and investment banks. The PRA will represent the UK on the new European Supervisory Authority (ESA) for banking and insurance.

The PRA will have a primary objective of promoting the stable and prudent operation of the financial system through the effective regulation of financial firms, to minimise the disruption caused by any firms which do fail.

The government is considering whether the rule-making function of the PRA should be subject to statutory process (including public consultation and the duty to carry out detailed cost-benefit analysis prior to the introduction of any new rules) as is currently the case for the FSA.

It is also envisaged that the PRA will reduce and simplify the FSA's rules and guidance to bring the UK into line with European standards.

Regulation of a firm's conduct towards their customers, and conduct of participants in the wholesale financial markets, will be carried out by the **Financial Conduct Authority (FCA)**.

The FCA will be solely responsible for the authorisation and supervision of all financial institutions not regulated by the PRA including intermediaries and investment exchanges. The FCA's role will be to ensure that the UK's financial markets function well and will continue the FSA's work of consumer protection, maintaining the integrity of the financial system and promoting competition.

The FCA will inherit the FSA's powers to investigate and prosecute insider dealing and market abuse and will take over as the UK Listing Authority (UKLA). It will also oversee the Financial Ombudsman Service (FOS), the Money Advice Service and (jointly with PRA) the Financial Services and Compensation Scheme (FSCS). The FCA and the PRA will each set the fees and make rules in respect of the activities under their remit.

This new regulatory framework has become known as **twin peaks** regulation. This means that the supervision of deposit takers, insurers and investment banks will be undertaken by two different supervisors; the PRA will focus on governance and the FCA will focus on conduct.

The FSA has already undergone internal reorganisation as part of the transition to the new structure, and replaced supervision and risk units with a Prudential Business Unit (PBU) and a Consumer and Markets Business Unit (CMBU) in readiness for the actual split, planned for early 2013.

Further consultations are planned to address the practicalities of the split, such as:

- amending the threshold conditions for authorisation to suit the twin peaks model;
- devising a supervisory framework to replace the current model, **Advanced Risk-Responsive Operating frameWork (ARROW)**;
- the memorandum of understanding between the PRA and FCA;
- reviewing the FSA Handbook to allocate the rules and responsibilities between the PRA and the FCA.

3. The FSA's Principles for Businesses and the Wider Obligations of Fair Treatment

Learning Objective 1.1.2

Understand the Principles for Businesses [PRIN 1.1.2 + 1.1.7 + 2.1.1] and the requirement to act honestly, fairly and professionally and to treat customers fairly [COBS 2.1]

3.1 The FSA's Principles for Businesses

If a firm breaches any of the Principles for Businesses it will be liable to disciplinary sanctions as they are legally binding on firms.

The 11 Principles for Businesses are:

1. **Integrity** – a firm must conduct its business with integrity.
2. **Skill, care and diligence** – a firm must conduct its business with due skill, care and diligence.
3. **Management and control** – a firm must take reasonable care to organise and control its affairs responsibly and effectively, with adequate risk management systems.
4. **Financial prudence** – a firm must maintain adequate financial resources.
5. **Market conduct** – a firm must observe proper standards of market conduct.
6. **Customers' interests** – a firm must pay due regard to the interests of its customers and treat them fairly.
7. **Communications with clients** – a firm must pay due regard to the information needs of its clients and communicate information to them in a way which is clear, fair and not misleading.

8. **Conflicts of interest** – a firm must manage conflicts of interest fairly, both between itself and its customers, and between customers and other clients.
9. **Customers: relationships of trust** – a firm must take reasonable care to ensure the suitability of its advice and discretionary decisions for any customer who is entitled to rely upon its judgment.
10. **Clients' assets** – a firm must arrange adequate protection for clients' assets when it is responsible for them.
11. **Relations with regulators** – a firm must deal with its regulators in an open and co-operative way and must disclose to the FSA appropriately anything relating to the firm of which the FSA would reasonably expect notice.

3.2 Fair Treatment

The concept of fair treatment is at the heart of the regulatory system. It is expressed in Principle 6 above, and also in an important conduct of business rule:

A firm must act honestly, fairly and professionally in accordance with the best interests of its client.

This rule is known as the 'client's best interests rule'.

An important part of the FSA's supervision of firms involves assessing how they are able to demonstrate fair treatment of clients. The firm's management culture should be ethical and have the clients best interests at the heart of the firm. A firm also needs to ensure it gathers sufficient management information to help it monitor how well it is adhering to these obligations, and to help it identify where it might be failing.

As part of its **Treating Customers Fairly (TCF)** initiative, the FSA defined six **consumer outcomes**. These are that:

1. Consumers can be confident that they are dealing with firms where the fair treatment of customers is central to the corporate culture.
2. Products and services marketed and sold in the retail market are designed to meet the needs of identified consumer groups and are targeted accordingly.
3. Consumers are provided with clear information and are kept appropriately informed before, during and after the point of sale.
4. Where consumers receive advice, the advice is suitable and takes account of their circumstances.
5. Consumers are provided with products that perform as firms have led them to expect, and the associated service is both of an acceptable standard and as they have been led to expect.
6. Consumers do not face unreasonable post-sale barriers imposed by firms to change product, switch provider, submit a claim or make a complaint.

4. The Statements of Principle and Code of Practice for Approved Persons

Learning Objective 1.1.3

Know the Statements of Principle 1 to 4 and Code of Practice for approved persons for all approved persons functions [APER 1.1.1, 1.2.3, 2.1.2, 3.1.1, 4.1, 4.2, 4.3.1, 4.4.1/3/4/9]

The FSMA recognises that certain roles within authorised firms are particularly important to the control or operation of the firm and to its capacity to meet its regulatory obligations. The roles are known as **controlled functions**, and a person has to apply to the FSA for approval to carry out the role before they can start. Hence, individuals performing controlled functions are known as **approved persons**.

Controlled functions are grouped under two headings:

1. **Significant influence functions** – functions that are governing or managerial. They include the directors of the firm and other key personnel.

2. **Customer functions** – functions involving interaction with the customers of the firm, such as investment advice or management.

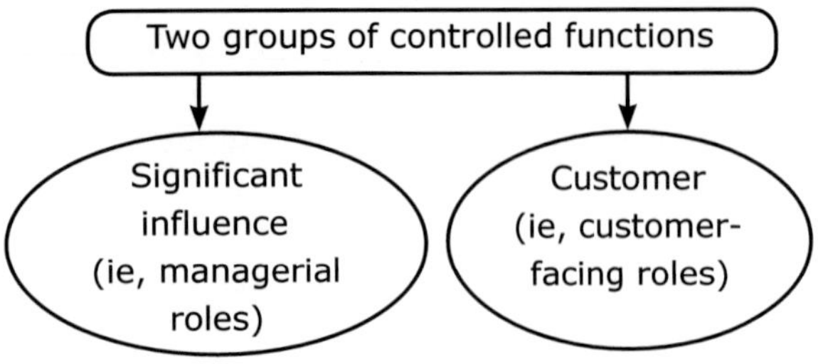

In a similar manner to the Principles for Businesses, the FSA Handbook details seven **Statements of Principle for Approved Persons** to observe as they carry out their duties.

4.1 Statements of Principle

There are seven Statements of Principle. The first four apply to all approved persons regardless of the controlled function that they perform. An approved person must:

1. act with **integrity** in carrying out his controlled function;
2. act with **due skill, care and diligence** in carrying out his controlled function;
3. observe **proper standards of market conduct** in carrying out his controlled function;
4. deal with the FSA and with other regulators **in an open and co-operative way** and must disclose appropriately any information of which the FSA would reasonably expect notice.

4.2 Code of Practice for Approved Persons – All Controlled Functions

Additionally, the FSA rules include a Code of Practice for Approved Persons. Paradoxically, the Code of Practice describes behaviours which, in the opinion of the FSA, do not comply with the Statements of Principle and also factors that should be taken into account in determining whether or not an approved person's conduct complies with a Statement of Principle.

4.2.1 Code of Practice for Statement of Principle 1

In the opinion of the FSA, any of the following is a failure to comply with the requirement for an approved person to **act with integrity** in carrying out his controlled function:

1. Deliberately misleading (or attempting to mislead) a client, the firm (including the firm's auditors or appointed actuary) or the FSA by either act or omission. This includes deliberately:
   - falsifying documents;
   - misleading a client about the risks of an investment;
   - misleading a client about the charges or surrender penalties of investment products;
   - misleading a client about the likely performance of investment products by providing inappropriate projections of future investment returns;
   - misleading a client by informing him that products only require a single payment when that is not the case;
   - mismarking the value of investments or trading positions;
   - procuring the unjustified alteration of prices on illiquid or off-exchange contracts;
   - misleading others within the firm about the creditworthiness of a borrower;
   - providing false or inaccurate documentation or information, including details of training, qualifications, past employment record or experience;
   - providing false or inaccurate information to the firm (or to the firm's auditors or appointed actuary);
   - providing false or inaccurate information to the FSA;
   - destroying, or causing the destruction of, documents (including false documentation) or tapes or their contents, relevant to misleading (or attempting to mislead) a client, the firm or the FSA;
   - failing to disclose dealings where disclosure is required by the firm's personal account dealing rules; and

- misleading others in the firm about the nature of risks being accepted.

2. Deliberately recommending an investment to a customer, or carrying out a discretionary transaction for a customer, if the approved person knows that he is unable to justify its suitability for that customer.
3. Deliberately failing to inform a customer, the firm (or its auditors or appointed actuary) or the FSA of the fact that their understanding of a material issue is incorrect. This includes deliberately failing to:
   - disclose the existence of falsified documents;
   - rectify mismarked positions immediately.
4. Deliberately preparing inaccurate or inappropriate records or returns in connection with a controlled function, such as:
   - performance reports for transmission to customers which are inaccurate or inappropriate (for example, by relying on past performance without giving appropriate warnings);
   - inaccurate training records or details of qualifications, past employment record or experience;
   - inaccurate trading confirmations, contract notes or other records of transactions or holdings of securities for a customer, whether or not the customer is aware of these inaccuracies or has requested such records.
5. Deliberately misusing the assets or confidential information of a client or the firm such as:
   - front running client orders ('front running' means handling the firm's own orders before those of its client, or before the firm's broker recommendations are released to clients, so as to benefit from price movements that may arise from client-dealing activity);
   - carrying out unjustified trading on client accounts to generate a benefit to the approved person (sometimes known as 'churning');
   - misappropriating a client's assets, including wrongly transferring cash or securities belonging to clients to personal accounts;
   - using a client's funds for purposes other than those for which they are provided;
   - retaining a client's funds wrongly;
   - pledging the assets of a client as security or margin in circumstances where the firm is not permitted to do so.
6. Deliberately designing transactions so as to disguise breaches of requirements and standards of the regulatory system.
7. Deliberately failing to disclose the existence of a conflict of interest in connection with dealings with a client.
8. Deliberately not paying due regard to the interests of a customer.
9. Deliberate acts, omissions or business practices that could be reasonably expected to cause consumer detriment.

4.2.2 Code of Practice for Statement of Principle 2

In the opinion of the FSA, any of the following is a failure to comply with the requirement for an approved person to **act with due skill, care and diligence** in carrying out his controlled function.

1. Failing to inform a customer or the firm (or the firm's auditors or appointed actuary) of material information in circumstances where he was aware, or ought to have been aware, of such information and the fact that he should provide it. Examples include:
   - failing to explain the risks of an investment to a customer;
   - failing to disclose details of the charges or surrender penalties of investment products;
   - mismarking trading positions;
   - providing inaccurate or inadequate information to the firm, its auditors or appointed actuary;
   - failing to disclose dealings where disclosure is required by the firm's personal account dealing rules.
2. Recommending an investment to a customer, or carrying out a discretionary transaction for a customer, where he does not have reasonable grounds to believe that it is suitable for that customer.
3. Undertaking, recommending or providing

advice on transactions without reasonable understanding of the risk exposure of the transaction to the customer. For example, recommending transactions in investments to a customer without a reasonable understanding of the liability of that transaction.

4. Undertaking transactions without a reasonable understanding of the risk exposure of the transaction to the firm. For example, trading on the firm's own account, without a reasonable understanding of the liability of that transaction.
5. Failing without good reason to disclose the existence of a conflict of interest in connection with dealings with a client.
6. Failing to provide adequate control over a client's assets, such as failing to segregate a client's assets or failing to process a client's payments in a timely manner.
7. Continuing to perform a controlled function despite having failed to meet the standards of knowledge and skills as required by the FSA.
8. Failing to pay due regard to the interests of a customer, without good reason.

4.2.3 Code of Practice for Statement of Principle 3

Statement of Principle 3 requires an approved person to **observe proper standards of market conduct** in carrying out his controlled function. In terms of interpreting what might be regarded as proper standards of market conduct, the FSA states that compliance with its Code of Market Conduct will tend to show compliance with Statement of Principle 3.

4.2.4 Code of Practice for Statement of Principle 4

Statement of Principle 4 requires an approved person to **deal with the FSA and other regulators in an open and co-operative way** and to disclose appropriately any information of which the FSA would reasonably expect notice. In the opinion of the FSA, an approved person is not complying with Statement of Principle 4 in the following circumstances:

1. Failing to report promptly in accordance with his firm's internal procedures (or, if none exists, direct to the FSA) information which it would be reasonable to assume would be of material significance to the FSA, whether in response to questions or otherwise.
2. Failing without good reason to:
   i. inform a regulator of information of which the approved person was aware in response to questions from that regulator;
   ii. attend an interview or answer questions put by a regulator, despite a request or demand having been made;
   iii. supply a regulator with appropriate documents or information when requested or required to do so and within the time limits attaching to that request or requirement.

4.3 Code of Practice for Approved Persons – Significant Influence Functions

Learning Objective 1.1.4

Know the Statements of Principle 5 to 7 and Code of Practice for approved persons in respect of Significant Influence Functions [APER 4.5.1/12/13/14 + 4.6.1/2/3/5/6/8 + 4.7.1/2/12/13]

Additionally, for significant influence functions there are three further principles:

An approved person must:

- take reasonable steps to ensure that the business of the firm for which he is responsible in his controlled function is organised so that it can be controlled effectively;
- exercise due skill, care and diligence in managing the business of the firm for which

he is responsible in his controlled function; and
- take reasonable steps to ensure that the business of the firm for which he is responsible in his controlled function complies with the relevant requirements and standards of the regulatory system.

4.3.1 Code of Practice for Statement of Principle 5

Statement of Principle 5 requires an approved person performing a significant influence function to take reasonable steps to ensure that the business of the firm for which he is responsible in his controlled function is organised so that it can be controlled effectively.

The FSA would expect this to include the following:

1. **Reporting lines** – the organisation of the business and the responsibilities of those within it should be clearly defined, with reporting lines clear to staff. If staff have dual reporting lines there is a greater need to ensure that the responsibility and accountability of each individual line manager is clearly set out and understood.
2. **Authorisation levels and job descriptions** – if members of staff have particular levels of authorisation, these should be clearly set out and communicated to staff. It may be appropriate for each member of staff to have a job description of which he is aware.
3. **Suitability of individuals** – if an individual's performance is unsatisfactory, then the appropriate approved person performing a significant influence function should review carefully whether that individual should be allowed to continue in that position. The approved person performing the significant influence function should not let the financial performance of the individual (or group) prevent an appropriate investigation into the compliance with the requirements and standards of the regulatory system.

Failure to comply with Principle 5 may include weaknesses and failings in any of these areas:

- failure to apportion responsibilities;
- poor systems and controls;
- failure to act upon relevant management information;
- failure to review the competence of individuals.

4.3.2 Code of Practice for Statement of Principle 6

Statement of Principle 6 requires an approved person performing a significant influence function to **exercise due skill, care and diligence** in managing the business of the firm for which he is responsible in his controlled function. In the opinion of the FSA, an approved person is not complying with Statement of Principle 6 when:

1. Failing to take reasonable steps adequately to inform himself about the affairs of the business for which he is responsible:
   - permitting transactions without understanding the risks;
   - permitting expansion of the business without assessing the risks;
   - inadequate monitoring of highly profitable or unusual transactions or practices;
   - not testing the veracity of explanations from subordinates; not obtaining independent, expert opinion where necessary.
2. Delegating the authority for dealing with an issue or a part of the business to an individual or individuals (whether in-house or outside contractors) without reasonable grounds for believing that the delegate had the necessary capacity, competence, knowledge, seniority or skill to deal with the issue or to take authority for dealing with that part of the business.
3. Failing to take reasonable steps to maintain an appropriate level of understanding about an issue or part of the business that he has delegated to an individual or individuals (whether in-house or outside contractors):
   - disregarding a delegated issue;
   - not obtaining adequate reports;
   - not testing the veracity of explanations from subordinates.
4. Failing to supervise and monitor adequately the individual or individuals (whether in-house or outside contractors) to whom

responsibility for dealing with an issue or authority for dealing with a part of the business has been delegated:
  - failing to take action where progress is unreasonably slow or unsatisfactory explanations given;
  - failing to review the performance of an outside contractor.

4.3.3 Code of Practice for Statement of Principle 7

Statement of Principle 7 requires an approved person performing a significant influence function to take reasonable steps to ensure that the business of the firm for which he is responsible in his controlled function **complies with the relevant requirements and standards of the regulatory system**. This can be achieved, in part at least, by establishing a competent and properly staffed compliance department – though that may well not suffice in and of itself. The following does not comply with Statement of Principle 7:

- Failure to implement and oversee appropriate compliance systems and controls.
- Failure to monitor compliance against regulatory requirements.
- Failure to stay informed about, investigate and provide effective remedy for compliance breaches.
- For the Money Laundering Reporting Officer, failure to discharge these duties.

5. The CISI Code of Conduct

Learning Objective 1.1.5

Know the Chartered Institute for Securities & Investment's Code of Conduct

Certain approved persons may, as well as having to comply with the FSA Statements of Principle, also be members of the **Chartered Institute for Securities & Investment (CISI)**. Membership of the CISI requires compliance with the CISI's own Code of Conduct – this includes an obligation to meet a set of standards set out within the **CISI Principles**.

These Principles impose an obligation on members to act in a manner which goes beyond mere compliance, and which is consistent with the underlying values of the CISI.

A material breach of the Code of Conduct is incompatible with continuing membership of the CISI.

Members who find themselves in a position which might require them to act in a manner contrary to the Principles are encouraged to do the following:

1. discuss their concerns with their line manager;
2. seek advice from their internal compliance department;
3. approach their firm's non-executive directors or audit committee;
4. if unable to resolve their concerns and having exhausted all internal avenues, contact the CISI for advice.

5.1 CISI Principles

1. To act honestly and fairly at all times when dealing with clients, customers and counterparties and to be a good steward of their interests, taking into account the nature of the business relationship with each of them, the nature of the service to be provided to them and the individual mandates given by them.
2. To act with integrity in fulfilling the responsibilities of your appointment and to seek to avoid any acts, omissions or business practices which damage the reputation of your organisation or the financial services industry.
3. To observe applicable law, regulations and professional conduct standards when carrying out financial service activities, and to interpret and apply them to the best of your ability, according to principles rooted in trust, honesty and integrity.
4. To observe the standards of market integrity, good practice and conduct required or expected of participants in markets when engaging in any form of market dealing.
5. To be alert to and manage fairly and

effectively and to the best of your ability any relevant conflict of interest.
6. To attain and actively manage a level of professional competence appropriate to your responsibilities, to commit to continuing learning to ensure the currency of your knowledge, skills and expertise and to promote the development of others.
7. To decline to act in any matter about which you are not competent unless you have access to such advice and assistance as will enable you to carry out the work in a professional manner.
8. To strive to uphold the highest personal and professional standards.

6. Senior Management Arrangements

Learning Objective 1.1.6

Understand the FSA's rules regarding Senior Management Arrangements, Systems and Controls for both common platform firms and non-MiFID firms: purpose [SYSC 1.2.1, 3.1.1, 4.1.1/2 + 19.2.1]

The FSA places certain requirements on financial services firms' directors and senior managers. These requirements are contained in the 'Senior Management Arrangements, Systems and Controls' (SYSC) part of the Handbook.

The purpose of these requirements is to:

1. encourage firms' directors and senior managers to take responsibility for their firm's arrangements on matters likely to be of interest to the FSA (because they are relevant to the FSA's ability to discharge its regulatory obligations);
2. amplify Principle for Businesses 3, under which a firm must take reasonable care to organise and control its affairs responsibly and effectively, with adequate risk management systems;
3. encourage firms to vest responsibility for an effective and responsible organisation in specific directors and senior managers, so that everyone knows who is responsible for what activities and so that functions are not, therefore, in danger of falling between stools (each director/manager regarding another as being accountable for a given activity or function, so that no one person assumes responsibility for its oversight); and
4. create a common platform of organisational systems and controls for firms.

The systems and controls requirements apply to firms in two ways.

- For firms that are subject to the Capital Requirements Directive (CRD) and MiFID, the requirements are known as the **common platform** of organisational systems and controls; they have the status of 'rule' and are legally binding on these firms and are expressed as 'must' in the Handbook text.
- For firms that are not subject to the CRD and MiFID (and hence not 'common platform' firms) some of the requirements have the status of 'rule' (for example, the provisions relating to financial crime) but other aspects apply as 'guidance'; guidance is not legally binding on firms and so is expressed as 'should' in the Handbook text and the FSA expects the firm to have regard to the guidance when designing and maintaining their arrangements.

The sections of SYSC that are relevant to investment firms are summarised below.

6.1 General Requirements (SYSC 4)

- **Sound governance:**
    - clear organisational structure and well-defined lines of responsibility;
    - adequate arrangements for business continuity to ensure that losses are minimised and essential data is preserved or recovered in a timely manner;
    - accounting policies and procedures to enable accurate and timely reporting to the FSA;
    - regular monitoring of the adequacy of

systems and controls, and measures taken to address deficiencies that are identified;
  - an audit committee to be established (if relevant to the scale and complexity of the business).
- **Persons who direct the business** must be of good repute and sufficiently experienced as to ensure the sound and prudent management of the firm. There must be at least two independent minds formulating policy and controlling the business.
- **Senior personnel** must receive frequent written reports (not less than annually) on compliance and internal audit (where relevant) measures for protecting against financial crime and risk management.
- **Apportionment of responsibilities** must be done in such a way as to ensure that it is clear who has which responsibility and the firm's business and affairs can be adequately monitored and controlled by its senior personnel and governors. Controlled function 8 – Apportionment and oversight must be specifically allocated.

6.2 Employees, Agents and Other Relevant Persons (SYSC 5)

The requirements of SYSC apply to all persons appointed to a firm, whether on an employed basis, self-employed, acting as agent, appointed representatives and those appointed under outsourcing arrangements. In addition to these provisions, there are specific qualifications and competence requirements for certain roles.

- **Skills, knowledge and expertise** – firms must employ personnel with the skills, knowledge and expertise necessary for the discharge of their responsibilities. This is a very important requirement and is known as the 'competent employees rule'.
- **Segregation of duties** – must be effective to ensure that persons performing several roles are able to perform each role soundly, honestly and professionally.
- **Awareness of procedures** – firms must ensure that persons are aware of the procedures that have to be followed for the performance of their duties.
- **Monitoring** – there must be regular evaluation of systems and controls specific to employee competence.

6.3 Compliance, Audit and Financial Crime (SYSC 6)

- **Compliance** – there must be adequate policies and procedures to ensure the firm's compliance with its obligations under the regulatory system, and to detect risk of failure. An effective compliance function must be maintained to monitor the firm's arrangements and to advise and assist personnel who conduct regulated activity. A compliance officer must be appointed. The compliance function must have the necessary authority, resources, expertise and access to relevant information and must be sufficiently independent. This means that, ideally, a person should not be involved in any activity that they monitor as part of the compliance function, but the FSA allows flexibility in this requirement for small firms where this may not be possible.
- **Internal audit** – the requirement to maintain an independent internal audit function applies in a proportionate manner, that is, if the scale, nature and complexity of a firm's business is such that an internal audit function is appropriate.
- **Financial crime** – firms must establish systems and controls to enable them to identify, assess, monitor and manage money laundering risk, and regularly evaluate the adequacy of the arrangements. The firm must allocate overall responsibility for mitigating financial crime risk to a director or senior manager, and a Money Laundering Reporting Officer (MLRO) must be appointed (who may be the same person).

6.4 Risk Control (SYSC 7 and 12)

- **SYSC 7 Risk Control** – expands on the general requirement to manage risk, and requires firms to have arrangements for identifying and assessing the risks the firm may be exposed to, and to set a level of risk tolerance for the firm. Risk management policies must relate to the firm's level of risk tolerance. Senior personnel must review risk management strategies and ensure they relate to the macroeconomic environment within which the firm operates.

- **SYSC 12 Group Risk Systems and Controls** – applies the risk control provisions to groups.

6.5 Outsourcing (SYSC 8)

Outsourcing is an arrangement between a firm and a provider concerning a function that the firm could otherwise have undertaken for itself, eg, where it has permission to safeguard client assets but chooses to outsource this to a third party custodian. This is a different situation from where a firm engages a provider for a service that the firm could not undertake for itself, eg, information technology (IT) support.

In either case, if a third party is engaged to provide operational support, the firm must ensure that it does not incur additional operational risk. If the arrangement counts as outsourcing, it must not compromise the quality of the firm's internal control nor the FSA's ability to monitor the firm.

The provisions in SYSC 8 differentiate between critical and non-critical operational functions. Critical functions are those where any defect would materially impair the continuance of sound regulated activity. Examples of non-critical functions on the other hand include:

- advisory services to the firm, eg, legal advice, training services, billing and security services;
- provision of market information/price feeds;
- telephone recording.

A firm that outsources a critical function or regulated activity remains fully responsible for the operation of that activity and its obligations under the regulatory system. Senior personnel may not delegate their responsibility, the firm's relationships with its clients must be unaltered and the conditions for the firm's authorised status must not be undermined or modified.

The due diligence conducted by the firm must ensure that the following conditions are satisfied:

- The service provider must be capable and have the necessary authority to perform the function.
- The firm must establish arrangements for monitoring effective performance of the function, ensuring that the service provider conducts internal supervision and risk management, and taking action if the service provider is not properly fulfilling the function.
- The firm must retain the necessary expertise to supervise and manage the risks of the outsourcing.
- The service provider must disclose any development that may impact on its continuing ability.
- The firm must be able to terminate the arrangement without detriment to its clients.
- The service provider must co-operate with the FSA, the firm and its auditors and allow access to its business premises and to relevant data.
- The service provider must protect confidential information concerning the firm and its clients.
- The firm and service provider must establish a contingency plan for disaster recovery and periodic testing of business continuity.
- Respective rights, obligations and authorities must be clearly allocated and subject to a written agreement.

The firm must notify the FSA when it intends to rely on a third party for the performance of critical operational functions.

6.6 Record-Keeping (SYSC 9)

This section requires firms to maintain orderly records of its business, internal organisation, services and transactions to enable the FSA to monitor the firm's compliance with regulatory requirements and its obligations towards its clients. Records for MiFID business must be retained for five years; the retention periods for other records vary and are specified in the rules relating to a particular record. Records must be retained in a durable medium that allows the following conditions to be met:

- The FSA must be able to access the record readily and be able to reconstitute each key state of processing a transaction.
- Corrections and amendments should be easily ascertained.
- It must not be possible for made records to be otherwise manipulated or altered.
- Generally, the records should be capable of being reproduced in English and on paper.

6.7 Conflicts of Interest (SYSC 10)

This section requires firms to maintain policies for identifying and managing conflicts of interest. This will be covered in detail in Chapter 4 when looking at Conduct of Business rules.

6.8 Remuneration (SYSC 19A)

All firms are required to establish remuneration policies that are consistent with and promote sound and effective risk management.

Additionally, some types of common platform firms are subject to the detailed requirements of the **Remuneration Code** in SYSC 19A.3.

The Code derives from the EU Capital Requirements Directive and originally only applied to the largest banks, building societies and broker-dealers. However, from 1 January 2011, the requirements extended to many other types of firm including asset managers, hedge fund managers and investment firms, as well as some firms that engage in corporate finance, venture capital, the provision of financial advice and stockbrokers.

In summary, the Code covers:

- **12 principles** – the Code contains 12 principles with which firms must comply in a proportionate way, depending on the size, internal organisation nature, scope and the complexity of the firm's activities.
- **Code staff** – these are senior management and anyone whose professional activities could have a material impact on a firm's risk profile. The onus is on firms to identify their code staff in the first instance, but their lists will be subject to review and challenge by the FSA. Code staff earning above a specified threshold are subject to specific restraints concerning bonus payments and a restriction on variable remuneration.
- **Guarantees** – firms must not offer guaranteed bonuses of more than one year. Guarantees may only be given to new hires for the first year of service in exceptional circumstances.
- **Strengthening of capital base** – firms must ensure that their total variable remuneration does not limit the ability to strengthen their capital base. Total variable remuneration must be significantly reduced in circumstances where the firm produces a subdued or negative financial performance.
- **Voiding provisions** – a new rule will be introduced which defines instances where breaches of the code may render a contract void and/or require recovery of payments made.
- **Severance payments** – should reflect performance over time and failure must not be rewarded.
- **Pensions** – CRD3 states that enhanced discretionary pension benefits should be held for five years in the form of shares or share-like instruments.

7. The Relationship Between the FSA and Various Other Bodies

Learning Objective 1.2.1

Know the regulatory infrastructure generated by the FSMA 2000 and the status of and relationship between the Treasury, the Office of Fair Trading, the Financial Services Skills Partnership and the FSA and also the relationship between FSA and the RIEs, ROIEs, DIEs, RCHs, MTFs and DPBs

The FSMA required that the FSA establish two schemes to provide protection for consumers: the Financial Ombudsman Service (FOS) and the Financial Services Compensation Scheme (FSCS). We will look at these before considering the relationship between the FSA and various other relevant bodies.

7.1 The Financial Ombudsman Service (FOS)

Part XVI of the FSMA provides for a single scheme for dealing with disputes between consumers and financial services firms. This single scheme replaced several ombudsman schemes that had previously existed. The FSMA required the FSA to establish a limited company (the Financial Ombudsman Service (FOS)) to administer the scheme and to make rules for its operation. The scheme is designed to provide quick resolution of disputes between **'eligible complainants'** and their product/ service providers with a minimum of formality, by an independent person.

The chairman and other directors of the FOS are appointed by the FSA, but the terms of their appointment must be such as to secure their independence from the FSA. The FSA requires an annual report on the scheme. The FOS also has some rule-making power, and any rules that the FOS makes must be approved by the FSA.

The FSA's rules specify who is eligible to use the FOS (the eligible complainant) and also requires financial services firms to set up and maintain complaints-handling and resolution procedures themselves. The hope is that most disputes will be resolved between the firm and the customer, and that the customer will not need to resort to the FOS.

If an eligible complaint does reach the FOS, the FOS is able to make judgements to compensate customers that are binding on the firm.

Consumers do not have to accept any decision the FOS makes and they can choose to go to court instead. But if they do accept the FOS decision, it is binding on them (and the firm). Further information on complaints-handling arrangements can be found in Chapter 5.

7.2 The Financial Services Compensation Scheme (FSCS)

Similarly, the FSMA required that the FSA establish a body, known as the Financial Services Compensation Scheme (FSCS), to provide a safety net for customers of financial services firms which become unable to repay them. This single scheme replaced several existing compensation schemes.

If an authorised financial services firm (eg, a bank) becomes insolvent, or appears likely to cease trading and fall insolvent, the customers of that firm (in our example, the people with money deposited at the bank) can make a claim under the FSCS for compensation for any loss – up to certain limits.

Details on the compensation limits are provided in Chapter 5.

As with the FOS, the FSA appoints the chairman and other board directors, with the terms of their appointment being designed to secure their independence from the FSA. The FSCS is required to make an annual report to the FSA.

7.3 The Office of Fair Trading (OFT)

The Office of Fair Trading (OFT) is a government department which carries out a wide range of functions, using powers given to it under various different pieces of legislation. Its overall aim is to ensure the fairness of a wide range of markets (financial and non-financial) for consumers. Most of its work comprises:

- analysing markets;
- enforcing consumer and competition law;

- administering the consumer credit licensing system;
- undertaking advocacy;
- delivering educational programmes to businesses and consumer.

Some of these areas overlap with the FSA's own areas of remit, for example:

- **Consumer credit licensed firms** – many of these are also likely to be authorised by the FSA because they are lending institutions such as banks/building societies, for example, or because they arrange or advise on consumer credit in their wider capacity as financial advisers.
- The OFT can take action to protect consumers under the **unfair contract terms** legislation; this aims to protect consumers if a firm's standard terms are unduly burdensome, unfair or hard to understand. The FSA also has powers under the unfair contract terms legislation.

Because of the areas of overlap between the OFT and the FSA, the two organisations work within a Memorandum of Understanding (MOU).

The MOU sets out procedures for approaching matters of common interest, to facilitate co-operation and prevent duplication.

7.4 The Financial Skills Partnership (FSP)

The Financial Skills Partnership (FSP) used to be called the Financial Services Skills Council (FSSC). Formerly it was responsible for the national occupational standards (NOS) and for maintaining the list of qualifications that were suitable for meeting the qualification standards of the FSA's Training and Competence (T&C) rules. This list is now maintained by the FSA. It forms part of the FSA's Handbook and is binding on firms.

However, the FSP now has a different remit and no longer covers regulated roles. It provides support for employers by:

- attracting staff into the financial services sector;
- representing employers' interests in terms of the planning and funding of finance sector staff training; and
- providing a forum for industry participants to exchange views and experiences.

7.5 The Bank of England

At one time, the Bank of England was a key regulator of the banking industry in the UK, supervising the commercial banks. However, in 1998, the Bank's regulatory role was withdrawn, and these functions were transferred to become a part of the FSA's responsibilities.

At the same time, the Bank of England was given an important role, under the Bank of England Act 1998, in effecting economic policy, by being given the ability to set interest rate levels through its **Monetary Policy Committee (MPC)**. A key interest rate, known as base rate, is reviewed monthly by the MPC and, if necessary, altered to keep inflation within the range determined by the government.

The Bank of England is also a member of the **Tripartite Standing Committee**, a framework within which it, the FSA and the Treasury co-ordinate their efforts to ensure appropriate action to prevent, or manage, crises in the financial system.

In addition, the Bank plays a part, in conjunction with the FSA and the Treasury, as one of the members of the Tripartite Standing Committee on financial stability. This committee considers risks to the stability of particular institutions or groups of institutions, and to the financial system and economy as a whole.

Under the new regulatory structure, the Bank of England (BoE) will once again have a role to play through its subsidiary, the Prudential Regulation Authority (PRA).

7.6 The Upper Tribunal (Tax and Chancery)

Learning Objective 1.2.2

Know the role of the Tax and Chancery Chamber of the Upper Tribunal

The Upper Tribunal (Tax and Chancery Chamber) is an agency of the Ministry of Justice. It aims to assist those who wish to appeal against decisions made by:

- first-tier Tribunal in tax or charity cases;
- the FSA;
- the Pensions Regulator.

7.6.1 Financial Services Cases

References can be made by the firm or the individual to whom the FSA or the Pensions Regulator notice is directed. The decision notices may cover a wide range of regulatory and disciplinary matters. Appeals can be made against the following types of FSA decision notice:

Authorisation and Permission

For example, FSA decisions not to authorise a firm, or if the FSA has invoked its power to withdraw authorisation, or vary the scope of a firm's permission.

Penalties for Market Abuse

The FSA may impose penalties for market abuse. The FSA is required to produce a code which helps to determine whether particular behaviour amounts to market abuse. Its decisions on market abuse by people (whether authorised or unauthorised) are referable to the Upper Tribunal.

Disciplinary Measures

The FSA may issue public statements about and/or impose penalties on authorised people who have failed to comply with requirements imposed by or under the Act. Such decisions are referable to the Upper Tribunal.

Official Listing

Certain decisions by the FSA in its role as competent authority are referable to the Upper Tribunal, for example, refusing to admit securities to the official list and suspending official listing of securities where necessary. The FSA is empowered to censure or impose penalties on issuers who breach listing rules.

Other Powers

The FSA will make decisions on the approval and discipline of employees and people who carry out certain functions on behalf of authorised people. They may prohibit certain people, including professionals, from carrying out particular functions.

7.7 HM Revenue & Customs (HMRC)

Learning Objective 1.2.3

Know HM Revenue & Customs' responsibility for issuing guidance on Treasury regulation for ISAs

Over the years, the government has provided a number of incentives for individuals to save money and invest money for the future, mainly by offering tax breaks and allowing tax-free savings, up to specified annual limits. These are known as Individual Savings Accounts (ISAs) and Junior ISAs (JISAs).

Her Majesty's Revenue & Customs (HMRC) is the body which administers, and issues guidance on, the Treasury's regulations in this area, including:

- what is eligible to be held within an ISA; and
- what is required of the firm offering the investments (the ISA manager).

Those firms wishing to offer and operate ISAs, therefore, also need – in addition to their FSA authorisation – to be approved to do so by HMRC and to operate them within the regulations and HMRC's guidance.

HMRC-approved ISA managers are able to conduct all aspects of ISA administration, including the reclaiming of tax on the income earned on certain investments held within their customers' ISAs.

It is important that such tax-favoured schemes are not abused, eg, by allowing people to invest more than is permitted under the limits – hence, the requirement that scheme managers are approved by the HMRC to operate them and that they follow the applicable regulations closely. HMRC not only maintains the lists of approved managers, but also audits their performance periodically to ensure that this is happening. Authorised firms that are also HMRC ISA managers must comply with HMRC procedures in addition to FSA rules for conducting business.

Note that the FSA does not make rules concerning how a firm should manage its tax affairs – nor does it give guidance on taxation such as VAT, for example. It is the responsibility of firms to ensure they are familiar with taxation matters relevant to their own business, and to seek guidance from their accountant and tax adviser and not the FSA.

8. The FSA Handbook

Learning Objective 1.2.4

Know the six types of provisions used by the FSA in its Handbook and the status of the FSA's approved industry guidance

8.1 Handbook Overview

The FSMA gives legal effect to the rules and guidance made by the FSA, which is set out in the FSA's Handbook. The Handbook covers the following areas:

- **Glossary** – this includes all the FSA-defined terms.
- **High-level standards** – ethics and expectations for governance and competence applicable to all firms.
- **Prudential standards** – financial resources.
- **Business standards** – conduct of business, including care of client assets and market conduct.
- **Regulatory processes** – authorisation, supervision, decision procedures and penalties.
- **Redress** – complaints handling procedures, the FOS, the FSCS and the scheme for making complaints about the FSA.
- **Specialist Sourcebooks** – for example, for regulated collective investment schemes, recognised investment exchanges and professional firms.
- **Listing, prospectus and disclosure rules.**
- **Handbook guides** – for specialist firms such as energy market participants, to direct them to which parts of the Handbook are relevant.
- **Regulatory guides** – for example, concerning enforcement, and perimeter guidance to establish whether an activity falls within the FSA regulation.

(Go to fsa.gov.uk/handbook to see the structure of the FSA's Handbook).

Within each section are a number of separate Sourcebooks and manuals (Handbook modules), that contain the FSA's main provisions. The modules all follow the same format. They commence with the application and purpose of the text, followed by the main body of the text and finally the schedules and transitional provisions:

- **Schedule 1** – record keeping requirements.
- **Schedule 2** – notification and reporting requirements.
- **Schedule 3** – fees and other payments (where relevant).
- **Schedule 4** – statutory powers exercised by FSA in making the provisions.
- **Schedule 5** – rights of actions for damages under s.150 of the FSMA, ie, whether or not a person may bring court actions for damages as a result of the provision.
- **Schedule 6** – rules that may be waived or modified.
- **Transitional provisions** – when rules are made or changed, the FSA typically allows a period of grace for firms to make the changes; or transitional provisions may provide for exemption from certain aspects of a rule, for a set period of time.

8.2 Status of Provisions

There are six different types of provisions, with each type being indicated by a single letter. The status of a provision is important because it determines the legal effect on a firm.

The six different types of provisions are:

R. Rules – rules are binding on authorised persons (firms) and, if a firm contravenes a rule, it may be subject to discipline. The

FSA's Principles for Businesses are given the status of rules.

E. Evidential provisions – these are rules but they are not binding in their own right. They will always relate to another, binding rule. Evidential provisions give the required evidence which is expected to show that a person has complied with, or contravened, a rule. For example, the qualifications tables have the status of evidential provisions and they relate to the rule that requires firms to ensure certain employees attain appropriate qualifications.

G. Guidance which may be used by the FSA to explain the implications of other provisions, to indicate possible means of compliance, or to recommend a particular course of action. Guidance is not binding, nor does it have 'evidential' effect. As a result, a firm cannot be disciplined for a failure to follow guidance.

D. Directions and requirements – dictate, eg, the form of content of applications for authorisation. They are binding on those to whom they are addressed.

P. The Statements of Principle for Approved Persons, binding on approved persons.

C. Conclusive behaviour that does not amount to market abuse. The letter 'C' is used because these types of behaviour are **conclusively not** market abuse (market abuse is covered in detail in Chapter 3).

Additionally, the Handbook text may include:

- **UK flag icon** – to indicate where non-FSA UK legislative material has been incorporated within the provision;
- **European Union (EU) flag icon** – to indicate where non-FSA EU legislative material has been incorporated.

8.3 FSA Confirmation of Industry Guidance

The FSA encourages the financial industry to develop its own best practice and will give official recognition to guidance that has been developed by the industry for the benefit of practitioners.

FSA-confirmed industry guidance does not create any new tier of regulation. It has the same status as the FSA's own guidance. That is: *'The FSA will not take action against a person for behaviour that it considers to be in line with guidance, other materials published by the FSA in support of the Handbook or FSA-confirmed Industry Guidance, which were current at the time of the behaviour in question.' (DEPP 6.2.1(4)G). Similarly, as Industry Guidance is not mandatory (and is one way, but not the only way, to comply with requirements), we do not presume that because firms are not complying with it they are not meeting our requirements'.*

However, where a breach has been established, industry guidance is potentially relevant to enforcement deliberations. For example, to:

1. help assess whether it could reasonably have been understood or predicted at the time that the conduct in question fell below the standards required by the Principles;
2. explain the regulatory context;
3. inform a view of the overall seriousness of the breaches, eg, it could decide that the breach warranted a higher penalty in circumstances where the FSA had written to chief executives in that sector to reiterate the importance of ensuring a particular aspect of its business complied with relevant regulatory standards;
4. inform the consideration of a firm's defence that it was judging the firm on the basis of retrospective standards; and
5. be considered as part of expert or supervisory statements in relation to the relevant standards at the time.

End of Chapter Questions

Think of an answer for each question and refer to the appropriate section for confirmation.

1. List three ways in which the FSMA 2000 provides enhanced consumer protection.

   Answer Reference: Section 1.1

   ....

   ....

   ....

2. To which government body is the FSA accountable?

   Answer Reference: Section 1.3

   ....

   ....

   ....

3. What is the regulatory status of a recognised investment exchange?

   Answer Reference: Section 1.4

   ....

   ....

   ....

4. What designation is given by the FSA to overseas-based exchanges that do not offer membership to UK firms?

   Answer Reference: Section 1.5

   ....

   ....

   ....

5. What are designated professional bodies?

   Answer Reference: Section 1.7

   ....

   ....

   ....

6. What is a multilateral trading facility?

   Answer Reference: Section 1.8

   ....

   ....

   ....

7. What are the FSA's four statutory objectives?

   Answer Reference: Section 2.1

   ....

   ....

   ....

8. Give three examples of the FSA's rule-making powers.

   Answer Reference: Section 2.2

   ....

   ....

   ....

9. List the 11 Principles for Businesses.

   Answer Reference: Section 3.1

   ....

   ....

   ....

10. What is the likely outcome for a firm that breaches a principle?

    Answer Reference: Section 3.1

    ....

    ....

    ....

11. What Statements of Principle apply to approved persons performing a significant influence function?

    Answer Reference: Sections 4.1 and 4.3

    ....

    ....

    ....

12. What are members of the CISI expected to do if they might be required to act in a manner contrary to the Principles?

    Answer Reference: Section 5

    ....

    ....

    ....

13. What is the purpose behind the FSA requirements for senior management?

    Answer Reference: Section 6

    ....

    ....

    ....

14. How do the requirements of SYSC apply to non-common platform firms?

    Answer Reference: Section 6

    ....

    ....

    ....

15. List five areas covered by SYSC.

    Answer Reference: Section 6

    ....

    ....

    ....

16. What is the relationship between the FSA and the FOS?

    Answer Reference: Section 7.1

    ....

    ....

    ....

17. What is the purpose of the FSCS?

    Answer Reference: Section 7.2

    ....

    ....

    ....

18. What is the interaction between the FSA and the OFT?

    Answer Reference: Section 7.3

    ....

    ....

    ....

19. What is the purpose of the Upper Tribunal and who does it report to?

    Answer Reference: Section 7.6

    ....

    ....

    ....

20. Who is responsible for providing regulation for ISA managers?

    Answer Reference: Section 7.7

    ....

    ....

    ....

21. What provision is indicated by the letters: G; D; P; E; R; C?

    Answer Reference: Section 8.2

    ....

    ....

    ....

22. What is the difference between a rule and an evidential provision in the FSA Handbook?

    Answer Reference: Section 8.2

    ....

    ....

    ....

23. What is the status of G provisions?

    Answer Reference: Section 8.2

    ....

    ....

    ....

24. What is the status of FSA-confirmed industry guidance?

    Answer Reference: Section 8.3

    ....

    ....

    ....

2

The Financial Services and Markets Act 2000

This syllabus area will provide approximately 7 of the 50 examination questions

The Financial Services and Markets Act 2000

1. Regulated and Prohibited Activities

Learning Objective 2.1.1

Know the regulated and prohibited activities (Part II/III of FSMA 2000, Regulated Activities Order 2001 and the under-noted guidance in the FSA's Perimeter Guidance Manual (PERG): authorised persons [PERG 2.2.3]; exempt persons [PERG 2.10] and FSMA Exemption Order 2001 [(SI 2001/1201)]; offences under the Act [PERG 2.2.1/2]; enforceability of agreements entered into with an unauthorised business [PERG 2.2.2]; defences available under the Act [PERG 2.2.1]

1.1 The General Prohibition

The FSMA is subdivided into 30 parts. Part II, **Regulated and Prohibited Activities**, includes the **general prohibition**, which simply states that no person can carry on a regulated activity in the UK, or purport to do so, unless he is either authorised or exempt. If a person contravenes the general prohibition it is a criminal offence; the maximum sanctions are up to two years' imprisonment and an unlimited fine.

A further effect of acting in contravention of the general prohibition is that any agreements made are unenforceable by the offending person against the other party. This is also the case for agreements made as a result of the activities of someone who was contravening the general prohibition, even if that person is not a party to the agreement.

The other party is entitled to recover any money or property transferred under the agreement, and to be compensated for any loss suffered.

It is a defence for a person to show that they took all reasonable precautions and exercised all due diligence to avoid committing the offence.

Example

Mrs X buys shares in ABC plc. The purchase is made following the recommendation of a firm of brokers, UNA Ltd. Mrs X subsequently discovers that UNA was not authorised under the FSMA.

Mrs X now has two choices: she can keep her shares in ABC and take no action against UNA, or she can sue UNA for the recovery of her money and damages (handing back her shares in ABC) because UNA Ltd has breached the general prohibition.

The relevant staff of UNA have also committed a criminal act, and will be liable to a potential punishment of up to two years in prison, plus an unlimited fine.

Chapter 1 gives examples of authorised and exempt persons. For a person to become authorised by the FSA, that person must first apply to the FSA for permission to perform particular regulated activities; if that person satisfies the FSA's criteria, the FSA will give it/him permission.

You should remember from the previous chapter that the term 'person' here means the trading entity or firm, which could be incorporated as a company – or could be an unincorporated entity such as a sole trader or partnership.

There are various provisions in the FSMA whereby a person can be exempt from the general prohibition when carrying on regulated activity. The provisions are, in summary:

- **s.39 FSMA and the FSMA (Appointed Representatives) Regulations 2001** – for appointed representatives;
- **s.285 FSMA** – for recognised investment exchanges and clearing houses;
- **s.312A FSMA** – for operators of multilateral trading systems, exercising certain rights;
- **s.316 FSMA** – special provisions for members of the Society of Lloyd's;
- **FSMA Exemption Order 2001** – for central banks, supranational bodies, local authorities, charities, industrial and provident societies and certain organisations that are subject to some oversight by the government;
- **Part XX FSMA** – the special regime for professional firms, subject to conditions.

Exempt persons are covered in more detail in Section 2 of this chapter.

1.1.1 Prohibition Orders

Learning Objective 2.1.2

Understand the FSA's actions in respect of prohibition orders and actions for damages and how private persons can sue for damages when a firm is declared in breach [FSMA 2000, s.56, 59, 71, 150]

Separately from the general prohibition, s.56 of the FSMA gives the FSA the power to make an order (prohibition order) prohibiting an individual from performing a specified function. The FSA may do this if it considers the individual is not a fit and proper person to perform the function. The prohibition order may relate to a particular regulated activity or regulated activity generally. If the individual breaches the order, they are guilty of a criminal offence and liable to a fine. It is a defence for the person to show they took all reasonable care and exercised due diligence to avoid breaching the order.

An authorised person (the firm) must take reasonable care to ensure that individuals for whom they are responsible do not breach prohibition orders.

Prohibition orders may also be made against exempt persons, and also exempt professional firms who are acting in accordance with the Part XX regime described in Chapter 1.

A person may apply to the FSA to have a prohibition order varied or revoked.

Section 59 states that a person cannot carry out certain controlling functions in a firm without approval by the FSA.

Section 71 of the FSMA provides for circumstances whereby a private person can sue a firm for damages if they suffer loss because the firm is found to be in breach of statutory duty in the following circumstances:

- an individual within a firm carries out a function in breach of a s.56 prohibition order;
- an individual carries out a controlled function but without prior approval (s.59).

Section 71 also provides for clients who are non-private persons (eg, businesses, trusts) to sue for damages as a consequence of negligence concerning prohibition orders, in prescribed circumstances.

Section 150 of the FSMA allows private persons to sue for damages as a result of the contravention of a rule.

Section 150 rights may also extend to persons who are not private persons, depending on the circumstances.

1.2 Regulated Activities

In order to understand whether someone is in breach of the FSMA general prohibition it is, of course, necessary to understand what the regulated activities themselves are. It is left to a separate statutory instrument, known as the **Regulated Activities Order 2001 (RAO)**, to clarify precisely what these regulated activities are. The FSMA provides that these will be defined by reference to two sets of criteria:

- a range of investments (including assets which we might typically think of as investments, such as shares and bonds, but also other assets such as deposits and contracts of insurance); and
- a range of activities which may be carried on in connection with those investments (such as dealing, managing or advising on investments, accepting deposits and effecting contracts of insurance).

Not all of the activities can be related to all the investments. Some are specific to just one type, eg, effecting a contract of insurance relates only to contracts of insurance.

If a person is performing one (or more) of these specified activities in relation to one (or more) of the specified investments, that person is performing a regulated activity and requires either authorisation or an exemption. It is the combination of carrying on a **specified activity**, in relation to a **specified investment**, which gives rise to **regulated activity**.

The investments and activities are detailed in secondary legislation issued under the FSMA – principally the RAO, as subsequently amended.

1.2.1 Specified Investments

Learning Objective 2.4.3

Know the investments specified in Part III of the Regulated Activities Order

The following are defined as specified investments within the RAO:

1. **Deposits** – money paid by one person to another, with or without interest being earned on it, and on terms that it will be repaid when a specified event occurs (eg, when a demand is made). The obvious example is deposits held with banks and building societies. For clarity, the RAO sets out certain exclusions – eg, electronic money (covered separately below), money paid in advance for the provision of goods or services and money paid as a security deposit.

2. **Electronic money** – monetary value (as represented by a claim on the e-money issuer) which is stored on an electronic device, issued on receipt of funds and accepted as a means of payment by third parties. In effect it is an electronic substitute for notes and coins.
3. **Rights under contracts of insurance** – includes both long-term insurance contracts (eg, life assurance or endowment policies) and general insurance (eg, motor or building insurance). The FSA gives guidance on identifying a contract of insurance (since this is not always as simple as you might think) in the Perimeter Guidance Sourcebook (PERG).
4. **Shares** – defined widely as shares or stock in any company (wherever incorporated) or in any unincorporated body formed outside the UK. The RAO definition excludes shares in open-ended investment companies (OEICs), since an OEIC is a collective investment scheme (CIS) and is captured under a separate definition. It also excludes some building society shares, since these can behave like – and are, therefore, captured under – the definition of deposits.
5. **Instruments creating or acknowledging indebtedness** – including debentures, debenture stock, loan stock and, as a 'mopping-up' clause, specifies also 'any other instrument creating or acknowledging debt'. Again, the definition is wide, so the RAO provides for some exclusions – eg, trade bills, cheques and other bills of exchange, and (because they are separately captured) contracts of insurance and government and public securities.
6. **Government and public securities** – eg, gilts and US treasuries and local authority loan stocks. Again, certain instruments are excluded, such as trade bills issued by government bodies, and National Savings & Investments (NS&I) deposits and products.
7. **Alternative finance investment bonds/ alternative debentures** – a form of Sharia'a-compliant bond or 'sukuk'.
8. **Instruments giving entitlements to investments** – essentially, warrants and similar instruments entitling the holder to subscribe for shares, debentures, government and public securities at a set price, and on or between set date(s) in the future.
9. **Certificates representing certain securities** – covers certificates which confer rights in (but are not themselves) other instruments such as shares, debentures, gilts and warrants. It includes, for example, American depositary receipts (ADRs), which typically give holders rights over a certain number of a UK companies shares. These ADRs are designed to offer the – typically US-based – investor a more convenient way to invest in UK shares, because they are dealt in, and pay dividends in, US dollars. Also covered here are other depositary receipts, such as global depositary receipts (GDRs).
10. **Units in a collective investment scheme** – covers holdings in any collective investment scheme, whether it is an authorised or an unregulated scheme. For example, it covers units in an authorised unit trust (AUT) or shares in an OEIC – which you may also see described as an investment company with variable capital (ICVC). This is why OEICs are specifically excluded from the heading of 'shares' above. Unregulated schemes can also take other legal forms, such as limited partnerships, and so rights in such partnerships fall within the scope of 'units in a collective investment scheme'.
11. **Rights under a stakeholder pension scheme** – stakeholder pensions are pension schemes set up under the Welfare Reform and Pensions Act 1999 which have to meet certain criteria and be run in a particular way.
12. **Rights under a personal pension scheme** – pensions designed for individuals who do not belong to a company scheme and/or who wish to take control of their own investment decisions for their pension provisions (for example, self-invested personal pensions (SIPPs). A wide range of investments may be held within a personal pension scheme.
13. **Options** – options (the right, but not the obligation, to buy or sell a fixed quantity of an underlying asset for a fixed price on or between fixed dates) are only covered if they relate to:
    - securities or contractually based

investments (eg, stocks, shares, bonds, or futures on similar instruments);
- currencies;
- certain precious metals, including gold and silver;
- options on futures contracts and other contracts for differences (see paragraph 15).

14. **Futures** – contracts for the sale/purchase of an asset where delivery and settlement will be made at a future date, at a price agreed when the contract is made. The RAO excludes futures agreed for commercial purposes as opposed to those made for investment/speculative purposes. Thus a contract to buy cocoa at an agreed price at some future date will not be caught if it is carried out by a chocolate maker to help him secure a certain price for the raw materials needed.
15. **Contracts for difference (CFDs)** – eg, spread bets, interest rate swaps. These are contracts where the investor's aim is to secure a profit (or avoid a loss) by making money by reference to fluctuations in the value of an index, or to the price of some other underlying property. The RAO excludes futures and options since these are separately caught.
16. **Lloyd's syndicate capacity and syndicate membership** – relates in the main to activities of Lloyd's members' agents and managing agents.
17. **Rights under a funeral plan contract** – ie, certain plans under which the customer pays for benefits which will pay for his (or someone else's) funeral upon their death.
18. **Rights under a regulated mortgage contract*** – ie, mortgage loans secured by first legal mortgages on property, at least 40% of which is to be used for the borrower's, or some related party's, dwelling. This specified investment also includes lifetime mortgages, a type of equity release transaction.
19. **Rights under a home reversion plan*** – another type of equity release transaction, whereby the customer sells part or all of his home to the plan provider in return for a lump sum or series of payments; he retains the right to stay in his home until he dies or moves into residential care.
20. **Rights under a home purchase plan*** – alternatives to mortgages, which allow people to buy their homes while complying with Islamic principles (financing via an interest-bearing mortgage is not permitted under a strict interpretation of these principles).
21. **Rights under a regulated sale and rent-back agreement*** – whereby a person sells all or part of qualifying interest in land/property but remains in occupation of at least 40% of the land/property.
22. **Rights to or interests in other specified investments** – rights in anything that is a specified investment listed, excluding rights in home finance transactions, are themselves a specified investment.

The investments marked * are collectively known as 'home finance transactions'.

1.2.2 Specified Activities

Learning Objective 2.4.1

Know the activities specified in Part II of the Regulated Activities Order

An activity is a regulated activity for the purposes of the FSMA if it is an activity of a specified kind which is carried on by way of business and relates to an investment of a specified kind; or, in the case of an activity of a kind which is also specified for the purposes of this paragraph, is carried on in relation to property of any kind. 'Investment' includes any asset, right or interest, and 'specified' means specified in an order made by the Treasury.

As we have already noted, the RAO defines regulated activities by reference:

- first to the range of specified investments; and
- then to the activities a firm might carry on in relation to those investments.

The specified activities themselves are as follows:

1. **Accepting deposits** – mainly the preserve of banks and building societies, but other firms may find themselves caught under this activity.
2. **Issuing e-money** – ie, acting as the issuer of e-money, as it is described in Section 1.2.1.
3. **Effecting or carrying out contracts of insurance as principal** – this essentially applies to insurers.
4. **Dealing in investments as principal or agent** – this applies only to certain of the specified investments. Dealing is buying, selling, subscribing for or underwriting the investments concerned.
   When the firm deals as principal (ie, on its own account), it applies only to those investments that are:
   - securities – shares, debentures and warrants, or
   - contractually based investments, such as options, futures, CFDs, and life policies.

   When the firm deals as agent (ie, on behalf of someone else), it applies to securities (as for dealing as principal) and relevant investments. Relevant investments include contractually based investments (as for dealing as principal) and additionally rights under pure protection and general insurance contracts.
5. **Arranging deals in investments** – covers:
   - bringing about deals in investments – that is, the involvement of the person is essential to bringing about/concluding the contract, and also
   - making arrangements with a view to transact in investments (which may be quite widely interpreted as any arrangement pursuant to transactions in investments, such as making introductions).

   The arranging activities relate only to specified investments which are:
   - securities (eg, shares, debentures or warrants);
   - relevant investments, eg, options, futures, CFDs and rights under insurance contracts;
   - underwriting capacity of a Lloyd's syndicate or membership of a Lloyd's syndicate; and
   - rights to or interests in any of the above.

   A typical example is a broker making arrangements for its client to enter into a specific insurance contract.
6. **Arranging home finance transactions** – the arranging and making of arrangements in relation to mortgages, home reversion or home purchase plans, and regulated sale and rent-back agreements are captured in the same way as arranging deals in investments.
7. **Operating a multilateral trading facility (MTF) –** this is a particular activity, see Section 1.8, Chapter 1.
8. **Managing investments** – this applies in respect of investments belonging to someone other than the manager, and when the manager exercises discretion over the management of the portfolio. The portfolio must include, or be able to include, securities or contractually based investments. A typical example is a portfolio manager. Non-discretionary management (when the firm does not make the final decision) is not covered under this heading: it is be captured under the separately defined regulated activities of dealing in investments and advising on investments.
9. **Assisting in the administration and performance of a contract of insurance** – this is activity carried on by an intermediary after conclusion of a contract of insurance, eg, loss assessors.
10. **Safeguarding and administering investments** – again, this applies in the context of securities (eg, shares, debentures) and contractually based investments (eg, options, futures, CFDs, qualifying insurance contracts). The firm must be holding the assets for someone else, and it must be both safeguarding and administering the assets to be caught under this heading. A typical example is a custodian bank, which might hold title documents to investments, hold dematerialised investments in its name, and administer the collection of interest/ dividends or the application of corporate actions.

11. **Sending dematerialised instructions** – covers firms which operate systems that allow for the electronic transfer of title in certain investments (again, securities and contractually based investments), and those which cause instructions to be sent on those systems. An example of such a system is CREST.
12. **Establishing, operating and winding up a collective investment scheme** – this activity captures persons who set up, operate/administer and wind up any type of CIS, whether an authorised scheme or an unregulated scheme. Acting as a trustee of an AUT, or as the depository or sole director of an OEIC, are also separate regulated activities.
13. **Establishing, operating and winding up a pension scheme** – captures those who set up, operate/administer and wind up stakeholder pension schemes and SIPPs. These activities may be carried out by the scheme trustees and/or the scheme administrators.
14. **Providing basic advice on stakeholder products** – this is a special regulated activity, for those who advise only on stakeholder products. Stakeholder products conform to certain criteria for cost and accessibility.
15. **Advising on investments** – this covers giving advice on securities and relevant investments. It does not extend to giving advice about deposits, nor to occupational pensions schemes, nor to generic advice (eg, 'invest in the US, not in Europe'). Neither does it extend to giving information – facts, which are not tailored to constitute a recommendation – instead of advice.
16. **Advising on home finance transactions** – advising on the merits of entering into, or varying the terms of, a regulated mortgage, a home reversion plan, a home purchase plan or a regulated sale and rent-back agreement is a regulated activity.
17. **Lloyd's market activities** – in addition to those mentioned above under arranging investments, there are three further Lloyd's-related regulated activities:
    - advising on syndicate participation;
    - managing underwriting capacity as a managing agent;
    - arranging deals in contracts of insurance at Lloyd's.
18. **Entering into a funeral plan contract** – a firm that enters into funeral plan contracts as provider (ie, being the person to whom the pre-payments are made) is conducting a regulated activity.
19. **Entering into and administering home finance transactions** – captures the activity of regulated mortgage lenders, home reversion providers, home purchase providers and regulated sale and rent-back agreement providers.
20. **Dormant account funds** – meeting repayment claims and managing dormant account funds are specified activities.
21. **Agreeing to carry on a specified activity** – is itself a regulated activity (and so a firm should not agree to carry on a regulated activity until it is properly authorised, notwithstanding that it may not intend to actually carry out that activity until it has its authorisation).

Advising, dealing and arranging activities when carried on in connection with a contract of insurance, and the activity of assisting in the administration and performance of a contract of insurance, are collectively known as 'insurance mediation activity' and subject to the provisions of the Insurance Mediation Directive.

Exercise

Have a look at your firm's scope of permission on the FSA's register. Go to ***fsa.gov.uk*** *and follow the links to the FSA Register. In 'Financial Services Firm Search' key in your firm's reference number or name. You can then view the scope of permission and other information about your firm and the approved persons.*

1.3 Exclusions

Learning Objective 2.4.2

Know the main exclusions from the need for authorisation under the FSMA 2000 [Regulated Activities Order]: dealing as principal [PERG 2.8.4]; advice in newspapers [PERG 2.8.12 & 7.1.2]; trustees, nominees and personal representatives [PERG 2.9.3]; employee share schemes [PERG 2.9.13]; overseas persons [PERG 2.9.15]

There are a significant number of exclusions provided in the FSMA; those carrying on regulated activities who fall entirely within the scope of an exclusion can conduct the activity without having to apply to the FSA for authorisation for the activity in question. Some key examples follow.

1.3.1 Exclusions from Dealing as Principal

Absence of Holding Out

Dealing in investments as principal is a regulated activity. This means that persons dealing for themselves in the hope of making profits are required to be authorised or exempt. However, this regulated activity is restricted to those persons who are holding themselves out as and acting as **market makers**, and who regularly solicit the public with the purpose of inducing them to deal. The result is that a wide range of activity is excluded from the regulated activity of dealing as principal.

This means that:

- firms which are professional dealers, such as market makers, and which hold themselves out as such, are carrying on a regulated activity; but
- individuals or companies which are not in the business of dealing in investments, and which invest only for themselves in the hope of making a profit, are excluded.

This exclusion relates to both securities (shares and bonds) and contractually based investments (futures, options and CFDs), as long as they are entered into by an unauthorised person.

Other Exclusions

There are other exclusions where dealing as principal is not classified as a regulated activity:

1. a bank providing finance to another person and accepting an instrument acknowledging the debt;
2. a company or other organisation issuing its own shares, warrants or debentures, or purchasing its own shares in accordance with certain provisions of the Companies Act 1985 (Treasury shares);
3. using options, futures and CFDs for risk management purposes, as long as the company's business is mainly unregulated activities and the sole or main purpose of the deals is to limit identifiable risks;
4. entering into transactions as principal for, or in connection with, the following:
    - while acting as bare trustee (or as nominee in Scotland);
    - the sale of goods or supply of services;
    - between members of a group or joint enterprise;
    - the sale of a body corporate;
    - an employee share scheme;
    - an overseas person;
    - an incoming electronic commerce provider.

1.3.2 Exclusions for Advice in Newspapers

There is a particular exclusion from the regulated activity of advising on investments and on home finance transactions, in relation to newspapers and other media. If a newspaper includes investment advice, and that advice is not the principal purpose of the newspaper, it is excluded from the regulated activity of advising on investments. The existence of 'money' and 'city' pages or subsections within a newspaper does not make the principal purpose of the paper anything other than the provision of news, so there is no need for authorisation.

If the principal purpose of a publication is the provision of investment advice, with a view to encouraging investors or prospective investors to undertake investment activity, authorisation is required. This is the case for periodicals that 'tip' certain investments and are often sold on a subscription basis. They are often referred to as 'tipsheets' and include publications like *Warrants Alert* (which highlights those warrants that offer good value to the investor).

1.3.3 Trustees, Nominees and Personal Representatives

There is an exclusion from the need for authorisation if the person carrying on the regulated activity is:

- acting as the representative of another party;
- not generally holding himself out as carrying on regulated activities; and
- not receiving additional remuneration for providing these investment services.

This exclusion can apply to the following types of regulated activity:

- dealing in investments as principal;
- arranging deals in investments and making arrangements with a view to transactions in investments;
- arranging a home finance transaction;
- managing investments;
- safeguarding and administering investments;
- sending dematerialised instructions;
- advising on investments or advising on a home finance transaction;
- assisting in the administration and performance of a contract of insurance;
- entering into, or administering a home finance transaction.

It is important to note that this exclusion is not available if the person is carrying on, dealing, arranging or advising activity in connection with a contract of insurance.

1.3.4 Employee Share Schemes

In order to encourage companies to set up schemes enabling their employees to hold shares in the company they work for, there are exclusions from the need to be authorised to operate such schemes. The exclusion covers four types of activity:

- dealing in investments as principal;
- dealing in investments as agent;
- arranging deals in investments and making arrangements with a view to transactions in investments; and
- safeguarding and administering investments.

1.3.5 Overseas Persons

There are a number of exclusions for overseas persons carrying on regulated activities, providing that they do not do so from a permanent place of business in the UK. These exclusions apply only if the business is done through an authorised, or exempt, UK person, or if they are the result of a **legitimate approach**, such as a UK client approaching an overseas person in an unsolicited manner.

The exclusions mainly cover the following types of activity:

- dealing in investments as principal;
- dealing in investments as agent;
- arranging deals in investments and making arrangements with a view to transactions in investments;
- arranging a home finance transaction;
- advising on investments;
- agreeing to carry on the regulated activities of managing investments, making arrangements with a view to transactions in

investments, assisting in the performance and administration of a contract of insurance, arranging deals in investments, safeguarding and administering investments or sending dematerialised instructions;
- operating a multilateral trading facility; and
- entering into, or administering a home finance transaction.

2. Exemptions

Learning Objective 2.1.1

Know the regulated and prohibited activities [Parts II/III of FSMA 2000, Regulated Activities Order 2001 and the under-noted guidance in the Perimeter Guidance Manual (PERG)]: authorised persons [PERG 2.2.3]; exempt persons [PERG 2.10] and FSMA Exemption Order 2001 [(SI 2001/1201)]; offences under the Act [PERG 2.2.1/2]; enforceability of agreements entered into with an unauthorised business [PERG 2.2.2]; defences available under the Act [PERG 2.2.1]

As mentioned previously, the FSMA provides for certain persons to be exempt from the general prohibition in the conduct of regulated activity. These exempt persons are summarised below.

2.1 Appointed Representatives

An appointed representative can be any type of person (ie, a natural person or any other legal person) who has entered into a contract with an authorised person (**the principal**) for the purpose of conducting regulated activity. The authorised person becomes the principal and accepts legal responsibility for the regulated activity conducted by the appointed representative. In this way, the appointed representative becomes an exempt person under the FSMA for the conduct of permitted regulated activity.

The FSA rules do not apply to appointed representatives because they are not authorised persons. However, any business conducted by the appointed representative for which the principal has accepted responsibility will be treated as having been conducted by the principal. The principal itself must have the permissions for the activity that is to be carried out by the appointed representative.

Additionally, some persons within the appointed representative firm must be approved for controlled functions, namely, the governors (directors, partners) and individuals who will be performing customer functions (CF30, see Section 5.3).

The FSA expects principals to conduct thorough reviews of the suitability and conduct of their appointed representatives. The exempt status that appointed representatives enjoy (s.39 FSMA and the FSMA (Appointed Representatives) Regulations 2001) comes at the price of ongoing supervision and monitoring by the principal.

The appointed representatives regulations only allow certain regulated activities to be conducted by appointed representatives on an exempt basis. These activities are:

- dealing in investments as agent (pure protection or general insurance contracts only);
- arranging deals in investments and making arrangements with a view to transactions in investments;
- arranging deals in home finance transactions and making arrangements with a view to home finance transactions;
- assisting in the administration and performance of a contract of insurance;
- arranging the safeguarding and administration of assets;
- advising on investments;
- giving basic advice on stakeholder products;
- advising on home finance transactions;
- agreeing to carry on a regulated activity.

In particular, appointed representatives are not permitted to deal in investments as principal or manage investments.

2.2 Recognised Investment Exchanges (RIEs) and Recognised Clearing Houses (RCHs)

Substantial amounts of trading in, and issuance of, securities is conducted through formal exchanges such as the LSE. There are often separate clearing systems connected to these formal exchanges that facilitate the settlement of the trades that take place. The firms operating these systems are referred to as **clearing houses**.

The FSMA gives the FSA the responsibility of recognising, regulating and supervising exchanges and clearing houses.

As we saw in Chapter 1, in order to be recognised by the FSA, these exchanges and clearing houses need to be fit and proper for their purpose. Once recognised, the exchanges are referred to as **recognised investment exchanges** (RIEs) and the clearing houses are referred to as **recognised clearing houses** (RCHs). RIEs and RCHs are exempt persons in that they do not need to seek authorisation from the FSA to do regulated activities – they are, instead, **recognised**.

2.3 FSMA Exemption Order 2001

The Treasury has established certain exemptions from the need to be authorised for particular persons. Some of these exemptions are restricted in that they only apply in certain circumstances.

For example supranational bodies of which the UK or another EEA member state is a member and central banks of the UK or another EEA member state are exempted from the need to be authorised to carry on any regulated activity, apart from effecting or carrying out contracts of insurance. Obvious examples are the Bank of England, the European Investment Bank (EIB) and the International Monetary Fund (IMF).

In contrast, certain bodies are exempted from the need to be authorised for the sole regulated activity of accepting deposits; these include municipal banks, local authorities and charities.

Certain persons are able to perform limited regulated activities without the need to be authorised or exempt. In effect, the general prohibition of the FSMA does not apply to them. Such persons include the members of Lloyd's insurance market and members of certain professional bodies (the DPBs), referred to in Section 1.7, Chapter 1.

2.3.1 Members of Lloyd's

Several activities carried on in connection with business at Lloyd's are regulated activities. These include:

- advising on syndicate participation;
- acting as a managing agent for one or more syndicates; and
- arranging deals in insurance contracts.

However, the FSMA disapplies the general prohibition for members of Lloyd's in relation to contracts of insurance written at Lloyd's. This is further extended to those members that ceased to be an underwriting member at any time on or after 24 December 1996; these former members can carry out insurance contracts underwritten at Lloyd's without the need for authorisation.

The reason why the general prohibition does not apply is because the FSA expects the activities at Lloyd's to be suitably supervised and executed by the Society of Lloyd's, and so additional FSA authorisation of members is unnecessary. The FSA does, however, have certain powers to impose rules on the members (or former members) of Lloyd's if it is felt necessary.

2.3.2 Members of the Professions

As seen in Section 1.7 of Chapter 1, Part XX (20) of the FSMA provides for five professions where individual firms are permitted to carry on particular regulated activities without the need to apply to the FSA. Firms are required to apply to their relevant professional body for permission to conduct these activities. The individual professions are accountants,

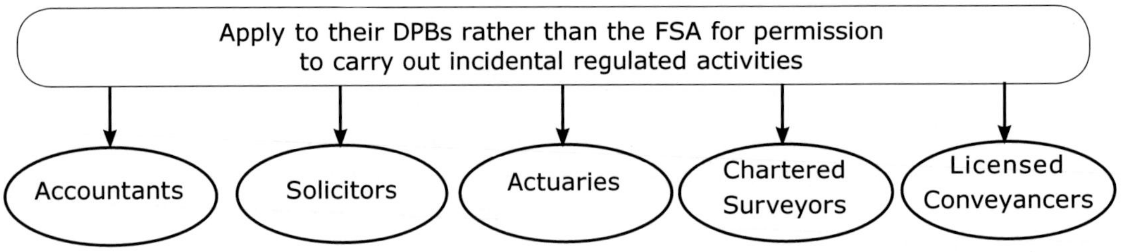

solicitors, actuaries, chartered surveyors and licensed conveyancers.

The professional bodies that are able to grant permissions are known as designated professional bodies (DPBs). They include the Institute of Chartered Accountants in England and Wales (ICAEW), the Law Society, the Institute of Actuaries and the Royal Institution of Chartered Surveyors.

The DPB must operate a set of rules with which its members must comply and the regulated activity must be incidental to the provision of professional services. For example, a firm of accountants providing tax advice might give a client advice as to which investments might best be sold to avoid the accrual of a tax liability.

In order to be able to rely on the Part XX regime, the activities carried out by member firms of DPBs are restricted. For example, such firms are allowed to receive pecuniary reward only from the client (ie, they must return to the client any commissions received from the providers of products held); and certain regulated activities may not be carried out by the members, namely:

1. accepting deposits;
2. dealing in investments as principal (ie, acting as market maker);
3. lending or administering home finance transactions (unless the firm is acting as trustee or personal representative);
4. establishing, operating or winding up a CIS;
5. establishing, operating or winding up a stakeholder pension scheme or a personal pension scheme;
6. acting as stakeholder pension scheme manager;
7. managing the underwriting capacity of a Lloyd's syndicate or advising on syndicate participation;
8. effecting or carrying out contracts of insurance (including Lloyd's business);
9. providing funeral plan contracts.

With regard to the regulated activity of managing investments, the firm may exercise discretion to sell investments but may only purchase investments where the decision is taken, or advice is given, by an authorised person.

Advising on investments can only be done in specified circumstances in order for it to be exempt.

3. Authorisation

Learning Objective 2.4.4

Know the authorisation procedures for firms: the need for authorisation [FSMA s.19, PERG 2.3, Annex 1 & 2, 2.10.9–16]; the threshold conditions for authorisation [FSMA sch.6, COND 2]

Persons wishing to carry on regulated activities in the UK, by way of business, need to be authorised or exempt, unless their activity falls wholly within the scope of one or more exclusions. **By way of business** broadly means holding oneself out as carrying on the activity on a commercial basis.

3.1 The Permissions Regime

The term **authorised person** includes those who have been authorised by the FSA and also other persons such as overseas firms, the

Society of Lloyd's and OEICs. This section looks at those who are authorised by the FSA.

Authorisation provided in this way is through the FSA's powers under Part IV of FSMA so is referred to as a **Part IV permission**. Part IV permission is given by the FSA and, once granted, the firm becomes an authorised person. As an authorised person, the firm can carry on regulated activities without breaching the general prohibition.

We have seen that there is a very wide range of specified investments and activities. The Part IV permission specifies precisely which activities the firm can carry on, the investments those activities may relate to, and any further requirements or special conditions attaching to the permission. For example, the holding or controlling of client money is not, in itself, a regulated activity. However, if a firm does not wish to hold client money the FSA will impose a requirement on the firm's scope of permission that the firm may not hold or control client money.

The activities which a firm is given permission to conduct can be limited. For example, it may be permitted to deal as principal, but only for a particular type of client.

3.2 The Authorisation Process

The applicant completes an application pack, available from the FSA's website. The packs are tailored depending on the type of activity that is to be applied for. The pack requires information on:

- core details – the applicant's legal form, summary details of ownership, accounting year end, organisational structure and IT systems;
- controllers – detailed information about the firm's owners and controllers;
- business supplement – a detailed form covering the business plan, type of activity, anticipated business levels, financial forecasts showing how the applicant will meet capital adequacy tests, details of professional indemnity insurance and compliance procedures;
- disclosure of significant events – if the firm has traded before (perhaps as an appointed representative), this questionnaire must be completed to disclose any trading issues;
- approved persons forms – each person who is to be carrying out a controlled function must send an individual form;
- checklist and declaration – including the application fee – this is £1,500 for straightforward cases (eg, advising and arranging) and £5,000 for moderately complex cases (eg, managing investments); this fee is not refundable in any circumstances.

A case officer is appointed to review the case and obtain further information from the applicant. The case officer prepares a report and this is then signed off by a committee and the applicant is notified that they are an authorised person with effect from a specified date. The FSA has statutory deadlines for determining cases: six months for complete cases and up to 12 months for incomplete cases.

If an authorised firm that was previously unincorporated (eg, sole trader, partnership) decides to incorporate (limited company or limited liability partnership (LLP)), the new entity will require authorisation. In these circumstances, and so long as there are no material changes and the activities are to be the same, the FSA allows a simplified pack to be submitted (change of legal status) with a reduced application fee.

3.3 The Threshold Conditions

In granting Part IV permission, the FSA is required to ensure that the applicant satisfies the minimum standards for being an authorised person. These are the **threshold conditions**, namely:

1. **Legal status** – the FSA broadly accepts individuals, companies, branches of companies, partnerships and unincorporated associations as authorised persons. However, there are some restrictions on the legal form that is acceptable for a firm wishing to undertake certain activities; for

example, an individual or partnership does not meet the criteria for banking deposits or insurance business.

2. **Location of offices** – the FSA requires companies established under UK law to have their head and registered offices in the UK if they are to be authorised. For firms other than companies, the FSMA stipulates that a *non-body corporate with its head office in the UK must carry on business in the UK*.
3. **Appointment of claims representatives** – this is only relevant to motor insurers who must have a claims representative in each EEA state for dealing with claims.
4. **Close links** – the FSA requires that firms applying for authorisation must not have close links which might make it difficult for the FSA to supervise their activities. The term 'close links' extends to controllers who own 20% or more of the applicant, and also other companies within a group structure (eg, a parent company or subsidiaries).
5. **Adequate resources** – the FSA will authorise only firms which have adequate resources. 'Adequate' means sufficient in terms of quantity, quality and availability, and 'resources' includes both financial and non-financial resources – cash, other liquid assets, physical resources and human resources.
6. **Suitability** – the firm is required to prove itself 'fit and proper' to be granted Part IV permission. The fit and proper requirement is considered in the context of all the firm's circumstances; this includes the range and nature of its proposed regulated activities, the need to be satisfied that its affairs are conducted soundly and prudently, and its connections with other persons. The FSA will assess an applicant's fit and proper status in the light of the specific activities it wishes to carry on. Just because an applicant is suitable to carry on one regulated activity, it does not mean that it is suitable to carry on all regulated activities.

4. Supervision

Learning Objective 2.4.5

Know the supervisory process: purpose of FSA's supervision arrangements [SUP 1.1.2/3]; focus on a firm's senior management [SUP 1.1.4, SYSC 1.2.1(1)/4.2.1/4.3.1]; FSA's risk-based approach to regulation – [SUP 1.3.1/2/3/4/5/8]; FSA's tools for supervision [SUP 1.4.1/2/4/5]; FSA's transaction reporting regime [SUP 17.1.4]

Under the FSMA, the FSA is required to maintain arrangements to supervise compliance with the requirements imposed on authorised persons.

The FSA's supervisory approach has to work to these principles to ensure the statutory objectives are met. Equally, there is also the need to ensure that supervision does not impose an unnecessary restriction or burden on firms. In this respect, the FSA also emphasises the role of senior management to organise and control the business for which they are responsible effectively. This includes implementing sound internal risk management systems and making sure that individuals are suitable and competent for the roles they are appointed to carry out. We looked at the main systems and controls requirements in Chapter 1. You may wish to review these in the context of FSA supervision.

The purpose of the FSA's supervision arrangements is to mitigate and manage risks to the statutory objectives. A structured approach is adopted (originally known as ARROW – Advanced Risk-Responsive Operating frameWork), which is designed to:

- **identify the main risks to objectives as they arise** – the FSA uses intelligence from a wide range of sources such as firm visits, enforcement actions, regulatory reporting, transaction monitoring, sector and environmental analysis; and consultation with market participants, consumer and practitioner panels, and the FOS for information on complaints trends;

- **measure the importance of the risk** – score the risk according to the impact on the FSA's objectives (were the risk to crystallise) and the probability of this happening;
- **mitigate the risk** – assess how to respond, having regard to costs and benefits, and the best use of supervisory resources;
- **monitor the progress of the risk** – reports are produced for FSA managers to assess that risks are being managed and that internal controls are adequate.

The FSA uses two basic approaches:

- **the Firms' Approach** – to assess risks in individual firms (the FSA refer to this as **vertical** supervision);
- **the Themes Approach** – to assess risks affecting several firms or markets (**horizontal** supervision).

The FSA assigns risk impact and probability scores to a firm or group of firms, and this determines the approach and the ongoing relationship between the firm and the FSA.

The **impact** of a firm is assessed in accordance with the FSA's regulatory objectives, namely:

- the extent to which **market confidence** would be damaged, should a risk materialise;
- the risks posed by a firm on the **stability of the UK financial system**;
- the effect on **consumers** as a result of prudential failure, misconduct, market malpractice or malfunction or the need to contribute to compensation schemes;
- the effect of **financial crime** perpetrated through or by the firm.

The **probability** of a firm posing a risk is assessed in terms of 'risk groups' within a firm, namely:

- its strategy;
- risks inherent within the firm's business model (eg, credit, market and operational risk);
- financial soundness;
- the nature of the firm's customers, products and services;
- compliance culture, systems and controls;
- governance – the firm's organisation and its capability to mitigate risk.

A risk impact rating is assigned, which governs the FSA's ongoing relationship with the firm.

- **Medium- and high-impact firms** – the FSA assigns a supervisor who carries out specified risk assessments on a cycle of one to four years. High-impact firms are also subject to a planned schedule of FSA visits throughout the regulatory period, for the FSA's supervisory team to work closely with the firm's managers. High-impact firms may also be subject to peer review.
- **Low-impact firms – generally small firms** – do not have specific risk assessments, set risk mitigation programmes or dedicated supervisors and the main point of contact with the FSA is the customer contact centre. However, the FSA recognises that 20,000 small firms could collectively pose risks to their objectives, and hence have developed the 'themes' approach referred to above. This involves analysing the data submitted on quarterly or six-monthly regulatory returns, eg, the GAthering Better Regulatory Information ELectronically (GABRIEL) reports, such as the Retail Mediation Activities Return (RMAR), and if the FSA need to investigate a matter further, it will conduct a series of themed visits and questionnaires. Results will be communicated via the Small Firms pages on the FSA's website, and via themed roadshows.

4.1 Tools of Supervision

The FSA has a range of supervisory tools available to it that it classifies under four headings:

1. **Diagnostic tools** – designed to identify, assess and measure risk such as those described in the impact and probability assessment above.
2. **Monitoring tools** – to track the development of identified risk, wherever this arises.
3. **Preventative tools** – to limit or reduce identified risks and so prevent them crystallising or increasing.
4. **Remedial tools** – to respond to risks when they have crystallised.

Four Supervisory Tools

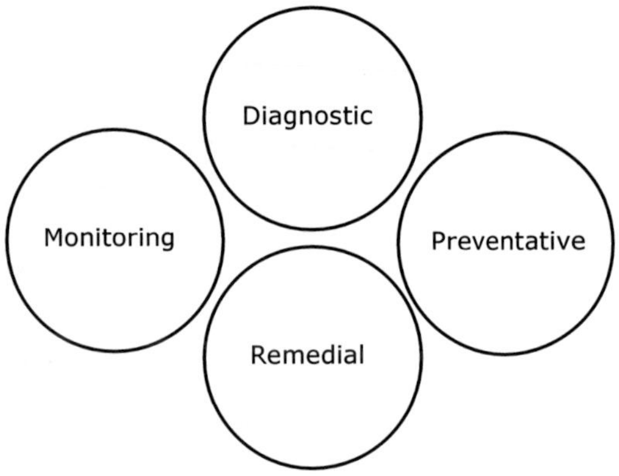

Some tools involve the FSA in a direct client relationship with firms, such as **supervisory visits** by FSA staff. Others do not involve the firms directly; for example, the FSA may make **public statements** to consumers about the risks of particular types of products.

For any given situation, the FSA has to consider which supervisory tools to use.

The FSA also has statutory powers under FSMA 2000 whereby it can impose certain requirements on firms. For example, it can change the scope of a firm's Part IV permission to prevent the conduct of activity that the FSA considers poses risks to its objectives.

The FSA uses a variety of methods for checking whether individual firms remain compliant. These include:

- desk-based reviews;
- liaison with other agencies and regulators;
- meetings with a firm's management;
- on-site inspections;
- analysis of periodic returns and notifications;
- reviews of past business;
- transaction monitoring;
- auditor's reports;
- skilled persons reports – under S.166 of FSMA 2000, the FSA can require a firm to appoint an independent skilled person to conduct a report on an aspect of the firm's business. The FSA defines the scope of the review, but the contract is between the firm and the skilled person.

4.2 Transaction Reporting

Firms that execute transactions in financial instruments or certain over-the-counter (OTC) derivatives are required to report details of the transaction to the FSA through an approved system. This helps the FSA's surveillance of market operations. The report must cover information about the:

- **reporting firm** – unique identification code and the capacity in which the firm dealt (principal or agent);
- **trade** – date, time, buy or sell;
- **instrument(s) as relevant** – identification code, type of instrument, maturity date, derivative details, put or call status;
- **price** – unit price, strike price of an option, price multiplier, price notation (currency);
- **quantity** – number and value of instruments;
- **counterparty**;
- **venue** – where the transaction was executed;
- **customer identification**;
- **other** – as required by the system.

Discretionary portfolio managers that send orders to other firms for execution do not have to make transaction reports themselves so long as they know the firm carrying out the order has to make such reports.

The transaction reporting regime is undergoing changes designed to harmonise transaction reporting across the EU.

5. The Process for Approved Persons

Learning Objective 2.4.6

Know the approval processes for Approved Persons: the application process [SUP 10.12.1/2/3]; the criteria for approval as an Approved Person [FIT 1.3, 2.1, 2.2, 2.3]

Section 59 of the FSMA requires persons fulfilling controlled functions to first be approved by FSA as fit and proper. This is the approved persons regime which we first encountered in Chapter 1. As we saw, approved persons – having been assessed as fit and proper – are also then expected to comply with the FSA's Statement of Principles and Code of Practice for Approved Persons.

5.1 The Approval Process

An individual may be permitted to perform a controlled function only after they have been granted approved person status by the FSA. The candidate completes a Form A and this is notified to the FSA by the firm. The Form A includes a comprehensive list of questions to establish a person's employment history and give the FSA the information it needs to conduct the assessment of fitness and propriety.

In certain circumstances an abbreviated form may be completed, for example if the person is already an approved person executing similar controlled functions.

The amount of time the FSA takes to determine an application varies depending on any additional checks that have to be made.

If adverse information about the candidate comes to light during the determination process, the firm must notify the FSA.

If a person does not wish to proceed with an application, the FSA must be formally notified using a Form B notification.

5.2 The Fit and Proper Test

The FSA may grant an application for approved person status only if it is satisfied that the candidate is a fit and proper person to perform the controlled function stated in the application form. Responsibility lies with the firm making the application to satisfy the FSA that the candidate is fit and proper to perform the controlled function applied for.

During the application process, the FSA may discuss the assessment of the candidate's fitness and propriety with the firm, and may retain notes of such discussions. In making its assessment, the FSA will consider the controlled function to be fulfilled, the activities of the firm and the permission which has been granted to the firm. If any information comes to light that suggests that the individual might not be fit and proper, the FSA will take into account how relevant and important it is.

In assessing the fitness and propriety of a person within the approved persons' regime, the FSA will look at a number of factors against a set of criteria, of which the most important will be the person's:

- honesty, integrity and reputation;
- competence and capability; and
- financial soundness.

The following criteria are among those which will be considered when assessing an individual's fitness and propriety. These are examples of the type of information that the FSA will want; it does not, however, constitute a definitive list of the matters which might be relevant.

5.2.1 Honesty, Integrity and Reputation

The FSA will have regard to whether a person has been:

- convicted of a criminal offence; particular consideration will be given to offences of fraud, dishonesty and financial crime;
- the subject of an adverse finding or settlement in a civil case, again with particular consideration given to cases involving financial businesses and fraud;
- the subject of previous investigation or disciplinary proceedings by the FSA or another regulatory authority;
- the subject of a justified complaint in relation to regulated activities;
- refused a licence to trade, or had a licence or registration revoked;
- involved in an insolvent business; or
- disqualified as a director, or dismissed from a position of trust.

The person must be able to demonstrate a readiness and willingness to comply with the requirements and standards of the regulatory system.

The FSA will treat each application on its merits, considering the seriousness and circumstances of any matters arising, as well as (in some cases) the length of time which has elapsed since the matter arose.

5.2.2 Competence and Capability

In assessing an applicant's competence and capability, the FSA will have particular regard to whether the person:

- satisfies the relevant requirements laid down in the FSA's Training and Competence Sourcebook (TC; covered in Section 6 of this chapter);
- has demonstrated the experience and training needed for them to fulfil the controlled function applied for; and
- has adequate time to perform the controlled function and meet the responsibilities associated with that function.

The FSA will consider previous convictions or dismissals/suspensions from employment for drug or alcohol abuse or other abusive acts only if they relate to the continuing ability of the person to perform the controlled function for which they are to be employed.

5.2.3 Financial Soundness

In assessing an applicant's financial soundness, the FSA will have particular regard to whether the person:

- has been subject to any judgement to repay a debt or pay another award that remains outstanding or was not satisfied within a reasonable period;
- has filed for bankruptcy, been adjudged bankrupt, had his assets sequestrated or made arrangements with his creditors.

The FSA will not normally require a statement of a person's assets and liabilities. The fact that a person may be of limited financial means will not of itself affect his suitability to perform a controlled function.

5.3 Controlled Functions

Learning Objective 2.4.7

Understand the FSA's controlled functions: the five functional areas, the required functions, the four areas of significant influence functions, the requirement for FSA approval prior to performing the function [SUP 10.5.1, 10.6.1, 10.7.1, 10.8.1, 10.9.1/2, 10.10.1/3 and the types of function listed under Table 10.4.5 FSMA s.59]

The FSA has identified five types of controlled functions:

1. **Governing functions** – these are the persons responsible for directing the affairs of the business. If the business is a company, they will be the directors of that company. If the business is a partnership, they will be the partners. It is important to remember, however, that the deciding factor is not just whether the person has the title of director – someone who acts as a director, even if they are not formally registered as such (eg, a 'shadow director') will also require FSA approval because of the influence they exert over the firm.
2. **Required functions** – these are specific functions which the FSA considers to be fundamental to effective control within an authorised firm, as appropriate to the nature of the business. For example, every firm should have appointed someone to fulfil the compliance oversight function and the money laundering reporting functions.
3. **Systems and control functions** – these functions are held by persons responsible for reporting to a firm's governors on its financial affairs, risk exposure and adherence to internal systems and controls.
4. **Significant management function** – this function occurs only in larger firms where there is a layer of management below the governing body which has responsibility for a significant business unit, for example, the head of equities, the head of fixed income and the head of settlements. The function also applies to a firm that conducts proprietary trading.

The above four groups of functions are collectively termed significant influence functions as the persons fulfilling these roles exercise a significant influence over the conduct of a firm's affairs.

5. **Customer function** – this function involves giving advice, dealing, arranging deals and managing investments. The individuals have contact with customers in fulfilling their role. Examples of customer functions are investment adviser or investment manager. The function only extends to activities carried on from a UK establishment.

Customer functions are not significant influence functions.

The table below sets out all the controlled functions.

5.3.1 The Scope of Controlled Functions CF1 and CF2

The scope of CF1 and CF2 extends beyond directors and non-executive directors in the authorised firm itself. Each of these functions also covers individuals within unauthorised parent undertakings or unauthorised holding companies, whose decisions, opinions or actions are regularly taken into account by the governing body of the authorised firm.

5.3.2 The Role of a Non-Executive Director CF2

The FSA considers the role of a non-exec to cover quite specific duties, including but not limited to:

- assisting executive colleagues within the firm's governing body in setting and monitoring the firm strategy;
- providing an independent perspective to the overall running of the business, scrutinising the approach of executive management and the firm's performance and standards of conduct; and
- carrying out other responsibilities as assigned by the board.

Non-executive directors (NEDs) are expected to have significant responsibilities in terms of challenging executive decisions and conduct and so contribute to sound governance of an authorised firm.

Type of function	CF	Description of controlled function
Governing functions*	1	Director function
	2	Non-executive director function
	3	Chief executive function
	4	Partner function
	5	Director of unincorporated association function
	6	Small friendly society function
Required functions*	8	Apportionment and oversight function
	10	Compliance oversight function
	10A	CASS operational oversight function
	11	Money laundering reporting function
	12	Actuarial function
	12A	With-profits actuary function
	12B	Lloyd's actuary function
Systems and control function*	28	Systems and controls function
Significant management function*	29	Significant management function
Customer function	30	Customer function
** significant influence functions*		

The FSA recognises that an influential but non-executive role may also be undertaken by other individuals within a firm, for example, the chairman, or chairman of specific functions. Therefore, a firm must ensure that additional controlled functions are allocated and approval sought if a person's role falls within the scope of one or more of the chairman's functions.

5.3.3 The CASS Oversight Function

The Client Asset Sourcebook (CASS) oversight controlled function (CF10A) applies to firms that hold client money and/or assets (CASS firms). Such firms have been categorised according to the amount of client money/and assets held, and all but the smallest firms must allocate CF10A to a senior person. The role includes general oversight of the firm's compliance with CASS, reporting to the firm's governing body in respect of that oversight and completing and submitting the monthly client money and assets return (CMAR).

5.3.4 Additional Information Pertaining to Approved Persons Applications

In March 2011, the FSA published a note saying that the implementation of the new significant influence functions has been deferred until further notice. The FSA remains committed to all of the proposals in its policy statement (PS 10/15: effective corporate governance – significant influence functions and the Walker Review) and will be pressing ahead with the other changes designed to promote corporate governance within firms and, in particular, those elements aimed at managing risk. The FSA has said that the deferral should not be interpreted as a change of policy on their part. It will ensure firms have two notices of the new implementation date.

6. Training and Competence

Learning Objective 2.4.8

Know the Training and Competence regime: the application of the systems and control responsibilities in relation to the competence of employees [SYSC 3.2.13/14/5.1.1]; the application of T&C for retail activities [TC 1.1.1/3/7]; assessing and maintaining competence [TC 2.1.1(1), 2.1.2]; the examination requirements before starting activities [TC 2.1.6/7(1)]; the firm must assess at the outset and at regular intervals the training needs of its employees [TC 2.1.11]; maintaining competence [TC 2.1.12/13]; activities to which the T&C rules apply [TC Appendix 1]

6.1 Overview

In Chapter 1 we saw that the Principles for Businesses require that firms take reasonable care to *"organise and control their affairs responsibly and effectively"*. To comply with this requirement, they must, clearly, ensure that any employee involved with a regulated activity achieves and maintains the competence needed for this role.

The Principles are built on further in the section of the Handbook dealing with senior management arrangements, systems and controls (SYSC). This stipulates a high-level competence requirement which applies to all UK authorised firms, whereby firms must employ personnel with the skills, knowledge and expertise necessary for the discharge of the responsibilities allocated to them.

Additionally, it is incumbent upon individuals who carry out significant influence functions to make sure that there are policies and procedures in place for reviewing the competence of personnel.

This high-level approach is then supplemented – for firms carrying on activities with or for retail clients – by the Training and Competence (TC) Sourcebook. This Sourcebook became effective on 1 November 2007 to bring the FSA's requirements into line with MiFID, and emphasises the outcomes achieved by firms through their internal training and competence arrangements, as opposed to prescribing how the arrangements should work.

The following activities fall within the scope of the TC Sourcebook, when they are conducted with or for retail clients:

- providing basic advice on stakeholder products;
- advising on/dealing in the following investments – securities*, derivatives*, packaged products, friendly society life policies, friendly society tax-exempt policies, long-term care insurance contracts, corporate finance advice, and advising on Lloyds syndicate participation*;
- acting as broker fund adviser*;
- acting as pension transfer specialist*; managing investments;
- overseeing CISs, safeguarding assets or client money, administrative functions relating to managing investments, administrative functions concerning contracts of insurance, and the operation of stakeholder pension schemes;
- advising on and overseeing various activities concerning regulated mortgages and equity release transactions;
- advising on non-investment contracts of insurance;
- advising on and overseeing regulated sale and rent-back agreements.

Note that, although all the activities involve dealing with retail clients, only those involving advising and dealing in investments require the person to be approved for CF30 Customer Function.

6.2 Assessing Competence

The TC Sourcebook requires that firms do not assess an employee as competent to carry on one of the specified activities until that employee has demonstrated the necessary competence to do so and has (if required) attained an appropriate qualification. The list of appropriate qualifications is an Appendix to the TC Sourcebook and has the status of 'evidential provision'.

For those activities marked with an asterisk in Section 6.1, the individual must have attained the full qualification before commencing the activity, even under supervision.

For the other activities requiring a qualification, as long as the person has attained the regulatory module of a qualification, they may commence the activity under supervision. The exception to this is the overseers' roles, as they may commence the activity under supervision without having attained any aspect of their qualifications.

But the overriding rule is that no-one conducting a specified activity is eligible for assessment as competent until they have attained the full qualification requirement. There is a time limit of 30 months for attaining a qualification – apart from the overseer roles, where this is a suggested time limit but is not mandatory.

If a person doesn't attain a qualification within 30 months they have to cease the activity to which the qualification relates and they may not re-commence the activity until they attain the qualification.

It is ultimately up to the firm to define precisely job roles and standards of competence and to conduct a proper assessment of competence. This may mean that a person has passed the required qualification but is still not deemed competent by the firm.

There is an exemption from the qualification requirements in certain circumstances, to help people who have been based overseas. These conditions are that the firm must be satisfied that the employee:

- has at least three years' up-to-date relevant experience in the activity, which he gained while employed outside the UK;
- has not previously been required to comply fully with the relevant examination requirements; and
- has passed the relevant module of an appropriate examination.

This exemption is not available for those roles (asterisked in Section 6.1) where the person must always attain the full qualification before commencing the activity. It may also not be available to a person who is benefiting from the **30-day rule**. This is a special dispensation for individuals who are largely based overseas and who spend no more than 30 days in the UK under appropriate supervision. In these circumstances, such a person does not have to apply for CF30 customer function.

From 31 December 2012 the **Retail Distribution Review (RDR)** standards of professionalism take effect, for those who advise on retail investment products. Retail investment products are:

- life policies (eg, investment bonds);
- units in regulated or unregulated collective investment schemes;
- stakeholder pension schemes/group stakeholder pension schemes;
- personal pension schemes (SIPPs) and group personal pension schemes;
- interest in investment trust savings schemes;
- security in investment trusts;
- structured capital at risk products;
- any other packaged investment product.

Retail investment advisers must obtain a **Statement of Professional Standing (SPS)** from an accredited body. Accredited bodies are those who have been recognised by the FSA for the purpose of providing independent verification of adviser competence. The following organisations have attained accredited status to date:

- The Chartered Financial Analyst (CFA) Society of the UK;
- The Chartered Insurance Institute (CII);
- The Institute of Financial Planning (IFP);
- The Chartered Institute for Securities and Investments (CISI);
- The Chartered Institute of Bankers in Scotland (CIOBS);
- The ifs School of Finance;
- The Institute of Chartered Accountants in England and Wales (ICAEW);
- The Pensions Management Institute (PMI).

If, by 31 December 2012, a person who was competent at 30 June 2009 has not obtained a SPS, they will be deemed to be non-competent. In order to obtain the SPS the adviser has to attain a higher level of qualification than they already hold. This means either taking top-up qualifications or filling gaps in examination syllabus content through structured and unstructured continuing professional development (CPD).

The other professionalism standards that take effect on 31 December 2012 are:

- **CPD** - competent advisers must complete a minimum of 35 hours' CPD per year, of which 21 must be structured;
- **Annual declaration** – advisers must confirm annually that they have complied with the Statements of Principle for Approved Persons, and have completed the required CPD.
- **Reporting requirements** – firms must send a quarterly report (the Professional Standards Data Submission Form) confirming the qualification status of each retail investment adviser; although no report is required if there are no changes since the previous report.

Firms are also required to notify the FSA if any of the following events occur:

- an adviser who was previously assessed as competent is no longer considered competent;
- an adviser has failed to attain an appropriate qualification within the prescribed time limits;
- an adviser has failed to comply with a Statement of Principle in carrying out his controlled function;

- an adviser has performed one of the specified activities before being assessed as competent, and without appropriate supervision.

6.3 Supervision

Further, firms must not allow an employee to carry on any of those specified activities without appropriate supervision. They are required to ensure that employees are appropriately supervised at all times. The Sourcebook states that the FSA expects that the level and intensity of that supervision will be significantly greater in the period before a firm has assessed its employee as competent than after. Firms should thus have clear criteria and procedures relating to the specific point at which their employees are assessed by them as being competent so as to be able to demonstrate when and why a reduced level of supervision was considered appropriate.

At all stages, firms are required to consider the level of relevant experience that an employee has in determining the level of supervision required.

Firms must ensure that supervisors have the necessary coaching and assessment skills, as well as the technical knowledge associated with the activity, so as to act as competent supervisors and assessors. In particular, firms should consider whether it is appropriate to require the supervisor to have attained an appropriate qualification. This is a mandatory requirement for supervisors of those who advise on retail investment products, who have not yet been assessed as competent.

6.4 Maintaining Competence

Firms are also required to review regularly their employees' competence – and to take appropriate action, where needed, to ensure that they remain competent for their role. In doing so, they should take account of:

- the individual's technical knowledge and its application;
- their skills and expertise; and
- changes in the market and to products, legislation and regulation.

Firms must assess their employees' training needs at the outset, and again at regular intervals (including if their role changes). They should also review the quality and effectiveness of their training.

7. Whistleblowing

Learning Objective 2.4.9

Know the legal and regulatory basis for whistleblowing [SYSC 18.1.2, 18.2.3]

The Public Interest Disclosure Act (PIDA) 1998, which came into force on 2 July 1999, introduced legislation to protect persons from retaliation, if they inform regulatory authorities of concerns that might come to their attention at their place of work; this is generally referred to as 'whistleblowing'. The FSA provides guidance to authorised firms as to how they might want to adopt internal procedures to facilitate whistleblowing as part of an effective risk management system.

PIDA makes any clause or term in an agreement between a worker and his employer void if it precludes the worker from making a 'protected disclosure' (sometimes known as 'blowing the whistle'). A protected disclosure is one, made in good faith, where information is revealed by a worker that shows that one of the following has been, is being, or is likely to be, committed:

- a criminal offence;
- a failure to comply with any legal obligation;
- a miscarriage of justice;
- the putting of the health and safety of an individual in danger;
- damage to the environment;
- deliberate concealment of any of the above.

It is irrelevant whether any of the above occurred in the UK or elsewhere, or whether the law is the law of the UK or any other country.

Firms are encouraged to consider adopting (and encouraged to invite their appointed representatives or, where applicable, their tied agents to consider adopting) appropriate internal procedures which will encourage workers with concerns to blow the whistle internally about matters which are relevant to the functions of the FSA.

Smaller firms may choose not to have as extensive procedures in place as larger firms. For example, smaller firms may not need written procedures. The following is a list of things that larger and smaller firms may want to do.

Appropriate internal procedures for larger firms include:

- a clear statement that the firm takes failures seriously;
- an indication of what is regarded as a failure;
- respect for the confidentiality of workers who raise concerns, if they wish this;
- an assurance that, if a protected disclosure has been made, the firm will take all reasonable steps to ensure that no person under its control engages in victimisation;
- the opportunity to raise concerns outside the line management structure, such as with the compliance director, internal auditor or company secretary;
- penalties for making false and malicious allegations;
- an indication of the proper way in which concerns may be raised outside the firm, if necessary;
- providing access to an external body such as an independent charity for advice;
- making whistleblowing procedures accessible to staff of key contractors.

Appropriate internal procedures for smaller firms include:

- telling workers that the firm takes failures seriously and explaining how wrongdoing affects the organisation;
- telling workers what conduct is regarded as failure;
- telling workers who raise concerns that their confidentiality will be respected, if they wish this;
- making it clear that concerned workers will be supported and protected from reprisals;
- nominating a senior officer as an alternative route to line management and telling workers how they can contact that individual in confidence;
- making it clear that false and malicious allegations will be penalised by the firm;
- telling workers how they can properly blow the whistle outside the firm if necessary;
- providing access to an external body such as an independent charity for advice; and
- encouraging managers to be open to concerns.

Firms should also consider telling workers (through the firm's internal procedures, or by means of an information sheet available from the FSA's website, or by some other means) that they can blow the whistle to the FSA, as the regulator prescribed in respect of financial services and markets matters under PIDA.

8. FSA Enforcement and Decision-Making Process

Learning Objective 2.2.1

Know the role of the FSA's enforcement division, the power of the FSA to make decisions by executive procedures and the role, scope and consequences of the Regulatory Decisions Committee's responsibility for decision making [DEPP 3.1–3.4, 4.1]

The FSA's criteria and procedures for making decisions concerning disciplinary matters are set out in a Handbook module called Decisions, Procedures and Penalties Manual (DEPP). This covers:

- the various statutory notices that the FSA may issue;
- the Regulatory Decisions Committee (RDC);
- settlements, penalties and the power to impose suspension or restrictions;
- the FSA's policy on assisting overseas regulators.

In addition, the FSA's Enforcement Guide (EG), which is in the same block, sets out the FSA's approach to how it exercises the main enforcement powers it has, both under the FSMA and under the Unfair Contract Terms Regulations, and how the FSA operates through the activities of its Enforcement Division.

The FSA reviewed its policy for enforcement and financial penalties in 2009/10 and implemented a tougher approach than formerly.

The FSA's approach to the enforcement of financial penalties supports its ongoing commitment to the principle of credible deterrence and the improvement of standards within firms in relation to market misconduct and their dealings with customers. The FSA created a structured framework, based on the following steps:

- removing profits made from the misconduct;
- setting a figure to reflect the seriousness of the breach;
- considering any aggravating and mitigating factors;
- achieving the appropriate deterrent effect;
- applying any settlement discount.

The settlement discount is designed to provide for earlier redress, protection to consumers and cost savings for both the FSA and the firm involved by allowing the firm to agree the amount of financial penalty and other conditions imposed by the FSA in return for a discount of up to 30%.

8.1 The Regulatory Decisions Committee (RDC)

In the interests of fairness, the FSMA requires that, when it makes decisions about the issue of warning and decision notices, the FSA follows procedures that are *'designed to secure, among other things, that the decision which gives rise to the obligation to give any such notice is taken by a person not directly involved in establishing the evidence on which that decision is based'*.

Thus, rather than allowing the FSA's enforcement team to make the decisions which are implemented in the statutory notices outlined above, these decisions are made by a relatively independent committee: the Regulatory Decisions Committee (RDC).

The RDC is a committee of the FSA's board, and is accountable to that board; however, it is independent to the extent that it is outside the FSA's management structure. Only the chairman is an FSA employee; the rest of the members represent the public interest and are either current or retired practitioners with financial services knowledge and experience, or non-practitioners.

The RDC meets either in its entirety, or as a panel – depending on the issue under review. In either case, the chairman or deputy must be present. The RDC also has its own legal function, so it is not advised on cases by the same legal team that advises the FSA's enforcement team who will have originally brought the case to the RDC.

The RDC has responsibility for statutory decisions, such as to:

- specify a narrower description of a regulated activity than that applied for in a Part IV permission, or to limit Part IV permission in a way which would make a fundamental change;
- refuse an application for Part IV permission, or to cancel an existing Part IV permission;
- refuse an application for approved person status, or withdraw an existing approval;
- make a prohibition order in relation to a person that will prohibit them from gaining approved person status, or to refuse to vary such an order;
- exercise the FSA's powers to impose a financial penalty, make a public statement on the misconduct of an approved person, issue a public censure against an authorised person, or make a restitution order against a person.

If a statutory notice decision is not made by the RDC, it will be made under the **executive procedures** of the FSA. These executive procedures enable the FSA to use statutory powers when individual guidance or voluntary agreement is felt to be inappropriate. A typical example of when these executive procedures might be used is if the FSA had particular concerns and, therefore, required a firm to submit reports, such as those on trading results, customer complaints, or detailing the firm's management accounts.

8.2 FSA Statutory Notices

Learning Objective 2.2.2

Know the outcomes of the FSA's statutory notices [DEPP 1.2], the regulatory enforcement processes: warning, decision, supervisory and final notices [DEPP 2.2 + 2.3] and the firm's right to refer to the tribunal [DEPP 2.3.2/3]

The FSMA gives the FSA the power to issue a variety of notices to authorised firms and/or approved persons, collectively referred to as 'statutory notices'. These are:

- **Warning notices** – give the recipient details about the action the FSA proposes to take and why it proposes to do so. They also give the recipient the right to make representations as to why the FSA should not take this action.
- **Decision notices** – give details of the action that the FSA has decided to take, leaving room for appeal by the recipient.
- **Further decision notices** – may follow the issue of a decision notice if the FSA has agreed with the recipient to take a different action to that proposed in the original decision notice. The FSA can issue a further decision notice only with the consent of the recipient.
- **Notices of discontinuance** – let the recipient know that, if the FSA has previously sent it a warning notice and/or a decision notice, it has decided not to proceed with the relevant action.
- **Final notices** set out the terms of the final action which the FSA has decided to take and the date that it is effective from. They are also – unlike warning and decision notices – published by the FSA on its website.
- **Supervisory notices** – give the recipient details regarding the action the FSA has taken, or proposes to take. A typical supervisory notice might limit a firm's Part IV permission with immediate effect (and hence it would seem reasonable for the FSA to alert the public to the fact that the firm is no longer permitted to carry on certain activities).

8.3 The Regulatory Enforcement Processes

Learning Objective 2.2.2

Know the outcomes of the FSA's statutory notices [DEPP 1.2], the regulatory enforcement processes: warning, decision, supervisory and final notices [DEPP 2.2 + 2.3] and the firm's right to refer to the tribunal [DEPP 2.3.2/3]

Regulatory enforcement measures are one of the ways the FSA can address instances of non-compliance with their requirements. There are three possible forms of formal disciplinary sanction:

1. public statements of misconduct (relating to approved persons, ie, individuals);
2. public censures (relating to authorised persons, ie, firms); and
3. financial penalties (fines).

The imposition of regulatory enforcement measures (such as fines and public statements/ censures) assists the FSA in meeting its statutory objectives.

In addition to these formal measures, you should remember that the FSA can take a lower-key approach if it feels this would be more appropriate. It could, for example:

- issue a private warning, or
- take supervisory action, such as:
  - varying or cancelling the firm's Part IV permissions, or removing its authorisation;
  - withdrawing an individual's approved person status;
  - prohibiting an individual from performing a particular role in relation to a regulated activity.

These might be used if the FSA considers it necessary to take protective or remedial action (rather than disciplinary action), or if a firm's ability to continue to meet its threshold conditions (see Section 3.3), or an individual approved person's fitness and propriety, is called into question.

When the FSA is considering formal discipline against an authorised firm and/or an approved person, it is required by the FSMA to issue one or more notices. These are the statutory notices we looked at in Section 8.2). As we saw, these notices fall into two categories: warnings and decisions.

Warnings are not in themselves disciplinary events, since for an action to be regarded as disciplinary action a decision must have been made – and a warning is just that, no more and no less. Indeed, the decision notices themselves may not be absolutely final – they may be:

- discontinued by the issue of a notice of discontinuance;
- varied with agreement in a further decision notice; or
- simply confirmed in a final decision notice.

8.3.1 Criteria for Disciplinary Action

In determining whether to take regulatory enforcement measures, the FSA will consider the full circumstances which may be relevant to the case. This would include, but not be limited to, the following:

- The nature and seriousness of the suspected breach.
  - Was it deliberate or reckless?
  - Does it reveal serious or systemic weakness of the management systems or internal controls of the firm?
  - How much loss, or risk of loss, was there to consumers and other market users?
- The conduct of the firm after the breach.
  - How quickly, effectively and completely was the breach brought to the attention of the FSA?
  - Has the firm taken remedial steps since the breach was identified? For example, by identifying and compensating consumers who suffered loss, taking disciplinary action against the staff involved, addressing systemic failures and taking action to avoid recurrence of the breach in the future.
- The previous regulatory record of the firm or approved person:
  - Has the FSA (or a previous regulator) taken any previous disciplinary action?

8.3.2 The Measures

1. **Private warnings** – these are issued by the FSA when it has concerns regarding the behaviour of the firm or approved person, but decide it is not appropriate to bring formal disciplinary action. It might include cases of potential (but unproven) market abuse, or where the FSA considered making a prohibition order but decided not to do so.

   In such circumstances, the FSA believes it is helpful to let the recipient know that they came close to disciplinary action and the private warning serves this purpose. The circumstances giving rise to a private warning might include a minor matter (in nature or degree), or where the firm or approved person has taken full and immediate remedial action. The benefit of a private warning is that it avoids the reputational damage that would follow from more public sanctions, such as a fine or public censure.

   The private warning will state that the FSA has had cause for concern but, at present, does not intend to take formal disciplinary action. It will also state that the private warning will form part of the FSA's compliance history and will require the recipient to acknowledge receipt and invite a response.

2. **Variation of permission** – the Part IV permission granted to the firm by the FSA can be varied on the FSA's own initiative. The FSA's powers to vary and cancel a person's Part IV permissions are exercisable in the same circumstances. However, the statutory procedure for the exercise of each power is different and this may determine how the FSA acts in a given case. When it considers how it should deal with a concern about a firm, the FSA will have regard to its regulatory objectives and the range of

regulatory tools that are available to it. It will also have regard to:

1. the responsibilities of a firm's management to deal with concerns about the firm or about the way its business is being or has been run; and
2. the principle that a restriction imposed on a firm should be proportionate to the objectives the FSA is seeking to achieve.

Examples of circumstances in which the FSA will consider varying a firm's Part IV permission because it has serious concerns about a firm, or about the way its business is being or has been conducted, include where:

1. in relation to the grounds for exercising the power under section 45(1)(a) of the Act, the firm appears to be failing, or appears likely to fail, to satisfy the threshold conditions relating to one or more, or all, of its regulated activities, because for instance:

    a. the firm's material and financial resources appear inadequate for the scale or type of regulated activity it is carrying on, for example, where it has failed to maintain professional indemnity insurance or where it is unable to meet its liabilities as they have fallen due; or
    b. the firm appears not to be a fit and proper person to carry on a regulated activity because:
        - it has not conducted its business in compliance with high standards which may include putting itself at risk of being used for the purposes of financial crime or being otherwise involved in such crime;
        - it has not been managed competently and prudently and has not exercised due skill, care, and diligence in carrying on one or more, or all, of its regulated activities;
        - it has breached requirements imposed on it by or under the Act (including the Principles and the rules), eg, in respect of its disclosure or notification requirements, and the breaches are material in number or in individual seriousness;
2. in relation to the grounds for exercising the power under section 45(1)(c), it appears that the interests of consumers are at risk because the firm appears to have breached any of Principles 6 to 10 of the FSA's Principles (see PRIN 2.1.1R) to such an extent that it is desirable that limitations, restrictions, or prohibitions are placed on the firm's regulated activity.

3. **Withdrawal of a firm's authorisation** – the FSA will consider cancelling a firm's Part IV permission in two major circumstances:
    a. where the FSA has very serious concerns about a firm, or the way its business is conducted; or
    b. where a firm's regulated activities have come to an end, but it has not applied for cancellation of its Part IV permission.

    The grounds on which the FSA may exercise its power to cancel an authorised person's permission under section 45 of the Act are the same as the grounds for variation. They are set out in section 45(1) and described in EG 8.1. Examples of the types of circumstances in which the FSA may cancel a firm's Part IV permission include:

    1. non-compliance with a FOS award against the firm;
    2. material non-disclosure in an application for authorisation or approval or material non-notification after authorisation or approval has been granted. The information which is the subject of the non-disclosure or non-notification may also be grounds for cancellation;
    3. failure to have or maintain adequate financial resources, or a failure to comply with regulatory capital requirements;
    4. non-submission of, or provision of false information in, regulatory returns, or repeated failure to submit such returns in a timely fashion;
    5. non-payment of FSA fees or repeated failure to pay FSA fees, except under threat of enforcement action;

6. failure to provide the FSA with valid contact details or failure to maintain the details provided, so that the FSA is unable to communicate with the firm;
7. repeated failures to comply with rules or requirements;
8. a failure to co-operate with the FSA which is of sufficient seriousness that the FSA ceases to be satisfied that the firm is fit and proper, eg, failing without reasonable excuse to:
   a. comply with the material terms of a formal agreement made with the FSA to conclude or avoid disciplinary or other enforcement action; or
   b. provide material information or take remedial action reasonably required by the FSA.

Section 45(2A) of the Act sets out further grounds on which the FSA may cancel the permission of authorised persons which are investment firms.

Depending on the circumstances, the FSA may need to consider whether it should first use its own-initiative powers to vary a firm's Part IV permission before going on to cancel it. Among other circumstances, the FSA may use this power if it considers it needs to take immediate action against a firm because of the urgency and seriousness of the situation.

4. **Withdrawal of approval** – as well as having the power to withdraw authorisation for the firm, the FSA has the power to withdraw the approval of particular individuals which allows them to fulfil controlled functions. The FSA is required to first issue a warning notice to the approved person and the firm, followed by a decision notice. The FSA's decision can be referred to the Tax and Chancery Chamber of the Upper Tribunal (Upper Tribunal) (see Section 8.4).

   The FSA recognises that withdrawing approval will often have a substantial impact on those concerned. When considering withdrawing approval it will take into account the cumulative effect of all relevant matters, including the following:

   - The competence and capability of the individual (embracing qualifications and training). Does he have the necessary skills to carry out the controlled function he is performing?
   - The honesty, integrity and reputation of the individual. Is he open and honest in dealings with consumers, market participants and regulators? Is he complying with his legal and professional obligations?
   - The financial soundness of the individual. Has he been subject to judgment debts or awards which have not been satisfied within a reasonable period?
   - Whether he failed to comply with the Statements of Principle, or was knowingly involved in a contravention of the requirements placed on the firm.
   - The relevance, materiality and length of time since the occurrence of any matters indicating the approved person is not fit and proper.
   - The degree of risk the approved person poses to consumers and the confidence consumers have in the financial system.
   - The previous disciplinary record and compliance history of the approved person.
   - The particular controlled function and nature of the activities undertaken by the approved person.

   The FSA will publicise the final decision notice in relation to the withdrawal of approval, unless this would prejudice the interests of consumers.

5. **Prohibition of individuals** – under Section 56 of the FSMA, the FSA has the right to make a prohibition order against an individual. This order can prohibit the individual from carrying out particular functions, or from being employed by any authorised firm if the FSA considers it necessary for the achievement of their four statutory objectives. The prohibition order may relate just to a single specified regulated activity, or to all regulated activities. It may also relate to the individual's ability to work for a particular class of firms, or to all firms.

Prohibition orders are generally used by the FSA in cases which it sees as more serious than those that merit mere withdrawal of approval, ie, there may be a greater lack of fitness and propriety. The FSA will consider all the factors listed above which could otherwise have resulted in a withdrawal of approval. It will also consider factors such as whether the individual has been convicted of, or dismissed or suspended from employment for, the abuse of drugs or other substances, or has convictions for serious assault. The FSA might feel it appropriate to issue a prohibition order against someone who continues to fulfil a controlled function after approval has been withdrawn.

As with withdrawal of approval, the FSA is required to first issue a warning notice to the approved person and the firm, followed by a decision notice. The FSA decision can be referred to the Tax and Chancery Chamber of the Upper Tribunal (see Section 8.4). Generally it will publicise the final decision notice in relation to the prohibition of an individual.

6. **Public censure and statement of misconduct** – the FSA is empowered under the FSMA to issue a public censure on firms it considers to have contravened a requirement imposed on them by, or under, the Act. For approved persons, FSMA may issue a public statement of misconduct where a person has failed to comply with the Statement of Principles, or has been knowingly involved in a firm's contravention of a requirement imposed on it by, or under, the Act. As with other disciplinary actions, the steps required of the FSA are to:
   - issue a warning notice (including the terms of the statement or censure the FSA is proposing to issue);
   - follow this by a decision notice;
   - subsequently provide the right to go to Upper Tribunal (see Section 8.4).

7. **Financial penalties** – as an alternative to public censures/statements of misconduct, the FSA is able to impose financial penalties on firms contravening requirements imposed on them by, or under, the FSMA, and on approved persons failing to comply with the Statements of Principle, or having been knowingly involved in a firm's contravention of requirements.

The FSA provides guidance as to the criteria used to determine whether to issue public censures/statements (and no fine), rather than impose a financial penalty. It includes the following factors:

- If the firm or person avoided a loss or made a profit from their breach, a financial penalty is more appropriate to prevent the guilty party from benefiting from its/his actions.
- If the breach or misconduct is more serious in nature or degree, a financial penalty is likely to be imposed.
- Admission of guilt, full and immediate co-operation and taking steps to ensure that consumers are fully compensated may lessen the likelihood of financial penalty.
- A poor disciplinary record or compliance history may increase the likelihood of a financial penalty, as a deterrent for the future.
- Whether FSA guidance has been followed by the firm.

As is usual for disciplinary matters, there will be a warning notice, decision notice and final decision notice and ordinarily the final decision will be made public by the FSA issuing a press release. However, in circumstances where it would be unfair on the person, or prejudicial to the interests of consumers, the FSA may choose not to issue a press release.

When the FSA publishes a notice of financial penalty on their website, it also publishes the rationale for the decision and the specific rules that were breached. Holders of significant influence functions should regularly review the notices to keep themselves informed of the FSA's approach and to help them mitigate against similar failings in their own firm.

8.4 The Upper Tribunal (Tax and Chancery)

Learning Objective 2.2.2

Know the outcomes of the FSA's statutory notices [DEPP 1.2], the regulatory enforcement processes: warning, decision, supervisory and final notices [DEPP 2.2 + 2.3] and the firm's right to refer to the tribunal [DEPP 2.3.2/3]

As has been noted previously, any person who receives a decision notice (including a supervisory notice) has the right to refer the FSA's decision to the Upper Tribunal. The individual or firm has 28 days in which to do so, and during this period the FSA cannot take the action it has proposed; it must give the person or firm the full 28 days to decide whether to refer the decision.

The Upper Tribunal is independent of the FSA and is appointed by the Government's Ministry of Justice (formerly the Department of Constitutional Affairs).

The Upper Tribunal will involve a full rehearing of the case and will determine on the basis of all available evidence whether the FSA's decision was appropriate. The rehearing may include evidence that was not available to the FSA at the time.

The Upper Tribunal's decision is binding on the FSA. While the Upper Tribunal has generally not overturned many of the FSA's decisions to date (indeed, it would be worrying if it had!), it has been known to do so – an important factor in demonstrating that it is independent in its decision-making and prepared to challenge the FSA where it sees fit.

It is possible for a firm or individual to appeal a decision of the Upper Tribunal itself (but only on a point of law: for this, permission is needed either from the Upper Tribunal itself or from the Court of Appeal).

See also Chapter 1, Section 7.6.

8.5 Financial Services Act 2010 – New Enforcement Powers

The Financial Services Act 2010 provided the FSA with additional enforcement powers, which are:

- short-selling disclosure rule-making power and the power to impose financial penalties on those who breach short-selling rules;
- power to suspend firms and individuals;
- power to impose financial penalties on individuals who have carried out controlled functions without approval;
- financial stability information-gathering power.

The FSA only intends to use the 'suspension power' if it considers that the imposition of a suspension will be a more effective and persuasive deterrent than the imposition of a financial penalty alone.

The non-approved persons power enables the FSA to impose a financial penalty on a person. Currently FSMA only permits the FSA to prohibit a person from working in the industry.

9. Information Required by the FSA

Learning Objective 2.3.1

Know the FSA's power to require information and to appoint persons to carry out investigations [FSMA 2000 s.165/7/8]

Under Section 165 of the FSMA, the FSA is given wide-ranging powers to require information. These powers extend to authorised persons, persons connected with authorised persons, RIEs and RCHs.

Essentially, the FSA is able to give written notice to an authorised person requiring information and/or documents to be provided within a reasonable period. Indeed, FSA staff (such as supervisors) are able to require documents and/or information without delay. This requirement applies only to information and documents reasonably required in connection with the exercise by the FSA of functions conferred on it by or under this Act.

Section 167 of the FSMA gives the FSA further information-gathering powers:

- It requires authorised firms (and certain persons connected with such firms) to appoint one or more competent persons to provide the FSA with a report on any matter about which the FSA has required or could require the provision of information under Section 167. The nature of that/those competent person/persons will depend on the issue being investigated – they are often solicitors or accountants. The purpose of the appointment by the FSA of a competent person/persons to carry out general investigations is to identify the nature, conduct or state of business of an authorised person or an appointed representative; a particular aspect of that business or the ownership or control of an authorised person (firm).

Section 168 of the FSMA permits the FSA to appoint competent persons (one or more) to carry out investigations on its behalf in particular cases, such as:

- if a person may be guilty of an offence under Sections 177/191 (offences) or 398(1) (misleading the FSA);
- if an offence has been committed under Section 24(1) (false claim to be authorised or exempt); or misleading statements and practices;
- if there may have been a breach of the general prohibition of regulated activities, market abuse may have taken place and there may have been a contravention of Sections 21 or 238 of the Act (Restrictions on Financial Promotions).

In addition, the FSA may undertake the appointment of a person to carry out investigations in particular cases where it appears to them that someone:

- may be carrying out authorised activities when they are not authorised to do so (s.20 of the FSMA);
- may be guilty of an offence under prescribed regulations relating to money laundering;
- may have contravened a rule made by the FSA;
- may not be a fit and proper person to perform functions in relation to a regulated activity carried on by an authorised or exempt person;
- may have performed or agreed to perform a function in breach of a prohibition order;

or if:

- an authorised or exempt person may have failed to comply with a prohibition order (s.56(6));
- a person for whom the FSA has given approval under s.59 (approval for particular arrangements) may not be a fit and proper person to perform the function to which that approval relates or a person may be guilty of misconduct for the purposes of s.66 (disciplinary powers).

10. Misleading Statements and Practices

Learning Objective 2.5.1

Know the purpose, provisions, offences and defences of FSMA s.397 (1)(2)(3)(4)(5) – misleading statements and practices

10.1 The Offences

Section 397 of FSMA makes it a criminal offence to make false, deceptive or misleading statements to induce another person to enter into an agreement relating to regulated activity and specified investments. The purpose of s.397 is to prevent the actions of investors being driven by reckless, misleading, deceptive or false actions of others; the overall aim is, therefore, to protect the integrity of the market.

For an offence to occur the offending behaviour must take place within the UK, or have an effect within the UK.

The sanctions are serious – a person found guilty of a s.397 offence is liable to:

- six months' imprisonment and/or a maximum fine of £5,000 if the matter is tried in a magistrate's court;
- seven years' imprisonment and/or an unlimited fine if the matter is so serious that it is tried in a Crown court.

The offences are where a person:

- makes a misleading, false or deceptive statement, promise or forecast;
- dishonestly conceals material facts in connection with a statement, promise or forecast made by him; or otherwise;
- recklessly makes (dishonestly or otherwise) a statement, promise or forecast which is misleading, false or deceptive.

There has to be intention, ie, the behaviour is done in order to induce another person to enter into a **relevant agreement** (ie, an agreement relating to regulated activity and specified investments) or exercise or refrain from exercising any rights conferred by specified investments.

Article 3 specifically creates an offence relating to the market or the price or value of investments, again where the behaviour is done with the intention of inducing a person to take action such as buying, selling, subscribing for or underwriting, exercising rights or refrain from doing any of these actions.

Example

A stockbroker might tell a potential investor that the shares in XYZ Plc (a property developer) are very cheap because XYZ has just won a major contract to build a shopping centre in central London. If the award of the contract to XYZ was false, the FSA could bring a criminal prosecution on the stockbroker under s.397 for making a false and misleading statement to persuade their client to purchase shares.

Example

A firm of fund managers might let the market know that it is very keen to buy substantial quantities of shares in ABC Plc, when actually they hold a smaller quantity of shares in ABC that they plan to sell. The fund manager's expressions of interest in buying ABC shares might mislead participants in the market to pay more money for the shares in ABC that the fund manager anonymously sells. The fund manager is guilty of misleading the market under s.397.

10.2 Defences

The potential defences to a charge under s.397 are:

- The person reasonably believed that his conduct would not create an impression that was false or misleading.
- The person was acting in conformity with the **price stabilisation rules** of the FSA. These allow market participants, such as investment banks, to support the price of a new issue of securities for their clients, with the aim of preventing the market from being excessively volatile. The rules themselves require certain disclosures to investors considering investing in the stabilised securities and restrict the support operation to a particular period.
- The person was acting in conformity with the **control of information** rules of the FSA. These rules relate to statements, actions or forecasts being made on the basis of limited information. The remainder of the information may be known to the firm, but it rests behind so-called Chinese walls, and is not known to the relevant individual.
- The person was acting in conformity with certain **EU provisions** with regards to stabilising financial instruments.

End of Chapter Questions

Think of an answer for each question and refer to the appropriate section for confirmation.

1. Is a bank deposit a specified investment as defined in the Regulated Activities Order?

   Answer Reference: Section 1.2.1

   ....

   ....

   ....

2. Would a firm that accepts deposits from customers need to be regulated and authorised by the FSA to carry out this activity?

   Answer Reference: Section 1.2.2

   ....

   ....

   ....

3. Is a market maker required to be regulated and authorised by the FSA when carrying on such activity for a firm?

   Answer Reference: Section 1.3

   ....

   ....

   ....

4. State three exclusions relating to regulated activity.

   Answer Reference: Section 1.3

   ....

   ....

   ....

5. How are appointed representatives exempt from the requirement to be regulated and authorised by the FSA?

   Answer Reference: Section 2.1

   ....

   ....

   ....

6. Name two types of exempt person under FSMA Exemption Order 2001.

   Answer Reference: Section 2.3

   ....

   ....

   ....

7. What are the threshold conditions for being granted Part IV permission?

   Answer Reference: Section 3.3

   ....

   ....

   ....

8. What is the purpose of the FSA's supervision arrangements?

   Answer Reference: Section 4

   ....

   ....

   ....

9. What factors are taken into account when assessing an individual as fit and proper for approval?

   Answer Reference: Section 5.2

   ....

   ....

   ....

10. State the five types of controlled function.

    Answer Reference: Section 5.3

    ....

    ....

    ....

11. Which type of firm must comply with the Training and Competence Sourcebook?

    Answer Reference: Section 6.1

    ....

    ....

    ....

12. True or false; a person who advises on derivatives may do so under supervision so long as they have passed a regulatory module?

    Answer Reference: Section 6.1

    ....

    ....

    ....

13. What is a Statement of Professional Standing?

    Answer Reference: Section 6.2

    ....

    ....

    ....

14. What are the qualification requirements for supervisors?

    Answer Reference: Section 6.3

    ....

    ....

    ....

15. Which act provides the legal basis for the protection of whistleblowers?

    Answer Reference: Section 7

    ....

    ....

    ....

16. What are the responsibilities of the RDC?

    Answer Reference: Section 8.1

    ....

    ....

    ....

17. What are the different types of statutory notices that the FSA can issue and what are their outcomes?

    Answer Reference: Section 8.2

    ....

    ....

    ....

18. What is the aim of a private warning made by the FSA to a firm?

    Answer Reference: Section 8.3.2

    ....

    ....

    ....

19. What does Section 165 of the FSMA permit the FSA to do?

    Answer Reference: Section 9

    ....

    ....

    ....

20. What is the offence under the FSMA Section 397 and what are the potential defences available?

Answer Reference: Section 10

....

....

....

3

Associated Legislation and Regulation

This syllabus area will provide approximately 12 of the 50 examination questions

CISI
CHARTERED INSTITUTE FOR SECURITIES & INVESTMENT

Associated Legislation and Regulation

1. Insider Dealing

1.1 Introduction

When a director of, or someone otherwise linked to, a listed company buys or sells shares in that company there is a possibility that they are committing a criminal act – insider dealing.

This would be the case, for example, if that director or other linked person bought in the knowledge that the company's last six months of trade were better than the market expected (and that information is price-sensitive and had not yet been made publicly available).

The person buying the shares has the benefit of this information because he is an 'insider' in the company. Under the Criminal Justice Act 1993 (CJA) this is a criminal act, punishable by a fine and/or a jail term.

1.2 Inside Information and the Insider

Learning Objective 3.1.1

Understand the meaning of 'inside information' and 'insider'; the offences and the instruments covered by the legislation [CJA 1993 s.52/56/57/58 + Schedule 2]

To be found guilty of insider dealing, a person must commit one of three specific offences; to do this, he must be an insider in possession of inside information.

The CJA defines both of these terms, as well as the offences that may be carried out.

Inside information is information which:

- relates to particular securities or to one or more particular issuers (ie, it is not so wide as to apply to securities or issuers of securities generally). It could, however, include information about the particular market or sector the issuer is active in;
- is specific or precise;
- has not been made public; and
- is price-sensitive (ie, if it were made public, it would be likely to have a significant effect on the price of any securities).

Some of these criteria may seem quite subjective; for example, what is 'specific' or 'precise'? In practice the meaning will be determined by the courts when cases come before them.

The CJA does give some assistance in interpretation, however; for example, it includes a (non-exhaustive) list of what **made public** means (from which we can work out when information has not been made public). For example, information becomes 'public' when it is:

- published in accordance with the rules of a regulated market to inform investors, eg, a UK-listed company publishing price-sensitive news through the LSE's Regulatory News Service (RNS); or
- contained within records open to the public (eg, a new shareholding that is reflected in the company's register of shareholders); or
- it can be readily acquired by those likely to deal in securities to which the information relates, or securities of an issuer to which it relates.

This tells us that it need not be actually published – it just needs to be available to someone who **exercises diligence or expertise** in finding it (ie, you might have to look quite hard for it). It may also be regarded as made public even if it has to be paid for.

Inside information Is often referred to as **unpublished price-sensitive information**, and the securities which may be affected by it are referred to as **price-affected securities**.

A person in possession of price-sensitive information is an insider if he knows that it is inside information and that it has been knowingly acquired from an **inside source**. He has obtained it from an inside source if he has got it:

- **because he is an inside source** himself (by being a director, employee or shareholder of an issuer of securities; and this need not necessarily be the company whose securities are the subject of the insider dealing); or
- **because he has access to the information by virtue of his employment, office or profession** (and, again, this need not necessarily be in relation to the company to which the information relates). An example might be the auditor, legal adviser or corporate finance adviser to a company; or
- **directly or indirectly from a person who obtained it in one of these two ways.** For example, a director's husband or wife will have information from an inside source if s/he sees confidential information at home about a takeover bid and then buys shares in the listed company which is the takeover target.

1.3 The Offences

Learning Objective 3.1.1

Understand the meaning of 'inside information' and 'insider'; the offences and the instruments covered by the legislation [CJA 1993 s.52/56/57/58 + Schedule 2]

Someone commits the offence of insider dealing if they:

- deal in price-affected securities when in possession of inside information;
- encourage someone else to deal in price-affected securities when in possession of inside information; or
- disclose inside information, otherwise than in the proper performance of their employment, office or profession.

For a deal (ie, an acquisition or a disposal of price-affected securities) to be caught under the insider dealing legislation, it must take place on a regulated market, or through a professional intermediary – otherwise, the legislation does not apply to it.

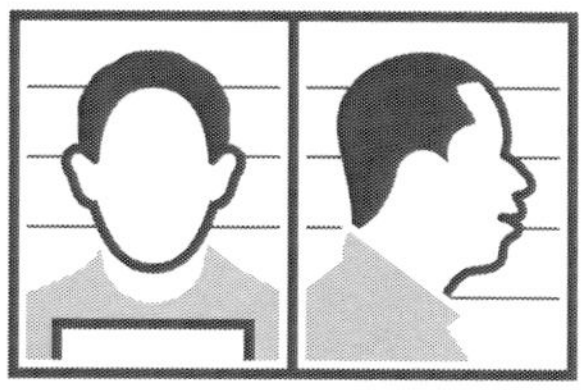

These offences can be committed only by an individual (and, of course, only then by someone holding inside information as an insider); a company cannot commit the offence. However, by arranging for a company to deal, an individual could commit the offence of 'encouraging' it to do so.

The offence of encouraging someone to deal need not result in an actual deal for the offence to have been committed (though it may be unlikely that the offence will come to light if no deal results).

1.4 The Instruments

Learning Objective 3.1.1

Understand the meaning of 'inside information' and 'insider'; the offences and the instruments covered by the legislation [CJA 1993 s.52/56/57/58 + Schedule 2]

Only certain investment instruments are caught under the insider dealing legislation; they are, for the purposes of the CJA, those described as 'securities' (note, you may find the term 'securities' defined differently in different legislation).

For the purpose of the CJA and insider dealing, securities are:

- shares;
- debt securities (issued by a company or a public sector body);
- warrants;
- depositary receipts;
- options (to acquire or dispose of securities);
- futures (to acquire or dispose of securities); and
- contracts for difference (CFDs) based on securities, interest rates or share indices.

You will see that this definition of securities does not embrace:

- commodities, and derivatives on commodities such as options and futures on agricultural products, metals or energy products;
- foreign exchange, and derivatives on foreign exchange, such as forward foreign exchange contracts. This is because these will not be price-sensitive or be affected in the same way as individual securities. The reason is that the price of the fund is determined by the prices of the underlying investments held;
- units or shares in open-ended collective investment schemes (CISs).

1.5 General Defences

Learning Objective 3.1.2

Know the general defences available with regard to insider dealing [CJA 1993 s.53]

The defences available to the defendant in an insider dealing case are as follows:

For the offence of **insider dealing**, or of **encouraging another to deal**, the defences are:

- the defendant did not expect the dealing to result in a profit (or avoid a loss) due to the information; or
- he believed, on reasonable grounds, the information had been sufficiently widely disclosed to ensure none of those taking part in the dealing would be prejudiced by not having the information; or
- he would have acted in the same way regardless of being in possession of the information.

For the offence of **disclosing only**, the defences are:

- he did not expect any person to deal; or
- although he may have expected a person to deal, he did not expect the dealing to result in a profit (or avoid a loss) due to the information.

1.6 Special Defences

Learning Objective 3.1.3

Know the special defences: market makers acting in good faith, market information and price stabilisation [CJA 1993 s.53 and Schedule 1 paras 1–5]

There are further defences available to defendants in particular circumstances ('special' defences). These are for market makers, in relation to market information and to price stabilisation activities.

1.6.1 Market Makers

As long as a market maker can show that he acted in good faith in the course of his business as a market maker, he will not be deemed guilty of insider dealing or encouraging another to deal. So, a market maker (or his employee) could have unpublished price-sensitive information as an insider and continue to make a market in that security.

A further defence is available if the market maker shows he was acting in connection with an acquisition or disposal where the price was under negotiation, and he acted in order to facilitate the deal. He would have to show that the information was market information arising directly out of the negotiations.

1.6.2 Market Information

Market information includes information such as the fact that the sale of a block of securities is under consideration, or the price at which such a transaction is likely to be done.

An insider is not guilty of dealing or encouraging others to deal if he can prove that the information he held was market information, and it was reasonable for him to act as he did despite having the information as an insider at the time. Whether or not the action was reasonable depends on:

- the content of the information;
- the circumstances in which he first had the information and in what capacity;
- the capacity in which he now acts.

A further defence is where a person can show that his dealing or encouragement of another person was in connection with an acquisition or disposal that was the subject of negotiation, and with a view to facilitating the acquisition or disposal; and that the market information in his possession arose directly out of the acquisition or disposal.

Example

A client had been discussing the possibility of purchasing a block of 10,000 shares in XYZ Plc with their broker. The client instructs the broker to buy. Clearly, the broker has the unpublished price-sensitive information that the buy order exists before he deals. However, this is market information and is a specific defence against a charge of insider dealing.

The defence would apply equally if it was market information relating to a client's planned disposal of securities.

1.6.3 Price Stabilisation

The FSA has a set of rules that allow the stabilisation of a security's price after a new issue in order to prevent too much volatility. These are known as the 'price stabilisation rules' and they provide a 'safe harbour' (see Chapter 1, Section 8.3) for a number of activities, including insider dealing. As long as a person can show that they are acting in conformity with these rules, they are not deemed to have undertaken insider dealing. The rules can be found in Chapter 2 of the FSA's Market Conduct Sourcebook (MAR).

1.7 FSA Prosecution Powers

Learning Objective 3.1.4

Know the FSA's powers to prosecute insider dealing [FSMA s.402, EG 12.7–10]

The FSA has been given the powers by the FSMA to prosecute certain criminal offences. In particular, it is able to institute proceedings for an offence, under Part V of the CJA, of insider dealing.

In deciding whether to bring a criminal prosecution under the CJA, the FSA uses the same principles as the Code for Crown Prosecutors. If the following aspects are present, the FSA may consider that a criminal prosecution is appropriate:

- the conduct is so serious that it would lead to a significant sentence;
- there are victims who have suffered significant and substantial loss;
- the misconduct has severely damaged markets or confidence;
- substantial profits have been achieved (or substantial loss avoided);
- grounds for believing the misconduct may be repeated;
- the person has a relevant history, whether criminal, civil or regulatory;
- the likelihood that prosecution may result in an effective remedy for the victims;
- lack of co-operation with the FSA in taking corrective measures;
- dishonesty or abuse of authority or trust is present;
- the person took a leading role in group activity (if relevant).

However, the importance of any of these factors will vary from case to case and the FSA will also have regard to the individual's circumstances. The FSA also has wide powers under the market abuse regime (see Section 2) and will not start a prosecution if it intends to bring disciplinary proceedings for the same misconduct.

2. Market Abuse

2.1 The Statutory Offence

Learning Objective 3.2.1

Understand the statutory offence of market abuse [FSMA 2000 s.118(1–8)]

Market abuse is a serious offence that damages investor confidence and the integrity of financial markets.

The **Market Abuse Directive (MAD)** was introduced to create a regime to tackle market manipulation in the EU and legislate for the proper disclosure of information to the market. It also aimed to update the then EU insider dealing legislation. MAD defines and prohibits market abuse and provides for a number of preventive measures such as prompt disclosure of inside information and management transactions or safeguards of impartiality of investment research.

The UK's own market abuse (an offence under the FSMA) regime came into force on 30 November 2001. However, the new regulations introduced by the directive came into effect on 1 July 2005. This required the FSA to make amendments to relevant rules such as the market conduct, UK listing rules and the price stabilisation rules.

Market abuse relates to 'behaviour' by a person, or a group of persons working together, which occurs in relation to **qualifying investments** on a **prescribed market** that satisfies one or more of the following three conditions. The behaviour as it is currently defined is:

1. based on information that is not generally available to those using the market and, if it were available, it would have an impact on the price; and
2. likely to give a false or misleading impression of the supply, demand or value of the investments concerned; and
3. likely to distort the market in the investments.

In all three cases, the behaviour is judged on the basis of what a **regular user** of the market would view as a failure to observe the standards of behaviour normally expected in the market.

The Treasury has determined the **qualifying investments** and **prescribed markets** – broadly, they are the investments traded on any of the UK's RIEs, investments where application has been made for trading on such markets, and related investments such as derivatives.

The behaviour will amount to market abuse as long as it relates to these investments, regardless of where it takes place. There is some overlap with the insider dealing legislation under the CJA, but:

- the CJA provides for a criminal regime, whereas the FSMA market abuse regime provides for civil penalties and, consequently, a lower required standard of proof; and
- the CJA insider dealing regime applies to a more restricted range of investments, whereas the FSMA market abuse regime extends its insider dealing provision to other markets, such as commodity and energy.

2.2 The FSA Code of Market Conduct

Learning Objective 3.2.2

Know the status of the FSA's Code of Market Conduct [FSMA 2000 s.119(1)-(3)]; the territorial scope of the legislation and regulation [FSMA s.118]

Learning Objective 3.2.3

Know the offences outlined in the Code of Market Conduct [MAR 1.2.2/7, 1.3.1, 1.4.1, 1.5.1, 1.6.1, 1.7.1, 1.8.1, 1.9.1, 1.2.22]

The FSA is tasked under FSMA s.118 to prepare and issue a code containing such provisions as they consider will give appropriate guidance to those determining whether or not behaviour amounts to market abuse. This is called the **'Code of Market Conduct'** and forms part of the FSA's Handbook. The FSA must have regard to European directives when formulating such guidance.

The Code provides guidance on what does and does not amount to market abuse and the factors which are taken into account in the determination of whether market abuse has occurred.

The territorial scope of FSMA s.118 is such that it only extends to the behaviour of market abuse undertaken in the UK or in relation to qualifying investments traded on any of the UK's Regulated Investment Exchanges (RIEs) which are either situated in the UK or which are accessible electronically in the UK.

The Code includes aspects of insider dealing as well as expanding on behaviours that constitute market abuse.

2.2.1 Code of Market Conduct Offences

The FSA's Code of Market Conduct Sourcebook explains the types of behaviour caught by the Market Abuse regime. They extend to seven circumstances:

1. **Insider dealing** – where an insider deals in, or attempts to deal in, a qualifying investment or a related investment on the basis of inside information. For market abuse purposes, an insider has inside information:
    a. as a result of his membership of the administrative, management or supervisory bodies of the issuer of the investment;
    b. as a result of his holding in the capital of the issuer of the investment;
    c. as a result of having access to the information through his employment, profession or duties;
    d. as a result of criminal activities; or
    e. which he has obtained by other means and which he knows, or could reasonably be expected to know, is inside information.
2. **Improper disclosure** – where an insider discloses inside information to another person otherwise than in the proper course of the exercise of his employment, profession or duties.

3. **Misuse of information** – where behaviour is not covered by 1 above (insider dealing) or 2 above (improper disclosure) but is based on information that is not generally available to those using the market and which a regular user would regard as relevant and a failure to observe the standard of behaviour reasonably expected.
4. **Manipulating transactions** – where the behaviour consists of effecting transactions or orders to trade that are not for legitimate reasons and in conformity with accepted practices on the relevant market, and which:
   a. give, or are likely to give, a false or misleading impression as to the supply or demand for, or the price of, the qualifying investment; or
   b. secure the price of such investments at an abnormal or artificial level.
5. **Manipulating devices** – behaviour that consists of effecting transactions or orders to trade which employ fictitious devices or any other form of deception or contrivance.
6. **Dissemination** – where the behaviour consists of the dissemination of information by any means which gives, or is likely to give, a false or misleading impression as to a qualifying investment by a person who knew, or could reasonably be expected to have known, that the information was false or misleading.
7. **Misleading behaviour and distortion** – where behaviour which is not covered by 4 above (manipulating transactions), 5 above (manipulating devices) or 6 above (dissemination):
   a. is likely to give a regular user a false or misleading impression as to the supply of, demand for, or price or value of, a qualifying investment: or
   b. would be regarded by a regular user as behaviour likely to distort the market in such investments.

In both circumstances, the regular user must view the behaviour as a failure to observe the standard of behaviour reasonably expected of a person in his position in relation to the market.

The practical examples given below for each of the seven circumstances are drawn from the FSA factsheet *'Why market abuse could cost you money'* published in June 2008.

Examples of Market Conduct Offences

Circumstances 1 and 2 – Insider Dealing and Improper Disclosure

An employee finds out that his company is about to become the target of a takeover bid. Before the information is made public, he buys shares in his company because he knows a takeover bid may be imminent. He then discloses the information to a friend. This behaviour creates an unfair marketplace because the person who sold the shares to the employee might not have done so if he had known of the potential takeover. The employee's friend also has this information and could profit unfairly from it.

Circumstance 3 – Misuse of Information

An employee learns that his company may lose a significant contract with its main customer. The employee then sells his shares, based on his assessment that it is reasonably certain the contract will be lost. This behaviour creates an unfair marketplace, as the person buying the shares from the employee might not have done so had he been aware of the information about the potential loss of the contract.

Circumstance 4 – Manipulating Transactions

A person buys a large number of a particular share near the end of the day, aiming to drive the stock price higher to improve the performance of their investment. The market price is pushed to an artificial level and investors get a false impression of the price of those shares and the value of any portfolio or fund that holds the stock. This could lead to people making the wrong investment decisions.

Circumstance 5 – Manipulating Devices

A person buys shares and then spreads misleading information with a view to increasing the price. This could give investors a false impression of the price of a share and lead them to make the wrong investment decisions.

Circumstance 6 – Dissemination

A person uses an internet bulletin board or chat room to post information about the takeover of a company. The person knows the information to be false or misleading. This could artificially raise or reduce the price of a share and lead to people making the wrong investment decisions.

Circumstance 7 – Distortion and Misleading Behaviour

An empty cargo ship that is used to transport a particular commodity is moved. This could create a false impression of changes in the supply of, or demand for, that commodity or the related futures contract. It could also artificially change the price of that commodity or the futures contract, and lead to people making the wrong investment decisions.

2.3 The Regular User

Learning Objective 3.2.4

Know the concept of effect rather than intention [MAR 1.2.3]; the concept of a reasonable regular user [MAR 1.2.20/21] and accepted market practices [MAR 1 Annex 2]

Whether or not behaviour amounts to market abuse does not require there to be an element of intention. Rather, it depends on how a hypothetical reasonable person (the regular user), familiar with the market in question, would view the behaviour. If a regular user would feel that the behaviour falls below the standards expected on the market in question, it will be market abuse.

In assessing whether the behaviour falls below the standards expected, the following will be considered:

- The characteristics of the market, the investments traded there and the users of that market.
- The rules and regulations of the market in question and any applicable laws (eg, if the behaviour occurred overseas, compliance with the law overseas will be a consideration).
- The prevailing market mechanisms, practices and codes of conduct applicable to the market in question.
- The standards reasonably expected of the person in the light of their level of skill and knowledge (eg, the standards expected of a retail investor may differ from those expected of an institutional investor).
- The need for market users to conduct their affairs in a manner that does not compromise the fair and efficient operation of the market as a whole, or damage the interests of investors.

It is not essential for the person responsible for the behaviour in question to have intended to commit market abuse, although the regular user test may determine that market abuse has not occurred unless the intention of the person was to engage in market abuse.

2.3.1 Accepted Market Practices

The FSA will take the following non-exhaustive factors into account when assessing whether to accept a particular market practice:

- The level of transparency of the relevant market practice to the whole market.
- The need to safeguard the operation of market forces and the proper interplay of the forces of supply and demand (taking into account the impact of the relevant market practice against the main market parameters, such as the specific market conditions before carrying out the relevant market practice, the weighted average price of a single session or the daily closing price).
- The degree to which the relevant market practice has an impact on market liquidity and efficiency.
- The degree to which the relevant practice takes into account the trading mechanism of the relevant market and enables market participants to react properly and in a timely manner to the new market situation created by that practice.
- The risk inherent in the relevant practice for the integrity of, directly or indirectly, related markets, whether regulated or not, in the relevant financial instrument within the whole EEA.

- The outcome of any investigation of the relevant market practice by any competent authority or other authority mentioned in Article 12(1) of MAD; in particular, whether the relevant market practice breached rules or regulations designed to prevent market abuse, or codes of conduct, be it on the market in question or on directly or indirectly related markets within the EEA.
- The structural characteristics of the relevant market, including whether it is regulated or not, the types of financial instruments traded and the type of market participants, including the extent of retail investors' participation in the relevant market.

2.4 Penalties

Learning Objective 3.2.5

Understand the enforcement regime for market abuse [MAR 1.1.4/5/6] and a firm's duty to report suspicious transactions [SUP 15.10.2]

The FSMA gives the FSA the power to impose a penalty, or to make a statement that a person has engaged in market abuse. These powers can be exercised if the FSA is satisfied that a person has engaged in market abuse, or if the person has taken (or refrained from taking) any action which required or encouraged another party to engage in behaviour that would amount to market abuse.

The penalties available to the FSA are essentially those outlined in Chapter 2 (ie, they are the sanctions that the FSMA empowers the FSA to use). They include:

- withdrawal of approval or authorisation;
- imposing an unlimited civil fine;
- making a public statement that a person has engaged in market abuse;
- applying to the court for an injunction to restrain threatened or continued market abuse, an injunction requiring a person to take steps to remedy market abuse or a freezing order;
- applying to the court for a restitution order; and
- requiring the payment of compensation to victims of the abuse.

However, if there are reasonable grounds for the person to believe that the behaviour in question did not amount to market abuse, or the person had taken all reasonable precautions and exercised all due diligence to avoid engaging in market abuse, the FSA cannot impose a penalty.

2.5 Reporting of Suspicions

Learning Objectives 3.2.5

Understand the enforcement regime for market abuse [MAR 1.1.4/5/6] and a firm's duty to report suspicious transactions (SUP 15.10.2)

The Supervision Manual (SUP) states that FSA-authorised investment firms and credit institutions, which arrange or execute a transaction with or for a client in a qualifying investment, and which have **'reasonable grounds'** to suspect that the transaction might constitute market abuse, must notify the FSA without delay. Qualifying investments are those admitted to trading on a prescribed market (SUP 15.10.2R).

Strictly, this obligation extends only to executed transactions and not to unexecuted orders – but a firm may voluntarily bring a suspicious order to trade to the FSA's attention. The provisions require that firms decide on a case-by-case basis whether there are reasonable grounds for suspecting that a transaction involves market abuse, taking into account the circumstances. Further, Principle 11 of the Principles for Businesses requires that a firm discloses to the FSA everything of which the FSA would reasonably expect notice, and many firms (or rather their employees) would interpret this as giving them grounds to report unexpected transactions as well.

2.6 Safe Harbours

Learning Objective 3.2.6

Know the statutory exceptions (safe harbours) to market abuse: [MAR 1.10.1–4 (excl. table 1.10.5)]

There are certain safe harbours against a charge of market abuse. Safe harbours outline situations where the behaviour in question is categorically not deemed to be market abuse.

1. **FSA rules** – some FSA rules make specific reference to the fact that behaviour conforming to the rules does not amount to market abuse. Therefore, people acting in accordance with these rules will not be deemed to be engaging in market abuse. They are:
   - the rules relating to Chinese walls (covered in more detail in the SYSC Sourcebook); and
   - the disclosure rules relating to the timing, dissemination or availability, content and standard of care applicable to the announcement, communication and release of information for listed companies.
2. **Takeover Code** – during the course of a takeover, both the predator company and its target have to comply with certain rules laid down in the Takeover Code. There are no rules in the Takeover Code that permit or require a person to behave in a way that amounts to market abuse. Specifically, as long as any announcements or the release of information conforms with the timing, dissemination and availability required by the rules of the Takeover Code, is expressly permitted or required by such rules and conforms with the Takeover Code's relevant general principle, it will not amount to market abuse.
3. **Price stabilisation and buy-backs** – price-support activities carried out in accordance with the price stabilisation rules will not amount to market abuse (you should remember that this was also the case with insider dealing; see Section 1.6.3).

2.7 Relationship with Other Legislation

Learning Objective 3.2.7

Understand the distinction between offences under market abuse, insider dealing [CJA] and under FSMA 2000 s.397

The first two behaviour types that are potentially market abuse, namely misleading (and the misuse of information) and behaviour which is likely to give a false or misleading impression of the supply, demand or value of the investments concerned, are, to an extent, already covered by the legislation relating to insider dealing (CJA, see Section 1) and the legislation relating to misleading statements and practices in Section 397 of FSMA (see Chapter 2, Section 10).

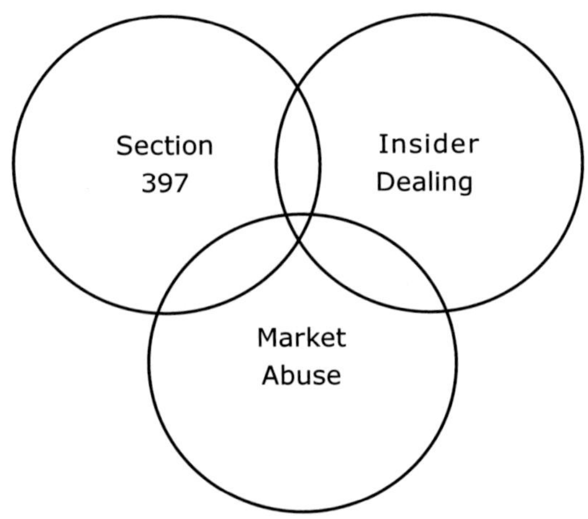

As we have already noted, the FSMA market abuse regime is designed to complement the criminal regime for insider dealing and misleading statements and practices. There will be cases where a possible breach of both the criminal law, as well as the market abuse regime, occurs and the FSA is required to assess whether it has sufficient evidence, and whether it is in the public interest, to commence criminal proceedings rather than impose sanctions for market abuse. The FSA has stated that it is its policy not to impose a sanction for market abuse if a person is being prosecuted for insider dealing or misleading statements and practices. Similarly, it will not commence criminal proceedings if it has brought, or is seeking to bring, disciplinary proceedings for market abuse.

2.7.1 Regulatory Developments

The following notes are for information only and will not be examined.

In October 2011 the European Commission (EC) published proposals for new criminal sanctions for insider dealing and market abuse. The new regulations will replace MAD, and will have a direct impact on member states, which means that there will be no need for national implementing legislation. The new regime may apply from 2014.

In summary, the proposals:

- extend the scope of the existing Directive to include multilateral trading facilities (MTFs), organised trading facilities (OTFs), financial instruments traded over-the-counter (OTC), spot commodity markets and emission allowances;
- amend the definition of inside information to include reference to specified instruments such as emission allowances and spot commodity contracts, and to introduce information that a reasonable investor would regard as relevant;
- include behaviours such as cancelling and amending orders, where the information used is inside information; attempted market abuse and attempted insider dealing;
- prohibit certain manipulative trading strategies (such as spoofing and quote stuffing);
- require controls for the prevention and detection of market abuse, including protection for whistleblowers;
- revise and extend disclosure requirements;
- require co-operation and co-ordination between the competent authorities in member states;
- specify heavy administrative sanctions, such as fines of up to 10% of annual turnover on firms, and up to €5,000,000 on individuals; and criminal sanctions, where insider dealing or market manipulation is intentional.

3. Money Laundering

Learning Objective 3.3.1

Understand the terms money laundering, criminal conduct and criminal property and the application of money laundering to all crimes [Proceeds of Crime Act 2002 s.340] and the power of the Secretary of State to determine what is 'relevant criminal conduct'

Learning Objective 3.3.2

Understand that the UK legislation on money laundering is found in the Proceeds of Crime Act 2002 (POCA), as amended by the Serious Organised Crime and Police Act 2005 (SOCPA), the Money Laundering Regulations 2007, the FSA Senior Management Arrangements, Systems and Controls Sourcebook [SYSC] and that guidance to these provisions is found in the Joint Money Laundering Steering Group guidance and understand the interaction between them

3.1 Introduction

Money laundering is the process of turning 'dirty' money (money derived from criminal activities) into money which appears to be from legitimate origins. Dirty money is difficult to invest or spend, and carries the risk of being used as evidence of the initial crime. Laundered money can more easily be invested and spent without risk of incrimination.

Increasingly, anti-money laundering provisions are being seen as the frontline against drug dealing, organised crime and the financing of terrorism. Much police activity is directed towards making the disposal of criminal assets more difficult and monitoring the movement of money.

The current rules and regulations in relation to money laundering come from a variety of sources:

- **The Proceeds of Crime Act (POCA) 2002** – POCA 2002 is widely drafted. It specifies that money laundering relates to criminal property – that is, any benefit (money or otherwise) that has arisen from criminal conduct. Property is criminal property only if the alleged offender knows or suspects it is criminal property. The broad requirement is for firms to report suspicions of money laundering to the authorities.
- **The Serious Organised Crime and Police Act (SOCPA) 2005** – this Act amended certain sections of POCA. In particular, one feature of POCA was that 'criminal conduct' was deemed to include anything which would have been an offence had it been done in the UK, regardless of where it had actually happened. This resulted in the often-cited 'Spanish bullfighter' problem. Bullfighting is illegal in the UK, but not in Spain, meaning that, arguably, a financial institution should regard deposits made by a Spanish bullfighter as the proceeds of crime, even if they represented his legitimate earnings in Spain. SOCPA addresses this difficulty – in part at least – in that there is a defence for alleged offenders if they can show that they know, or believe on reasonable grounds, that the conduct was not criminal in the country where it happened. However, the Secretary of State has reserved the right to prescribe certain offences as 'relevant criminal conduct' that might be legal where they occurred but would be illegal in the UK and still need to be reported. For example, the government may specify serious tax evasion or drug cultivation as types of criminal conduct which do need to be reported, despite occurring overseas.
- **The Money Laundering Regulations (ML Regs)** – these are relatively detailed regulations, implemented as the result of EU directives, which deal predominantly with the administrative provisions that firms need to have to combat money laundering. For example, they deal with firms' requirements for systems and training to prevent money laundering and their obligations to check the identity of new customers. The most recent version was issued in 2007.
- **The FSA Senior Management Arrangements, Systems and Controls (SYSC) Sourcebook** – this provides high-level rules and guidance for authorised firms in formulating their anti-money laundering policies and controls. However, the FSA no longer provides rules for procedures but rather refers firms to the Joint Money Laundering Steering Group (JMLSG) guidance.
- **The Joint Money Laundering Steering Group (JMLSG) guidance** – this is provided by a combination of UK trade associations including the British Bankers' Association (BBA), the Council of Mortgage Lenders (CML) and the Association of British Insurers (ABI). Guidance is provided to firms on how they should interpret and implement anti-money laundering provisions. They are not mandatory but do highlight industry best practice and provide procedural guidance for firms to follow. They are also approved by the Treasury, which means that if a firm can show that it adhered to them, the courts will take this into account as evidence of compliance with the legislation.

3.2 The Stages of Money Laundering

Learning Objective 3.3.4

Understand the three stages of money laundering

There are three stages to a successful money laundering operation.

1. **Placement** – introduction of the money into the financial system; typically, this involves placing the criminally derived cash into a bank or building society account, a bureau de change or any other type of enterprise which can accept cash, such as, for example, a casino.
2. **Layering** – involves moving the money around in order to make it difficult for the authorities to link the placed funds with the ultimate beneficiary of the money. This might involve buying and selling foreign currencies, shares or bonds in rapid succession, investing in CISs, insurance-based investment products or moving the money from one country to another.
3. **Integration** – at this final stage, the layering has been successful and the ultimate beneficiary appears to be holding legitimate funds (clean money rather than dirty money). The money is regarded as integrated into the legitimate financial system.

Broadly, the anti-money laundering provisions are aimed at identifying customers and reporting suspicions at the placement and layering stages, and keeping adequate records which should prevent the integration stage being reached.

3.3 The Offences

3.3.1 Money Laundering Regulations 2007

Learning Objective 3.3.3

Understand the main offence set out in the Money Laundering Regulations (internal controls), which includes obligations on firms for adequate training of individuals on money laundering

The Money Laundering Regulations 2007 impose obligations on a wide range of businesses – from financial services firms to casinos – to apply customer due diligence when establishing a business relationship or carry-out transactions. If there is any suspicion of money laundering or terrorist finance or doubt about the veracity of the customer's identity, the firm has to take action.

The obligations can be summarised as:

1. **Administrative** – carry out certain identification procedures, implement certain internal reporting procedures for suspicions and keep records in relation to anti-money laundering and terrorist financing activities.
2. **Training** – adequately train staff in the law relating to money laundering and terrorist financing, and how to recognise and deal with suspicious transactions.
3. **Preventative** – ensure the establishment of internal controls appropriate to identify and prevent money laundering and terrorist financing. This is a catch-all requirement.

It is an offence, liable to a maximum jail term of two years and an unlimited fine, for firms to fail to comply with the Money Laundering Regulations. It is a defence for a person to show that he took all reasonable steps and exercised due diligence to avoid committing the offence. This means that the court may consider whether the firm followed the relevant guidance at the time.

3.3.2 Proceeds of Crime Act (POCA) 2002

Learning Objective 3.3.5

Understand the main offences set out in POCA Part 7 Sections 327, 328, 329, 330, 333A, 342 (Assistance ie, concealing, arrangements, acquisition, use and possession; failure to disclose; tipping off) in the regulated sector and the implications of Part 7 regarding the objective test in relation to reporting suspicious transactions; that appropriate disclosure [internal for staff and to the Serious Organised Crime Agency (SOCA) for the firm] is a defence

The Proceeds of Crime Act (POCA) 2002 establishes five offences:

1. **Concealing (s.327)** – it is an offence for a person to conceal or disguise criminal property.
2. **Arrangements (s.328)** – that is, being 'concerned in' an arrangement which the person knows, or suspects, facilitates the acquisition, retention, use or control of criminal property for another person. Being concerned in an arrangement may be widely interpreted – it could include a person working within a financial organisation giving advice on a transaction, for example.
3. **Acquisition, use and possession (s.329)** – acquiring, using or having possession of criminal property. The person must know or suspect that the property arose out of criminal conduct.

These offences are punishable by a fine and a jail term of up to 14 years.

4. **Failure to disclose (s.330)** – there is a duty on employees in the regulated sector to make reports if they know or suspect that another person is engaged in money laundering or terrorist financing activity. It is an offence for employees to fail to disclose such information. Three conditions need to be satisfied for this offence:
   a. the person knows or suspects (or has reasonable grounds to know or suspect) that another person is committing an offence;
   b. the information giving rise to the knowledge or suspicion came to them during the course of business in a regulated sector (such as the financial services sector); and
   c. the person does not make the required disclosure to a nominated officer (NO), such as the firm's money laundering reporting officer (MLRO), as soon as is practicable.

These offences are punishable by a fine and a jail term of up to five years.

5. **Tipping off (s.333A)** – this is a particular offence applying only to persons in working in the regulated sector, and it involves disclosing a suspicious activity report or investigation. It is committed if a person knows or suspects that by disclosing the information this is likely to prejudice the investigation, and the information came to them in the course of business in the regulated sector. It is possible to commit this offence even if you do not know that a report has actually been made.

These offences are punishable by a fine and a jail term of up to five years.

As further detailed below, a person has a defence against the first three offences (concealing, arrangements, and acquisition, use and possession) if they make the required disclosure to the MLRO or, if the person was the MLRO, to the Serious Organised Crime Agency (SOCA).

The offence of failure to disclose suspicions of money laundering may be committed, not only when the person knows or suspects money laundering, but also when there are reasonable grounds to know or suspect money laundering (even if the person did not know or suspect it). The test as to whether there are reasonable grounds is called the **'objective test'**; whether a **reasonable person** would have known or been suspicious, even though the offender protests their innocence.

Part 7 of POCA concerns investigations, and s.342 describes the offence of prejudicing investigations, which applies generally, that is not only to those working in the regulated sector. A person commits this offence if they:

- make a disclosure that is likely to prejudice an investigation; or
- falsify, conceal, destroy or otherwise dispose of documents relevant to an investigation, or permit such falsification.

The offence is not committed if:

- the person did not know or suspect that the disclosure would prejudice an investigation;
- the disclosure was made in the performance of a duty under POCA or other similar enactment;
- the person is a legal adviser acting in his professional capacity in advising his client or in contemplation of legal proceedings (apart from where the disclosure is made with the purpose of furthering a criminal purpose);
- the person did not know or suspect that documents were relevant to the investigation;
- the person did not intend to conceal from an investigator any facts disclosed by the documents.

These offences are punishable by a fine and a jail term of up to five years.

3.4 Systems and Controls in Relation to Money Laundering

3.4.1 The FSA's Requirements

Learning Objective 3.3.6

Understand the approach adopted by the FSA as covered by the Senior Management Arrangements, Systems and Controls Sourcebook [SYSC], in particular, the systems and controls that the FSA expects firms to have adopted, the role of the Money Laundering Reporting Officer, Nominated Officer and the Compliance function [SYSC 3.2.6, 3.2.6 (A)–(J), 3.2.7, 3.2.8, SYSC 6.3]

The FSA's expectations for investment firms concerning financial crime systems and controls are set out in SYSC 6.3. In summary, the requirements are that firms establish and maintain effective systems and controls for compliance with the various requirements and standards under the regulatory system and for countering the risk that the firm might be used to further financial crime. The provisions are principles-based as opposed to prescribing detail as to how firms must do this, and it is up to firms to implement arrangements that are proportionate to the nature, scale and complexity of the business.

Firms are required to ensure that their systems and controls enable them to identify, assess, monitor and manage **money laundering risk**. They must carry out regular assessments of the adequacy of these systems and controls.

Money laundering risk is the risk that a firm may be used to launder dirty money. Failure by a firm to manage this risk effectively will increase the risk to society of crime and terrorism. When considering whether a breach of its rules on systems and controls against money laundering has occurred, the FSA will look to see if the firm has followed relevant provisions in the guidance for the UK financial sector provided by the JMLSG.

In identifying its money laundering risk, and in establishing its systems and controls, a firm should consider a range of factors, including:

- its customer, product and activity profiles;
- its distribution channels;
- the complexity and volume of its transactions;
- its processes and systems; and
- its operating environment.

A firm should ensure that the systems and controls include appropriate:

- training for its employees in relation to money laundering;
- provision of information to its governing body and senior management, including a report at

least annually by the firm's MLRO (see below) on the operation and effectiveness of those systems and controls;
- documentation of its risk management policies and risk profile in relation to money laundering;
- measures to ensure that money laundering risk is taken into account in its day-to-day operation and also with the development of new products, the taking on of new customers, and changes in its business profile; and
- measures to ensure that new client identification procedures do not unreasonably deny access to persons who may not be able to produced detailed evidence of identity.

Each authorised firm must give a director or senior manager (who may also be the MLRO) overall responsibility for the establishment and maintenance of effective anti-money laundering systems and controls.

A firm must also appoint an MLRO, who is responsible for receiving and assessing internal suspicion reports, and determining – after a proper investigation – whether to report them on to SOCA. Acting as MLRO is a controlled function (CF11) and so the individual holding this role is subject to the approved persons' regime. The firm must ensure that its MLRO has an appropriate level of authority and independence within the firm and access to resources and information sufficient to enable them to carry out their responsibilities. The MLRO acts as a central point for all activity within the firm relating to anti-money laundering and should be based in the UK.

Depending on the nature, scale and complexity of its business, it may be appropriate for a firm to have a separate compliance function. This function may be heavily involved in monitoring the firm's compliance with its anti-money laundering procedures. The organisation and responsibilities of a compliance function should be documented. A compliance function should be staffed by an appropriate number of competent staff who are sufficiently independent to perform their duties. It should be adequately resourced and should have unrestricted access to the firm's relevant records.

3.4.2 The Joint Money Laundering Steering Group (JMLSG) Requirements

Learning Objective 3.3.7

Understand the standards expected by the JMLSG Guidance particularly in relation to: risk-based approach; requirements for directors and senior managers to be responsible for money laundering precautions; need for risk assessment; need for enhanced due diligence in relation to politically exposed persons (JMLSG 5.5.1–5.5.29); need for high level policy statement; detailed procedures implementing the firm's risk-based approach [JMLSG 1.20, 1.27, 1.40–1.43, 4.17–4.18]; financial sanctions regime [JMLSG Part III 4.1–4.10]

As mentioned in Section 3.1, the primary source of procedural guidance for firms is the JMLSG Guidance Notes. The JMLSG notes are in three parts:

- **Part I** is general guidance applicable to all types of firms in the financial sector. This part also explains the international context and the UK legislative framework.
- **Part II** is sectoral guidance where each chapter is specific to a particular type of firm, such as retail banking, wealth management, execution-only stockbrokers, wholesale markets, and so on.
- **Part III** is specialist guidance, for example relating to electronic payments (wire transfers); this section also contains the UK financial sanctions regime.

The JMLSG approach is essentially risk-based that is, firms must identify the risks that their own business faces in conducting financial transactions, and then implement arrangements and controls to mitigate against the risk that the firm will be used for financial crime.

In 2009, the JMLSG issued revised guidance notes setting out how authorised firms should manage their risk in terms of money laundering and terrorist financing. The revised notes reflected the changes introduced under the

Money Laundering Regulations 2007, which were, in summary:

- some new or revised definitions, including to beneficial owners of businesses and trusts, and politically exposed persons (PEPs);
- expansion of the guidance on customer due diligence measures to be applied in various circumstances, and how to operate a risk-based approach;
- an explanation of the extent to which reliance may be placed on the customer due diligence work of other regulated firms;
- the setting out of situations where simplified customer due diligence measures may be applied;
- guidance for when enhanced due diligence must be applied in higher-risk situations, eg, with individuals who are PEPs, on the basis that these people may be more vulnerable or susceptible to corruption; in non-face-to-face situations, and in connection with correspondent banking.

Politically Exposed Persons (PEPs)

A 'politically exposed person' is defined in the JMLSG guidance as *"an individual who is or has, at any time in the preceding year, been entrusted with prominent public functions and an immediate family member, or a known close associate, of such a person"*.

This is only if the person holds such office outside the UK, or in an EC institution or other international body. For example:

- heads of state, heads of government, ministers and deputy or assistant ministers;
- members of parliaments;
- members of supreme courts, constitutional courts or other high-level judicial bodies whose decisions are not normally subject to further appeal;
- members of courts of auditors or on the boards of central banks;
- ambassadors, chargés d'affaires and high-ranking officers in the armed forces;
- members of administrative, management or supervisor boards of state-owned enterprises.

However, it does not normally include middle-ranking or junior officials, although firms must apply a risk-based approach and take enhanced measures if the person's political exposure places them on a basis similar to national level.

Immediate family members are spouses, partners, children and their spouses or partners, and parents. Close associates include someone who is known to have joint beneficial ownership of a legal entity or other arrangement, or any other close business relationship with a PEP, and extends to a person who has sole beneficial ownership of a legal entity or arrangement known to have been set up for the benefit of a PEP. Enhanced due diligence is required because a PEP or connected person may be vulnerable to corruption, and so this makes them a higher money laundering risk than the norm. PEP enhanced due diligence involves procedures for:

- determining whether or not a person is a PEP or is connected to a PEP – note that firms only need to have regard to information that is in their possession or publicly known to establish the connection;
- obtaining senior management approval for establishing a business relationship with the person;
- establishing the source of wealth and source of funds; and
- conducting enhanced monitoring of the business relationship.

These procedures are not prescribed; it is up to firms to make their own arrangements, having regard to the scale and complexity of the firm's activity. The JMLSG guidance suggests that firms use internet search engines, published reports and databases such as the Transparency International Corruption Perceptions Index, which ranks around 150 countries in order of perceived corruption.

Although technically a person ceases to be a PEP after one year, firms are encouraged to continue enhanced due diligence and monitoring and to take a risk-based approach in deciding whether the higher risks associated with the person's position have abated to allow normal procedures to be applied. Different types of due diligence are covered in Section 3.4.3.

Senior Management Responsibilities and Policy Statement

Senior management of FSA-regulated firms must appoint an appropriately qualified senior member of staff who will have overall responsibility for the maintenance of the firm's anti-money laundering systems and controls.

Firms must also have an anti-money laundering policy statement in place. This provides a framework to the firm and its staff and must identify named individuals and functions responsible for implementing particular aspects of the policy. The policy must also set out how senior management undertakes its assessment of the money laundering and terrorist financing risks the firm faces and how these risks are to be managed.

The firm's policy statement might include such matters as:

- **Guiding principles:**
  1. customers' identities need to be satisfactorily verified before the firm accepts them;
  2. a commitment to the firm 'knowing its customers' appropriately – both at acceptance and throughout the business relationship – through taking appropriate steps to verify a customer's identity and business;
  3. staff will need adequate training and need to be made aware of the law and their obligations;
  4. recognition of the importance of staff reporting promptly their suspicions internally.
- **Risk mitigation approach:**
  1. a summary of the firm's approach to assessing and managing its money laundering and terrorist financing risk;
  2. allocation of responsibilities to specific persons and functions;
  3. a summary of the firm's procedures for carrying out appropriate identification and monitoring checks on the basis of their risk-based approach; and
  4. a summary of the appropriate monitoring arrangements in place to ensure that the firm's policies and procedures are being carried out.

The Sanctions Regime

An important aspect of the JMLSG guidance concerns the UK **financial sanctions** regime. Sanctions can take the form of any restrictive or coercive measure on another state, business or individual, including trade embargoes. When an embargo is in place this means that the firm must not do business with the state, entity or business in question. The sanctions regime requires absolute compliance – which means that firms need to keep fully updated with the latest sanctions lists and have robust arrangements in place to prevent business being conducted in breach of the sanctions regime. Anyone guilty of an offence in breach of the sanctions regime may be imprisoned and/or fined.

The responsibility for the UK sanctions regime lies with:

- HM Treasury;
- the Foreign and Commonwealth Office; and
- the UK Department for Business Innovation and Skills.

HM Treasury regularly publishes consolidated lists: www.hm-treasury.gov.uk/fin_sanctions_index.htm.

3.4.3 JMLSG Guidance on Know Your Customer

Learning Objective 3.3.8

Understand the money laundering aspects of know your customer (Joint Money Laundering Steering Group's Guidance for the Financial Sector [Para 5.1.1–5.1.14])

Chapter 5 of the JMLSG guidance explains that the requirement to conduct **customer due diligence (CDD)** derives from the Money Laundering Regulations 2007. The requirements are there for two broad reasons:

- to help the firm be satisfied that the customers know who they say they are and that there are no legal reasons preventing the relationship;
- to assist law enforcement.

The CDD requirements should be applied by firms having regard to the risks associated with different types of business relationship. There are three aspects to CDD at the outset of a new business relationship:

- identify the customer – obtain their name, address and date of birth; for non-personal customers the beneficial owners must be identified;
- obtain verification of the customer's identity – conduct additional checks to verify the information;
- obtain information about the intended nature of the business relationship.

This is **standard due diligence**, and Chapter 5 of the JMLSG notes gives practical guidance to the due diligence required for different types of customer. For personal customers, standard verification requirements may be satisfied by the production of a valid passport or photocard driving licence. For non-personal customers, such as companies, partnerships and clubs, it will be necessary to conduct checks on public registers such as Companies House.

Enhanced due diligence is where the firm conducts more checks than for standard cases. This is obligatory in three circumstances:

- where the client is a PEP – see Section 3.4.2;
- where the client is not physically present (non-face-to-face cases); and
- in respect of a correspondent banking relationship.

But the firm may choose to conduct enhanced due diligence for any case where this is deemed necessary.

Simplified due diligence means not having to conduct due diligence at all, and is permissible if the customer falls into one of the following types:

- certain regulated financial services firms;
- listed companies;
- beneficial owners of pooled accounts held by notaries or legal professionals;
- UK public authorities;
- community institutions;
- certain products/arrangements where the risk of their being used for money laundering is inherently low: life assurance, e-money products, pension funds, child trust funds and other low risk products.

If simplified due diligence does not apply, then satisfactory identification evidence for the customer should be obtained, and verified, as soon as is reasonably practicable after first contact between the firm and the customer. If there is a delay between the forming of the business relationship and the verification of the customer's identity (eg, in the case of non-face-to-face business) firms' risk management procedures should limit the extent of the relationship. They could do this, eg, by placing restrictions on the transactions the customer can enter into, or on the transfer of funds, until verification is complete.

If a firm cannot satisfactorily verify a customer's identity, it should not proceed with the business relationship, and should consider whether this should cause it to make a report to SOCA. If it is simply the case that the customer cannot produce the correct documents or information, the firm may consider whether there is any other way it can satisfy itself as to their identity.

The chapter also deals with Know Your Customer requirements in the context of multipartite relationships, eg, where one firm introduces a customer to another, or where more than one firm is involved in providing the service to the customer. In such cases, a firm may rely on the due diligence conducted by another regulated firm.

Regardless of the type of due diligence conducted at the outset, in all cases the firm must conduct ongoing monitoring of the business relationship, and this is considered next.

3.5 The Money Laundering Reporting Officer (MLRO) and the Nominated Officer

Learning Objective 3.3.6

Understand the approach adopted by the FSA in August 2006 as covered by the Senior Management Arrangements, Systems and Controls Sourcebook [SYSC], in particular, the systems and controls that the FSA expects firms to have adopted, the role of the Money Laundering Reporting Officer, Nominated Officer and the Compliance function [SYSC 3.2.6, 3.2.6 (A)-(J), 3.2.7, 3.2.8, SYSC 6.3]

Learning Objective 3.3.9

Understand the importance of ongoing monitoring of business relationships and being able to recognise a suspicious transaction and the requirement for staff to report to the MLRO and for the firm to report to the Serious Organised Crime Agency (SOCA)

Under POCA 2002, it is an offence to fail to disclose a suspicion of money laundering. Obviously, this requires the staff at financial services firms to be aware of what constitutes a suspicion, and there is a requirement that staff must be trained to recognise and deal with what may be a money laundering transaction. Firms are also required to ensure that business relationships are understood, and monitored, sufficiently well that their staff will recognise patterns of activity which are not in keeping with the customer's anticipated profile.

The disclosure of suspicions is made, ultimately, to the legal authorities, namely SOCA; however, disclosure goes through two stages. Firstly, the employee with a suspicion should disclose that suspicion within the firm to the MLRO – a required controlled function. It is the MLRO who reviews matters, and decides whether the suspicion should be passed on to SOCA.

It is important to appreciate that, by reporting to the MLRO, the employee with the suspicion has fulfilled their responsibilities under the law – they have disclosed their suspicions. Similarly, by reporting to SOCA, the MLRO has fulfilled their responsibilities under the law.

The main part of FSA's Handbook which relates to the MLRO is the Senior Management Arrangements, Systems and Controls (SYSC) Sourcebook. As an approved person, the MLRO is subject to the approved persons' regime. The MLRO is primarily responsible for ensuring a firm adequately trains staff in knowing and understanding the regulatory requirements and how to recognise and deal with suspicious transactions.

3.5.1 MLRO or Nominated Officer?

Under the FSA rules, all firms (except for sole traders, general insurance firms and mortgage intermediaries) must appoint an MLRO with responsibility for oversight of their compliance with the FSA's rules on systems and controls against money laundering.

The Money Laundering Regulations require all affected firms to appoint a **nominated officer** to be responsible for receiving internal money laundering disclosures from staff members, and to make external reports to SOCA where necessary. The nominated officer is also responsible for receiving internal disclosures under POCA and the Terrorism Act 2000.

Although the obligations of the MLRO under the FSA requirements are different from those of the nominated officer under POCA, the Terrorism Act or the Money Laundering Regulations 2007, in practice the same person tends to carry on both roles – and is usually known as the MLRO.

3.5.2 The FSA's Principles-Based Approach to Money Laundering Prevention

The FSA approach to supervision is primarily an **outcomes-focused** approach. This approach has already been extended to its requirements of firms in the context of the prevention of money laundering. As a consequence, it has abandoned its earlier, relatively prescriptive Sourcebook on money laundering and replaced it with higher-level requirements. These are set out in the Systems and Controls Sourcebook (SYSC).

These high-level requirements place obligations on firms' senior management to ensure that they have systems and controls in place which are appropriate to the business for the prevention of money laundering and terrorist financing. The JMLSG Guidance Notes aid firms in interpreting and dealing with these obligations in the context of their specific types of business.

In order to determine the arrangements and controls needed by a firm for these purposes, its senior management needs to have carried out a **risk assessment**. This should consider such factors as:

- the nature of the firm's products and services;
- the nature of its client base and geographical location; and
- the ways in which these may leave the firm open to abuse by criminals.

3.6 Terrorism and Money Laundering

Learning Objective 3.3.10

Know what activities are regarded as 'terrorism' in the UK [Terrorism Act 2000 Part 1] the obligations on regulated firms under the Counter-Terrorism Act 2008 [money laundering of terrorist funds] [Part 5 section 62 and s.7 parts 1–7] and the Anti-Terrorism Crime & Security Act 2001 Schedule 2 Part 3 [Disclosure of Information] and where to find the sanction list for terrorist activities

In light of the **war against terrorism**, legislation in the form of the Terrorism Act 2000 has defined what amounts to terrorism:

Terrorism is the use or threat of action where it:

- involves serious violence against a person or serious damage to property;
- endangers a person's life, other than the person committing the action;
- creates serious risk to the health or safety of the public (or a section of the public);
- is designed to seriously interfere or disrupt an electronic system.
- is designed to influence the government or intimidate the public (or a section of the public);
- is made for the purpose of advancing a political, religious or ideological cause.

Note, if the threat or action involved firearms or explosives it is terrorism, regardless of whether it was designed to influence the government or intimidate the public (or a section of the public).

Many of the requirements of anti-terrorism legislation are similar to the anti-money laundering provisions encountered earlier. A person commits an offence if he enters into, or becomes concerned with, an arrangement that facilitates the retention or control of terrorist property by concealment, removal from the jurisdiction, transfer to nominees or in any other way. The person may have a defence if he can prove that he did not know, and had no reasonable cause to suspect, that the arrangement related to terrorist property.

There is a duty to report suspicions and it is an offence to fail to report where there are reasonable grounds to have a suspicion. The Terrorism Act 2000 and **Anti-Terrorism Crime Security Act 2001** specify that a failure to report is liable to a term of up to five years in jail, plus a fine.

The **Counter-Terrorism Act (CTA)** became law on 26 November 2008, adding further to the Government's armoury of legislation to tackle terrorism. Of particular interest is **Schedule 7,** which gives new powers to the Treasury to issue directions to firms in the financial sector.

In summary, directions can be given to individual firms, to firms that fit a particular description, or to the sector as a whole, concerning individuals or institutions who are doing business or are resident in a particular non-EEA country or regarding the government in that country. Directions can relate to customer due diligence (CDD) and ongoing monitoring, systematic reporting on transactions and business relationships, and limiting or ceasing business, as follows:

- **Customer due diligence and monitoring** – the provisions are broadly similar to the requirements already imposed under the Money Laundering Regulations. However, the Treasury is now able, for example, to direct that CDD be undertaken again or completed **before** entering into a business relationship (where it might otherwise have been conducted in parallel), or that enhanced measures be carried out. It may also direct that specific activity monitoring be carried out.
- **Systematic reporting** – until now, reporting orders have only been available to law enforcement agencies and must be obtained through the courts. Under the CTA, the Treasury itself can now require information to be provided concerning business relationships and transactions involving the specified person(s), on a one-off or periodic basis.
- **Limiting or ceasing business** – the Treasury's powers under the present Money Laundering Regulations (Regulation 18) are limited to where the Financial Action Task Force (FATF) has applied countermeasures. The CTA powers are more flexible and allow directions to be imposed in a wider range of situations (see below). Under CTA, the Treasury may issue directions when one or more of the following are met:
  - the FATF has advised that countermeasures should be applied to a country (as per the Money Laundering Regulations);
  - the Treasury reasonably believes that money laundering/terrorist financing activities are being carried on in the country, by its government or by persons resident/incorporated there, which pose a significant threat to the UK's national interests;
  - the Treasury reasonably believes that the country is developing or producing nuclear or chemical weapons, or doing anything to facilitate that, and poses a significant threat to the UK's national interests.

While directions to individual firms will be served upon them, it is not yet clear how orders that apply to specified types of firm or the whole sector (which will require secondary legislation each time) will be publicised. It may or may not be via the sanctions mechanism or something similar – this issue is still being clarified with the Treasury.

Meanwhile, the Treasury regularly publishes lists of individual names and countries that have been identified as unacceptable and with whom UK firms may not conduct business.

3.6.1 The Differences Between Money Laundering and Terrorist Financing

Learning Objective 3.3.11

Understand the importance of preventative measures in respect of terrorist financing and the essential differences between laundering the proceeds of crime and the financing of terrorist acts [JMLSG Guidance 2007 paras 1.38 – 1.39, Preface 9 as amended December 2011] and the interaction between the rules of FSA, the Terrorism Act 2000 and the JMLSG Guidance regarding terrorism [JMLSG Guidance 2007 Preface 27, 28, 29 – as amended December 2011]

Because terrorist groups can have links with other criminal activities, there is inevitably some overlap between anti-money laundering provisions and financing terrorist acts. However, there are two major difficulties when terrorist funds are compared to other money laundering activities:

1. Often, only quite small sums of money are required to commit terrorist acts.
2. If legitimate funds are used to fund terrorist activities, it is difficult to identify when the funds become 'terrorist property'.

Financial services firms need to ensure that their preventative measures take account of the different nature of terrorist financing in order comply with the FSA's requirements for combating financial crime.

The JMLSG Guidance provides a sound basis for firms to meet their obligations under POCA, the Terrorism Act, the Money Laundering Regulations and the FSA's rules. The extent to which a firm has followed the guidance is a material factor for offences brought before the courts. Similarly, the FSA will have regard to whether a firm has followed the guidance in deciding whether to prosecute a breach of the Money Laundering Regulations, or whether to take action against a firm for a rule breach.

4. The Model Code for Directors

Learning Objective 3.4.1

Know the main purpose and provisions of the FSA's Model Code on share dealing by directors and other persons discharging managerial responsibilities, including close periods; undisclosed inside information; chairman's approval; dealings by the chairman; short-term dealing; exceptional circumstances; application and record-keeping

The FSA fulfils the role of the UK Listing Authority (UKLA). This means that it is the competent authority to set the requirements for shares or other securities to be **'listed'**. Listing allows, for example, a company to have its shares traded on a recognised investment exchange, such as the LSE.

As part of its listing rules, the UKLA has produced the **'Model Code'**. Listed companies must comply with the Model Code restricting the ability of their senior managers and officers (**restricted persons**) to deal in the company's securities. Equally, the Code sets out how restricted persons may deal in the securities of the company they work for without falling foul of the insider dealing or market abuse regimes.

Firstly, the Model Code requires restricted persons to seek **clearance** before buying or selling securities. Normally, it is the chairman of the company who gives this clearance. If the chairman himself seeks permission, the clearance will be given by the chief executive officer (CEO); if chairman and CEO are the same person, then the clearance will be given by the board.

Restricted persons who are not directors can seek clearance from the company secretary or a designated director.

A response to a request for clearance must be given within five business days of the request. Once clearance has been given, the person must deal as soon as possible and in any event within two days of receiving clearance.

There are prescribed circumstances when clearance must be refused:

- on **short-term** considerations; investments with a maturity of one year or less are always considered short-term;
- during any period where **inside information** may exist;
- during a **close period**.

A close period is any of the following:

- the 60 days leading up to a preliminary announcement of the company's annual results;
- the 60 days leading up to publication of the company's annual financial report;
- if the company reports on a half-yearly basis, the period from the end of the relevant financial period until the time of publication;
- the 30 days leading up to the publication of quarterly results.

If a person is in severe financial difficulty, or there exists some other exceptional circumstance, clearance may be given to sell (but not buy) when the Code would otherwise have prohibited the sale. The person must not be in possession of inside information, and clearance can only be given by a designated director. The Code states that the FSA should be consulted over requests to deal in exceptional circumstances. A tax liability is not normally considered an exceptional circumstance (unless the person has no other way of settling the liability); but a court order or some other legal obligation to sell the securities may meet the exceptional test.

The company must keep a record of the response to a request to deal and any clearance given, and provide the restricted person with a copy of the response and the clearance.

5. The Disclosure and Transparency Rules

Learning Objective 3.5.1

Know the purpose of the Disclosure and Transparency rules and the control of information [DTR 2.1.3, 2.6.1]

The Disclosure and Transparency rules (DTR) are part of the FSA's Handbook. The Disclosure Rules are made by the FSA in its role as UKLA, and the Transparency Rules give effect in the UK to the Transparency Directive. Both sets of rules apply to issuers of securities listed to trade on certain markets.

The purpose of the **Disclosure Rules**, in accordance with EU provisions for dealing with inside information and preventing market abuse, is to:

- promote prompt and fair disclosure of relevant information to the market;
- set out specific circumstances in which an issuer can delay the public disclosure of inside information; and
- set out requirements to ensure that such information is kept confidential in order to protect investors and prevent insider dealing.

The purpose of the **Transparency Rules** is to implement the requirements of the Transparency Directive and to ensure there is adequate transparency of and access to information in the UK financial markets.

5.1 Control of Inside Information

The Disclosure Rules set out the requirements for the control of inside information, in two respects:

- **Denying access** – An issuer must establish effective arrangements to deny access to inside information to persons other than those who require it for the exercise of their functions within the issuer.
- **Breaches of confidentiality** - An issuer must have measures in place that enable public disclosure to be made via an FSA-approved regulated information service (RIS) as soon as possible, in cases where the issuer is unable to ensure the confidentiality of the inside information. These measures should include a 'holding announcement' to be used if a breach of confidentiality occurs when the issuer is legitimately delaying disclosure of inside information to protect its own interests, in accordance with FSA rules that permit this. The holding announcement must give as much detail as possible, state why a full announcement can't be made, and undertake to announce further details as soon as possible.

6. The Data Protection Act

Learning Objective 3.6.1

Know the eight Data Protection Principles; the need for notification of data controllers with the Information Commissioner; the record-keeping requirements of FSA-regulated firms [DPA Schedule 1, Part 1 & COBS Schedule 1 – record-keeping requirements and SYSC 3 & 9]

6.1 Data Protection Principles

The Data Protection Act 1998 provides for the way in which 'personal data' must be dealt in order to protect the rights of the persons concerned. Personal data is data which relates to living individuals.

Any firm determining the way personal data is held and processed is known as a 'data controller' and is, therefore, responsible for compliance with the Data Protection Act. All data controllers must be registered with the Information Commissioner.

The Data Protection Act lays down **eight principles**, which must be complied with:

1. Personal data shall be processed fairly and lawfully.
2. Personal data shall be obtained for one or more specified and lawful purposes, and shall not be further processed in any manner that is incompatible with those purposes.
3. Personal data shall be adequate, relevant and not excessive in relation to the purpose or purposes for which it is processed.
4. Personal data shall be accurate and, where necessary, kept up-to-date.
5. Personal data shall not be kept for longer than is necessary for its purpose or purposes.
6. Personal data shall be processed in accordance with the rights of the subject under the Act.
7. Appropriate technical and organisational measures shall be taken against unauthorised or unlawful processing of personal data, and against accidental loss or destruction of, or damage to the personal data.
8. Personal data shall not be transferred to a country or territory outside the EEA, unless that country or territory ensures an adequate level of protection in relation to the processing of personal data.

Clearly, these principles of data protection will apply to personal data maintained by financial services firms (who often have a duty to **'know their customers'**) and to the personal data maintained by the FSA itself (in relation to its approved persons' regime).

In addition, firms should have regard for the provisions of this Act when considering their record-retention policies. The FSA imposes a number of record-keeping requirements and firms will not be contravening data protection requirements by complying with an FSA rule. Other than this, firms must comply with data protection in not keeping data longer than necessary, and keeping current data accurate, including, for example, in connection with training and competence records for employees).

The Information Commissioner has the authority and power to fine investment firms that do not comply with its requirements in respect of data security.

6.2 Record-Keeping Requirements

The FSA's high-level rules for records maintained by authorised firms are set out in SYSC. Firms must arrange for orderly records to be kept of their business and internal organisation, including all services and transactions undertaken by them. The medium for holding records is not prescribed, but the records should be capable of being reproduced in English and on paper. This includes a requirement to provide a translation if the record is retained in a language other than English. The general principle for retention periods is that they should be retained for as long as relevant to the purpose for which the record was made.

However, in addition to these high-level requirements there are more specific record-keeping rules pertaining to certain types of business. For example, investment firms must retain all records in relation to MiFID business for a period of at least five years, and in relation to non-MiFID business the record-keeping requirement is three years.

Each Handbook module specifies, in Schedule 1 to the module, any detailed record-keeping requirements for that particular module. For example, the Conduct of Business Sourcebook (COBS) has detailed record-keeping requirements relating to specific activities undertaken by firms, such as:

- **COBS 2.3 (Inducements)** – fee, commission or non-monetary benefits received;
- **COBS 3.8 (Client categorisation)** – client classification notice to client, client agreements and the firm's evidence to support the category;
- **COBS 4.11 (Communicating with clients, including financial promotions)** – financial promotion, telemarketing scripts and compliance of financial promotions;
- **COBS 6.2 (Information about the firm)** – scope and range of service for packaged products;
- **COBS 8.1 (Client agreements)** – client agreements;
- **COBS 9.5 (Suitability, including basic advice)** – suitability report, and information supporting the report;
- **COBS 10.7 (Appropriateness for non-advised services)** – appropriateness test and information used in the assessment;
- **COBS 11.5 (Dealing and managing)** – detailed records concerning client orders and decisions to deal in portfolio management;
- **COBS 11.6 (Dealing and managing)** – prior and periodic disclosure on the use of dealing commission;
- **COBS 11.7 (Dealing and managing)** – personal account dealing records;
- **COBS 12.4 (Research recommendations)** – basis of substantiation of research recommendation;
- **COBS 15.3 (Cancellation)** – where the client has exercised the right to cancel;
- **COBS 16 (Reporting information to clients)** – trade confirmation and periodic statements;
- **COBS 19 (Pensions)** – execution-only pension transfer or opt-out; record of why a promotion of a personal pension scheme was justified.

7. Prudential Standards

Learning Objective 3.8.1

Know the purpose of the FSA's Capital Adequacy Requirements [GENPRU 1.2.12/13]

7.1 Capital Adequacy Requirements

Principle 4 establishes that: *'a firm must maintain adequate financial resources'.* 'Financial resources' include both capital resources, and liquidity resources, so that the firm can meet its liabilities as they fall due. The standards differ according to the activities undertaken by the firm and whether the firm's activities also fall within the scope of the Markets in Financial Instruments Directive (MiFID). The standards for investment firms are set out in three FSA Handbook modules:

- **The General Prudential Sourcebook (GENPRU)** – high-level standards, principles and capital adequacy requirements for firms that are subject to the Capital Requirements Directive (CRD);
- **The Prudential Sourcebook for Banks, Building Societies and Investment firms (BIPRU)** – additional provisions for CRD firms, setting out standards for calculating capital to meet specified risks and for maintaining adequate liquidity resources;
- **Interim Prudential Sourcebook for Investment Businesses (IPRU-INV)** – capital adequacy rules for investment firms that are not subject to the CRD.

The CRD created an EU-wide common framework for financial resources and risk management to minimise the risk of a firm's financial failure. The CRD framework is based on the concept of three 'Pillars':

- **Pillar 1** – minimum capital requirements for credit, market and operational risks.
- **Pillar 2** – firms and supervisors decide whether additional capital should be held to cover risks not covered in Pillar 1.

- **Pillar 3** – disclosure of information about risks, capital and risk management, to improve market discipline.

BIPRU gives additional guidance for assessing risks:

- **credit risk** – the risk of default on loans to which the firm is exposed;
- **operational risk** – the risk of loss resulting from failed processes, people or systems, or from external events including legal risk;
- **market risk** – this is broken down into very specific risks associated with various positions a trading firm may take;
- **group risk consolidation** – risks associated with group arrangements, especially groups containing firms in different sectors (eg, investment, banking and insurance);
- **securitisation risk** – where capital resources held for securitised assets prove inadequate;
- **concentration risk/large exposures** – such as where the firm has made a large loan to a single borrower, or has large exposure to a single counterparty;
- **residual risk** – the risk that techniques the firm uses to mitigate credit risk are less effective than envisaged;
- **insurance risk** – uncertainty as to occurrence, timing and amount of insurance liabilities;
- **business risk** – arising from changes to its business, risk that the firm may not be able to carry out its strategy, risk arising from remuneration policies;
- **interest rate risk** – trading book and non-trading book;
- **pension obligation risk** – arising out of the firm's obligation to make contractual pension contributions or payments;
- **liquidity risk** – the risk that a firm may not be able to meet its liabilities as they fall due without borrowing at excessive cost.

Firms are required to provide detailed reports to the FSA on their capital adequacy; the frequency of reporting depends on the size of the firm and whether it is subject to the CRD or not. Additionally, if at any time a firm knows that its capital resources have fallen below the prescribed minimum, then it must notify the FSA immediately.

Firms subject to the CRD must also comply with provisions relating to the quality of capital that is held. That is, a firm must have regard to the loss absorbency of instruments it wishes to use to meet its capital resource requirements. Capital is broadly split into three types (tiers) for this purpose:

- **Core Tier One capital** – such as permanent share capital, reserves, externally verified interim profits.
- **Tier Two capital** – such as long-term subordinated debt and revaluations reserves.
- **Tier Three capital** – such as short-term subordinated debt and interim trading book profit and loss.

There are restrictions as to how much Tier Two and Tier Three capital may be used to meet the capital resource requirements.

The rules also require firms to 'stress-test' the capital that is, to formulate financial models to assess how well the capital resources stand up against a range of adverse scenarios over specified time periods.

Firms that are not subject to the CRD must adhere to the FSA's rules in IPRU-INV. Such firms include:

- authorised professional firms;
- certain types of securities and futures firms not directly subject to MiFID;
- Lloyd's underwriting agents and members' advisers;
- fund managers, including operators of personal pension schemes (SIPP operators);
- exempt Capital Adequacy Directive (CAD) firms or local firms (firms that conduct a limited type of business under MiFID, or are exercising passporting rights);
- service companies;
- personal investment firms that are operating under a MiFID exemption, eg, financial advisory firms;
- credit unions that provide child trust funds (CTFs).

The way that IPRU-INV applies depends on the activity that is conducted by the firm; consequently, if an investment firm's activity changes, this may mean that the firm must comply with different aspects of IPRU-INV (or even GENPRU and BIPRU if the change brings it within the scope of the CRD). Each type of firm has prescribed capital adequacy tests, and all firms must comply with two over-arching requirements:

- firms must at all times have available the amount and type of financial resources required by the FSA's rules;
- firms must notify the FSA immediately they become aware that they are in breach of, or expect shortly to be in breach of, the relevant financial resources rule.

From December 2013 the capital resources tests are changing for personal investment firms that are not subject to the CRD. The test is changing from an 'own funds' test of £10,000 to an expenditure-based test, and the amount of subordinated loan that can be used to meet capital will also be restricted.

The changes are being introduced in a staged manner as follows:

- **31 December 2013** – the test will become one month's expenditure with a minimum capital floor of £15,000;
- **31 December 2014** – the test is two months' expenditure and subordinated loans will be restricted to 400%;
- **31 December 2015** – the test is three months' expenditure with a minimum capital floor of £20,000, and subordinated loans will be restricted to 200%.

7.2 Basel III

The EU capital adequacy framework has its foundations in the Basel Accord of 1988, agreed by the Basel Committee on Banking Supervision (BCBS). The intention was to strengthen the stability of the international banking system through prescribed capital ratios. The concept of the three Pillars of capital adequacy was introduced by Basel II and implemented through the CRD as described above.

The financial crisis of subsequent years has prompted a further strengthening of the framework and CRD II and CRD III have already been implemented within the UK.

Basel III measures include:

- enhancing the quality and quantity of capital;
- increasing the Pillar 1 requirement for counterparty risk and market risk;
- a new leverage ratio as a backstop to risk-based capital;
- two new capital buffers – one for capital conservation and one to act as a counter-cyclical capital buffer;
- an enhanced liquidity regime.

Basel III is a long-term strategy that will be implemented through a 'CRD IV package'. This includes Capital Requirements Regulation (CRR) (Pillar 1 and Pillar 3) and a Capital Requirements Directive for Pillar 2, supervisory review and buffers. An EU-wide single rule book for financial services is also being developed. The CRD IV package is likely to become binding on banks, building societies and credit institutions on 1 January 2013 with a transition period until 2021.

7.3 Liquidity Standards

Learning Objective 3.8.2

Know the purpose, scope and application of the FSA's liquidity framework requirements and how they apply to regulated firms (BIPRU 12.1.1, 12.2.12/4/5/7 + 12.3.4/5)

In October 2009 the FSA implemented a revised framework for managing liquidity risk. Liquidity risk is the risk that a firm may not be able to meet its liabilities as they fall due, without borrowing at excessive cost.

The requirements apply to all types of firms that are covered by the CRD but they apply in a proportionate manner. For example, the largest, most complex firms need more sophisticated liquidity management arrangements than the small private client discretionary firms.

7.3.1 Adequacy of Liquidity Resources

The overarching rule (BIPRU 12.2.1) at the heart of the FSA's liquidity framework regime stipulates that firms must at all times maintain liquidity resources which are adequate, both as to amount and quality, to ensure that there is no significant risk that its liabilities cannot be met as they fall due. All firms must comply with this fundamental requirement for self-sufficiency.

A firm may not include liquidity resources that can be made available by other members of its group and may not include liquidity resources that may be made available through emergency liquidity assistance from a central bank.

The overall liquidity adequacy rule is expressed to apply to each firm on a solo basis. However, the FSA does recognise that there will be circumstances in which it may be appropriate for a firm or a branch to rely on liquidity support provided by other entities within the group or from elsewhere within the firm. A firm wishing to rely on support of this kind may only do so with the consent of the FSA – given by way of a waiver under section 148 (Modifications or Waiver Rules) of the Act to the overall liquidity adequacy rule.

Lehman Brothers demonstrated that during a severe liquidity crisis it is the individual position of the various legal entities within a group that matters most. The FSA has to be satisfied with the liquidity position of the locally incorporated entity or local branch.

The FSA's liquidity policy can be considered as having four key strands:

- **Individual liquidity adequacy standards** – a framework for liquidity management for many of the larger and more complex firms that the FSA supervise. This framework is based on firms being able to survive liquidity stresses of varying magnitude and duration.
- **Systems and controls** – a systems and controls framework based on the recent work of the BCBS and the European Banking Authority (EBA).
- **Group-wide and cross-border management of liquidity** – firms may deviate from self-sufficiency if this is appropriate and will not result in undue risk to consumers and other stakeholders.
- **Regulatory reporting** – to enable the FSA to collect granular, standardised liquidity data at an appropriate frequency so that they can form firm-specific, sector-specific and market-wide liquidity risk exposures.

Each of these strands is expanded below.

Individual Liquidity Adequacy Standards (ILAS)

The purpose of ILAS is to ensure that firms are better able to manage their liquidity position than has been the case in the past. Firms that are subject to ILAS must regularly submit detailed information to the FSA and have to complete an Individual Liquidity Adequacy Assessment (ILAA), including a contingency funding plan to demonstrate how the firm would maintain its liquidity against various stressed scenarios.

Systems and Controls Requirements

The FSA requires firms:

- to have in place sound, effective and complete processes, strategies and systems that enable it to identify, measure, monitor and control liquidity risk;
- to ensure that its processes, strategies and systems are comprehensive and proportionate to the nature, scale and complexity of a firm's activities;
- to ensure that a governing body establishes the firm's risk tolerance. The governing body is ultimately responsible for the liquidity risk assumed by the firm and the manner in which this risk is managed;
- to ensure that the governing body undertakes a review (at least annually), confirming that the firm's arrangements remain adequate;
- senior management continuously to review the firm's liquidity position, including its compliance with the overall liquidity adequacy rule and report to its governing body on a regular basis adequate information as to that;
- to have appropriate contingency funding plans approved by their governing body;

- to conduct regular stress tests so as to identify sources of potential liquidity strain; ensure that current liquidity exposures continue to conform to the liquidity risk tolerance established by that firm's governing body; and identify the effects on the firm's assumptions about pricing. The FSA expects that the extent and frequency of such testing should be proportionate to the size of the firm and of its liquidity risk exposures. A firm's governing body must review regularly the stresses and scenarios tested to ensure that their nature and severity remain appropriate and relevant to that firm.

The objective of the rules is to ensure that firms actively monitor and control liquidity risk exposures and funding needs within and across legal entities, business lines and currencies. Firms are subject to rigorous supervisory review of their governance arrangements, measurement tools, methods and assumptions used in the stress tests, mitigating strategies, business planning assumptions and contingency funding plans.

Group-Wide and Cross-Border Management of Liquidity

Every firm is subject to the overall liquidity adequacy rule, meaning that every firm is required to be self-sufficient in terms of liquidity adequacy and to be able to satisfy this rule, relying on its own liquidity resources.

However, the FSA recognises that there may be circumstances in which it will be appropriate for a firm to rely on liquidity resources which can be made available to it by other members of its group, or for a firm to rely on liquidity resources elsewhere in the firm for the purposes of ensuring that its UK branch has adequate liquidity resources in respect of the activities carried on from the branch.

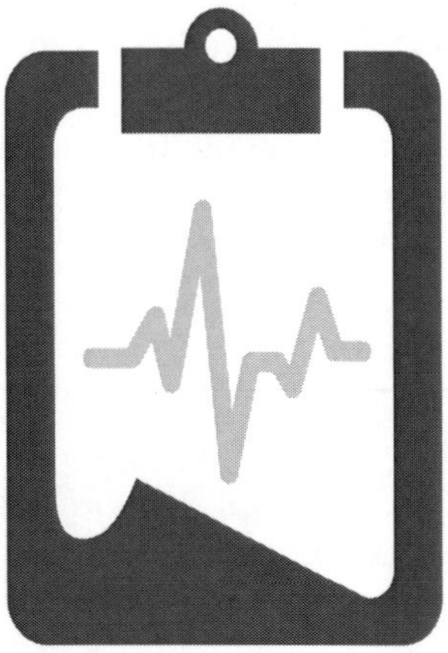

If the FSA is satisfied that the statutory tests in Section 148 (Modifications or Waiver of Rules) of the Act are met, it will consider modifying the overall liquidity adequacy rule to permit reliance on liquidity support of this kind.

Regulatory Reporting

The reporting requirements are proportionate to the nature and scale of the firm's activities. Larger firms must report in more detail and more frequently than smaller firms conducting a more restricted range of activity. The report for this latter type of firm is an annual systems and controls questionnaire.

8. Relevant European Regulation

Learning Objective 3.7.1

Know the relevant European Union Directives and the impact on the UK financial services industry in respect of: passporting within the EEA (MiFID); home vs host state regulation (MiFID); selling cross-border collective investment schemes (UCITS); selling securities cross-border (Prospectus Directive)

As a member of the EU, the UK plays a part in the attempt to create a single market across Europe for financial services. Primarily, this is achieved by the European Parliament issuing directives to the member states, and their implementation into national legislation.

8.1 MiFID – Passporting within the EEA

The Investment Services Directive (ISD) was issued in 1993. Broadly, it specified that, if a firm had been authorised in one member state to provide investment services, this single authorisation enabled the firm to provide those investment services in other member states without requiring any further authorisation.

This principle was, and still is, known as the 'passport'.

The state providing authorisation is where the firm originates and is commonly referred to as the home state. States outside the home state where the firm offers investment services are known as host states.

The ISD was repealed and replaced by another EU Directive, the Markets in Financial Instruments Directive (MiFID). MiFID provisions came into force in the UK from 1 November 2007.

One of the key aims of MiFID was to provide investor protection rules across the European Economic Area (EEA). Investor protection is ensured, inter alia, via the obligation to obtain the best possible result for the client, information disclosure requirements, client-specific rules on suitability and appropriateness and rules on inducements. As a general principle, MiFID places significant importance on the fiduciary duties of firms. That is why MiFID established a general obligation for firms to act in the client's best interest.

MiFID has been designed to support two key policy goals of the EU. These are:

- extending the scope of the passport to include a wider range of services; and
- removing a major hurdle to cross-border business, by way of the application of host state rules to incoming passported firms.

Previously, under the ISD, firms had only been able to passport a limited range of investment services into other host states. MiFID widens the range of passportable activities – for example, it now includes:

- investment advice (which under ISD was only permitted if it was an 'ancillary service' to some other core service being provided – eg, dealing in investments);
- some underwriting activities;
- operating an MTF (see Section 1.8, Chapter 1);
- investment activities relating to commodity derivatives, credit derivatives and contracts for difference, since MiFID has extended the scope of the passport to cover these instruments for the first time;
- investment research, if it is an ancillary service to some other core service.

8.1.1 MiFID Activities and UK-Regulated Activities

Whilst MiFID replaced the ISD, it did not replace any existing UK-regulated activity. If a UK investment firm wishes to exercise passporting rights under MiFID, it must already have Part IV permission to conduct the equivalent UK-regulated activity as shown in the table below.

MiFID activity	Broadly equivalent to UK-regulated activity
Receipt and transmission of orders in relation to one or more financial instruments	Arranging deals in investments
Execution of orders on behalf of clients	Dealing as principal Dealing as agent
Dealing on own account	Dealing as principal
Portfolio management	Managing investments
Investment advice	Advising on investments
Underwriting of financial instruments and/or placing of financial instruments on a firm commitment basis	Dealing as principal Dealing as agent
Placing of financial instruments without a firm commitment basis	Dealing as agent Arranging deals in investments
Operation of multilateral trading facilities	Operating a multilateral trading facility (formerly known as an alternative trading system)

MiFID ancillary activity	UK-regulated activity
Safekeeping and administration of financial instruments for the account of clients, including custodianship. Also related services such as the management of cash and collateral	Safeguarding and administering investments Sending dematerialised instructions Agreeing to carry on regulated activities
Lending to investors to allow them to effect a transaction in one or more financial instruments when the lender is involved in the transaction	N/A
Advice to undertakings on capital structure, industrial strategy and related matters; also, advice/services relating to mergers and the purchase of undertakings	Dealing as principal Dealing as agent Arranging deals in investments Advising on investments Agreeing to carry on regulated activities
Foreign exchange services (but only if these are connected with the provision of investment services)	Dealing as principal Dealing as agent Arranging deals in investments Advising on investments Agreeing to carry on regulated activities
Investment research and financial analysis, or other forms of general recommendation in relation to transactions in financial instruments	Advising on investments Agreeing to carry on regulated activities
Services in relation to underwriting	Arranging deals in investments Advising on investments Agreeing to carry on regulated activities
Investment services and activities, and ancillary services, related to the underlying assets of certain derivatives when these are connected to the provision of investment or ancillary services.	Dealing as principal Dealing as agent Arranging deals in investments Operating a multilateral trading facility Managing investments Advising on investments Agreeing to carry on regulated activities

8.1.2 Ancillary Activities

The same principle applies to MiFID's range of ancillary activities – UK firms must already have the relevant activity within their Part IV permission. Additionally, an ancillary activity cannot be passported in its own right – it can only be passported if it is being provided in conjunction with one of the main activities from the previous table. See the table above.

8.1.3 Financial Instruments Covered by MiFID

MiFID applies only to activities in relation to a specified list of financial instruments. These are:

- transferable securities;
- money market instruments;
- units in collective investment undertakings;
- derivatives relating to securities, currencies, interest rates or yields, or other financial indices or measures which may be settled physically or in cash;

- commodity derivatives that must be settled in cash or may be settled in cash at the option of one of the parties (other than by default or termination);
- commodity derivatives that can be physically settled provided they are traded on a regulated market and/or an MTF;
- commodity derivatives which can be physically settled, which are not for commercial purposes, and which are similar to other derivatives in certain criteria;
- credit derivatives;
- financial CFDs; and
- derivatives relating to climatic variables, freight rates, emission allowances or inflation rates or other statistics, and certain other derivatives.

Therefore, when exercising passporting rights the firm must also specify the financial instruments that are to be included within the passport. These are broadly equivalent to some (but not all) of the specified investments that are within a UK firm's Part IV permission.

Financial instruments not covered by MiFID include:

- bank accounts;
- foreign exchange (unless it relates to the provision of an investment activity or service, eg, buying/selling an option on FX).

8.2 MiFID – Home vs Host State Regulation

Not all firms authorised by the FSA are directly subject to the requirements of MiFID: whether they are or not, will depend on the nature of the regulated activities that they have within their Part IV permission. If the activity is the same as a MiFID activity, then the firm will be 'caught' by MiFID.

Broadly, the range of UK firms which are classified as MiFID firms is as follows:

- investment banks;
- portfolio managers;
- stockbrokers and broker-dealers;
- many futures and options firms;
- firms operating an MTF;
- venture capital firms that meet certain criteria;
- energy market participants, oil market participants and commodity firms which meet certain criteria;
- corporate finance firms which meet certain criteria;
- certain advisers;
- credit institutions which carry on MiFID business; and
- exchanges, UCITS investment firms and some professional firms.

However, there are two important exemptions for investment firms:

Article 3 exemption - this is available for firms that:

- only provide investment advice and receive/transmit orders;
- do not hold client funds or securities;
- only transmit orders to other MiFID firms and certain other institutions.

This exemption is widely used by financial advisory firms. If a firm is relying on the Article 3 exemption and wishes to exercise a MiFID passport, it must first apply to the FSA to vary its UK Part IV permission to remove the exemption.

Article 2.1(c) incidental exemption – this is available for professional firms if the investment service provided is incidental to the professional practice of their firm.

Firms that do not conduct investment services at all are not within the scope of MiFID. They include insurance undertakings, employee schemes, people administering their own assets, and any firms which do not provide investment services and/or perform investment activities.

As mentioned above, the concept of passporting under MiFID relies on the concept of 'home state' and 'host state' regulators. In essence, the home state is where the firm carrying on activities is established; the host state is the state in which it is providing services as a 'guest'. Firms can either establish a branch in another state, or they can conduct activities from their home state on a cross-border basis.

MiFID requires a high degree of co-operation between regulators to ensure that the investor remains fully protected when activities are conducted on a passported basis. In general terms the home state regulator retains responsibilities for the firm's prudential regulation (financial resources, governance) and the host state regulator applies its rules to the firm's conduct of business in the host state. However, there are some exceptions to this general arrangement.

8.2.1 Regulatory Developments

The following notes are for information only and will not be examined.

The European Commission (EC) is reviewing MiFID, to ensure that it stays relevant in the face of new markets and products. The revisions are being called 'MiFID II', and the main proposals are:

- extension of the scope, to include commodity firms, data providers and third country firms (institutions based in non-EEA states and authorised by non-EEA competent authorities) operating in EEA states;
- an equivalence decision to be made before third country firms can operate in EEA states, and to require such firms to at least establish branches;
- to include additional financial instruments, such as structured deposits and emissions allowances;
- new requirements for the trading of derivatives, and the introduction of a new venue called 'organised trading facilities' (OTFs), which will require separate permission;
- extension of disclosure requirements and additional transaction reporting;
- enhanced investor protection – a prohibition on commission for independent advisers and portfolio managers; independent firms must know the customer well enough to ensure they match a customer's profile and interests with the products provided; structured UCITS funds will no longer be classed as 'non-complex' instruments, and so will become subject to the non-advised appropriateness test;
- enhanced powers for national regulators to enable them to permanently ban products and to limit a firm's position in certain products, such as commodity derivatives.

It is unlikely that MiFID II will be implemented before 2015.

8.3 UCITS Directives – Selling Cross-Border Collective Investment Schemes

UCITS stands for Undertakings for Collective Investments in Transferable Securities, and the family of UCITS directives established a set of regulatory standards for open-ended funds across the EU – again, with the aim of facilitating cross-border trade.

Put simply, if a collective fund is set up in accordance with the UCITS rules, it should be able to be sold across the EU, subject only to local tax and marketing laws. So, a UCITS scheme can gain a single authorisation from its home state regulator, and need not apply for further authorisation in other member states before being sold to the public there.

The original UCITS Directive was approved in 1985 and adopted by the UK in 1989. It aimed to provide common standards of investor protection for publicly promoted collective investment schemes across the EU. However, only a relatively limited range of scheme types could qualify as UCITS and be freely marketed throughout the EU. The requirements which needed to be satisfied included:

- the scheme had to be solely invested in transferable securities;
- no more than 10% of the fund could be in the shares or bonds of a single issuer;
- no more than 5% of the assets of the scheme were allowed to be invested in other CISs;
- the scheme was only able to hold money in bank deposits as 'ancillary liquid assets' and not as a major part of the investment strategy of the scheme;
- the scheme was only able to invest in, or utilise, financial derivatives for efficient portfolio management or hedging purposes.

Demand for a wider variety of funds, marketable throughout the EU, rendered these investment restrictions somewhat out of date. As a result, two new UCITS directives were introduced:

- **the Management Directive** – dealt mainly with the management companies operating UCITS funds – eg, the degree to which they can delegate activities, their capitalisation, internal administration and accounting requirements;
- **the Products Directive** – widened previous investment powers of UCITS schemes, to enable them to invest in money market instruments, other CISs, deposits and financial derivatives. It also allowed certain UCITS to use strategies designed to replicate the performance of stock market indices (index tracker funds).

The most recent UCITS directive – **UCITS IV** – was implemented in the UK on 1 July 2011. UCITS IV repealed previous UCITS directives, and introduced the following changes:

- **Passporting for management companies** – management companies no longer have to be established in the same member state of the fund(s) they operate.
- **Key Investor Information Documents (KIIDs)** – replaced the simplified prospectus; the KIID is a concise document – not exceeding two sides of A4 – containing standardised product information.
- **Improved cross-border marketing of authorised funds** – a more streamlined process for allowing funds to access the market of another member state without delay.
- **Mergers** – a single framework for cross-border fund mergers, and standardised investor information.
- **Master-feeder structures** – whereby one fund can invest the majority of its assets into another.
- **Improved supervisory co-operation** – between regulators of different member states.

8.4 Prospectus Directive – Selling Securities Cross-Border

The Prospectus Directive is another directive aimed at creating common standards across the EU, this time with the aim of simplifying the issue of a prospectus throughout the EEA.

It was implemented in the UK in July 2005.

The Prospectus Directive sets out common standards in terms of the information that must be provided about the issuer and the securities being issued or admitted for listing. It can be thought of as a single passport for issuers. It means that once a prospectus has been approved by a home state listing authority, it must be accepted for the purpose of listing or public offers throughout the EU. The purpose of the Prospective Directive is therefore to make it easier and cheaper for companies (issuers) to raise capital in Europe.

8.5 Regulatory Developments

The following will not be examined as part of the syllabus; however candidates should be aware these matters.

8.5.1 Alternative Investment Fund Managers Directive (AIFM)

The AIFM Directive effectively introduces a regulatory framework for managers of any collective investment undertaking that is not covered by the UCITS Directive, if the manager is domiciled in the EU, or if the fund is domiciled or marketed within the EU.

This covers a wide range of funds, for example, hedge funds, private equity funds, commodity, real estate and infrastructure funds, closed-ended funds (such as investment trusts in the UK), non-retail UCITS Retail Scheme (NURS) funds in the UK, and Qualified Investor Schemes (QISs).

The directive imposes a number of requirements including authorisation, capital requirements, conduct of business and organisational requirements (including the appointment of service providers; an independent valuator and depository for each AIF), and specific initial and ongoing disclosure to investors and regulators.

The AIFM Directive has been passed by the European Parliament; member states must transpose the directive into national law/legislation by 22 July 2013.

8.5.2 EU Financial Supervision

The regulation of financial services across Europe is overseen by three European Supervisory Authorities (ESAs), which work with the European Systemic Risk Board (ESRB) to ensure financial stability. The ESAs are:

- the **European Securities and Markets Agency** (ESMA);
- the **European Banking Agency** (EBA); and
- the **European Insurance and Occupational Pensions Authority** (EIOPA).

The ESA's aim is to create a single EU rule book with which national supervisors and firms must make every effort to comply. The ESAs have power to investigate national supervisors that may be failing to apply EU law, or be in breach of EU law. They can also temporarily ban certain financial activities and, in a crisis, the ESAs will provide EU-wide co-ordination.

9. The Bribery Act 2010

9.1 Bribery Act 2010

The Bribery Act 2010 received Royal Assent on 8 April 2010. Bribery poses very serious threats to sustained economic progress in developing and emerging economies and to the proper operation of free markets more generally. The Bribery Act 2010 is intended to respond to these threats and to the extremely broad range of ways that bribery can be committed. It does this by providing robust offences, and enhanced sentencing powers for the courts, raising the maximum sentence for bribery committed by an individual from seven to ten years' imprisonment.

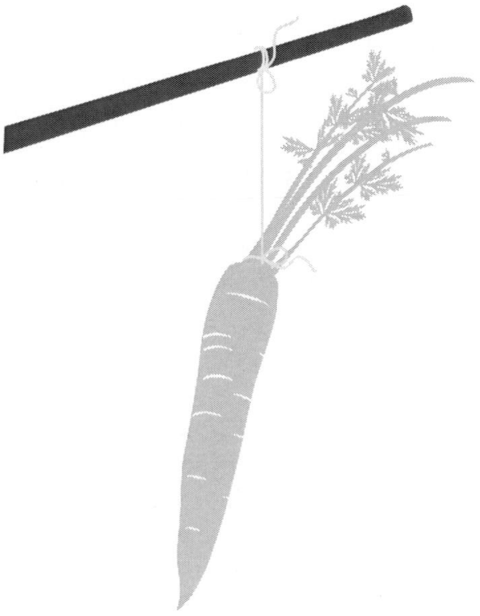

The Act contains two general offences covering the offering, promising or giving of a bribe (**active bribery**) and the requesting, agreeing to receive or accepting of a bribe (**passive bribery**). It also sets out two further offences which specifically address **commercial bribery**. Section 6 of the Act creates an offence relating to **bribery of a foreign public official** in order to obtain or retain business or an advantage in the conduct of business, and Section 7 creates a new form of **corporate liability for failing to prevent bribery on behalf of a commercial organisation**.

Section 9 of the Act requires the Secretary of State to publish guidance about procedures which commercial organisations can put in place to prevent persons associated with them from bribing.

Section 12 of the Act provides that the courts will have jurisdiction over the Sections 1, 2 or 6 offences committed in the UK, but they will also have jurisdiction over offences committed outside the UK if the person committing them has a close connection with the UK by virtue of being a British national or ordinarily resident in the UK, a body incorporated in the UK or a Scottish partnership. However, as regards Section 7, the requirement of a close connection with the UK does not apply.

9.2 Bribery Offences

Section 1 of the Act (offences of bribing another person) makes it an offence for a person ('P') to offer, promise or give a financial or other advantage to another person in one of two cases:

- **Case 1** applies if P intends the advantage to bring about the improper performance by another person of a relevant function or activity or to reward such improper performance.
- **Case 2** applies if P knows or believes that the acceptance of the advantage offered, promised or given in itself constitutes the improper performance of a relevant function or activity.

Improper performance is defined at Sections 3 (functions or activity to which bribe relates), 4 (improper performance to which bribe relates) and 5 (expectation test). In summary, this means performance which amounts to a breach of an expectation that a person will act in good faith, impartially, or in accordance with a position of trust. The offence applies to bribery relating to any function of a public nature, connected with a business, performed in the course of a person's employment or performed on behalf of a company or another body of persons. Therefore, bribery in both the public and private sectors is covered.

For the purposes of deciding whether a function or activity has been performed improperly, the test of what is expected is a test of what a **reasonable person** in the UK would expect in relation to the performance of that function or activity. If the performance of the function or activity is not subject to UK law (for example, it takes place in a country outside UK jurisdiction) then any local custom or practice must be disregarded – unless permitted or required by the written law applicable to that particular country.

Section 6 creates a stand-alone offence of **bribery of a foreign public official**. The offence is committed if a person offers, promises or gives a financial or other advantage to a foreign public official with the intention of influencing the official in the performance of his or her official functions. The person offering, promising or giving the advantage must also intend to obtain or retain business or an advantage in the conduct of business by doing so. However, the offence is not committed if the official is permitted or required by the applicable written law to be influenced by the advantage.

Bona fide **hospitality** and promotional or other business expenditure which seeks to improve the image of a commercial organisation, better to present products and services or establish cordial relations, is recognised as an established and important part of doing business and it is not the intention of the Act to criminalise such behaviour.

Section 7 of the Act creates a new offence which can be committed by commercial organisations which fail to prevent persons associated with them from committing bribery on their behalf. A commercial organisation will be liable to prosecution if a person associated with it bribes another person intending to obtain or retain business or an advantage in the conduct of business for that organisation. The commercial organisation will have a full defence if it can show that, despite a particular case of bribery, it nevertheless had adequate procedures in place to prevent persons associated with it from bribing.

End of Chapter Questions

Think of an answer for each question and refer to the appropriate section for confirmation.

1. Insider dealing is an offence under which act?

   Answer Reference: Section 1.1

   ....

   ....

   ....

2. What is inside information?

   Answer Reference: Section 1.2

   ....

   ....

   ....

3. What is the offence of insider dealing?

   Answer Reference: Section 1.3

   ....

   ....

   ....

4. What financial instruments are caught by insider dealing legislation?

   Answer Reference: Section 1.4

   ....

   ....

   ....

5. What are the defences against insider dealing?

   Answer Reference: Sections 1.5 & 1.6

   ....

   ....

   ....

6. What is market abuse?

   Answer Reference: Section 2.1

   ....

   ....

   ....

7. What are the three types of behaviour that give rise to the offence of market abuse?

   Answer Reference: Section 2.1

   ....

   ....

   ....

8. How does the FSA provide guidance on what constitutes market abuse?

   Answer Reference: Section 2.2

   ....

   ....

   ....

9. What behaviours are caught by the FSA's market abuse regime?

   Answer Reference: Section 2.2.1

   ....

   ....

   ....

10. What is a regular user in the context of market abuse?

    Answer Reference: Section 2.3

    ....

    ....

    ....

11. What are the penalties for market abuse?

    Answer Reference: Section 2.4

    ....

    ....

    ....

12. What reporting requirements exist for market abuse?

    Answer Reference: Section 2.5

    ....

    ....

    ....

13. List three rules that can be used as safe harbours against the charge of market abuse?

    Answer Reference: Section 2.6

    ....

    ....

    ....

14. What is the link between market abuse and insider dealing?

    Answer Reference: Section 2.7

    ....

    ....

    ....

15. Name the main sources of rules and regulations governing money laundering.

    Answer Reference: Section 3.1

    ....

    ....

    ....

16. What is the activity of money laundering?

    Answer Reference: Section 3.1

    ....

    ....

    ....

17. How many stages are there in money laundering?

    Answer Reference: Section 3.2

    ....

    ....

    ....

18. The Money Laundering Regulations 2007 place various requirements on firms. What are they?

    Answer Reference: Section 3.3.1

    ....

    ....

    ....

19. What defence can be used for the offences under the Proceeds of Crime Act 2002?

    Answer Reference: Section 3.3.2

    ....

    ....

    ....

20. What is the UK financial sanctions regime?

    Answer Reference: Section 3.4.2

21. What three types of customer due diligence are set out in the Joint Money Laundering Steering Group notes?

    Answer Reference: Section 3.4.3

22. What are the responsibilities of the MLRO?

    Answer Reference: Section 3.5

23. What is the definition of terrorism under the Terrorism Act 2000?

    Answer Reference: Section 3.6

24. What are the main differences between money laundering and terrorist financing activities?

    Answer Reference: Section 3.6.1

25. From whom must directors obtain permission before dealing in their own company's shares?

    Answer Reference: Section 4

    ....

    ....

    ....

26. What is the purpose of the Disclosure and Transparency rules?

    Answer Reference: Section 5

    ....

    ....

    ....

27. State the eight principles of good practice under the Data Protection Act 1998.

    Answer Reference: Section 6.1

    ....

    ....

    ....

28. What is the record retention period for a firm undertaking MiFID investment business?

    Answer Reference: Section 6.2

    ....

    ....

    ....

29. What is the purpose of the capital adequacy requirements?

    Answer Reference: Section 7.1

    ....

    ....

    ....

30. What is liquidity risk?

    Answer Reference: Section 7.3

    ....

    ....

    ....

31. What is passporting?

    Answer Reference: Section 8.1

    ....

    ....

    ....

32. What responsibilities are imposed by MiFID on home state and host state regulators?

    Answer Reference: Section 8.2

    ....

    ....

    ....

33. What are the aims of the UCITS Directive?

    Answer Reference: Section 8.3

    ....

    ....

    ....

34. What is the purpose of the Prospectus Directive?

    Answer Reference: Section 8.4

    ....

    ....

    ....

4

The FSA's Conduct of Business and Client Assets Sourcebooks

This syllabus area will provide approximately 24 of the 50 examination questions

CISI
CHARTERED INSTITUTE FOR SECURITIES & INVESTMENT

The FSA's Conduct of Business and Client Assets Sourcebooks

1. Application and General Provisions of COBS

1.1 The Conduct of Business Sourcebook (COBS)

The Conduct of Business Sourcebook (COBS) is contained within the Business Standards block of the FSA Handbook. It came into force on 1 November 2007, replacing the old Conduct of Business rules which were referred to as 'COB'.

The aim of COBS is to move the regulatory approach towards a better focus on outcomes rather than compliance with detailed and prescriptive rules. It also implements the provisions of the Markets in Financial Instruments Directive (MiFID) that relate to conduct of business. The provisions of MiFID are high-level. MiFID sets standards for business conduct but does not prescribe how firms should achieve those standards.

COBS contains provisions for investment firms that are not subject to MiFID and also those that are. If the provision is derived from MiFID, the relevant part of MiFID is quoted next to the provision.

1.2 Firms Subject to COBS

Learning Objective 4.1.1

Know the firms subject to the FSA Conduct of Business Sourcebook [COBS 1.1.1–1.1.3, COBS Annex 1 Part 3, section 3]

Learning Objective 4.1.3

Know the impact of location on firms/activities of the application of the FSA Conduct of Business Sourcebook: permanent place of business in UK [COBS 1.1.1–1.1.3 & Annex 1, Part 2 and Part 3 (1–3)]

The **general application** rule is based on geographical location and states that firms are subject to COBS if they carry on any of a range of activities from an **establishment maintained by them or their appointed representative in the UK**.

Furthermore, COBS generally applies to a firm which carries on business with a client in the UK from an establishment overseas (unless the overseas person meets certain criteria which allow some activities to be excluded from COBS' scope).

There is a special rule (called the **EEA territorial scope rule**) that overrides the general position where this is necessary to be compatible with EU law. This is relevant to a firm that is conducting business subject to MiFID, in circumstances where there is a cross-border element or the firm has established a branch in another EEA state, both of which can be done using passporting rights.

In summary:

- COBS applies to UK firms conducting MiFID business for UK clients within the UK (as for other investment firms);
- COBS applies to UK firms that may have established a branch in another EEA state, but who are conducting MiFID investment business outside of that state's territory (whether this be the UK or another state);
- For an EEA firm that has established a branch in the UK, COBS applies where the business is carried on within the territory of the UK.

There is an exception for investment research and personal account dealing, where the COBS rules apply on a home state basis only. This means that these aspects of COBS apply to UK firms regardless of where they are conducting business and, in the same vein, an EEA firm conducting MiFID investment business within the UK is not subject to COBS for these rules, but is subject to the equivalent rules of its home state regulator.

1.3 Activities Subject to COBS

Learning Objective 4.1.2

Know the activities which are subject to the FSA Conduct of Business Sourcebook including Eligible Counterparty Business and transactions between regulated market participants [COBS 1.1.1–1.1.3, Annex 1, Part 1(1) & (4)]

The activities that are subject to COBS are:

- designated investment business;
- long-term insurance business in relation to life policies;
- accepting deposits – in part, eg, financial promotion rules, and rules on preparing and providing product information.

Certain of the COBS rules are disapplied for specific types of activity. For example, a range of COBS rules are disapplied, in certain cases, for firms carrying on 'eligible counterparty business' (see Section 2.1). These include:

- **A large part of COBS 2** – general conduct of business obligations.
- **Much of COBS 4** – communicating with clients (including financial promotions).
- **COBS 6.1** – provision of information about the firm, its services and its remuneration.
- **COBS 8** – client agreements.
- **COBS 10** – appropriateness (for non-advised services).
- **Certain parts of COBS 11** – best execution, client order handling and use of dealing commission.
- **Parts of COBS 12** – labelling of non-independent research.

- **COBS 14.3** – information relating to designated investments.
- **COBS 16** – reporting requirements to clients.

Additionally, members and participants in a regulated market do not have to comply with COBS 11.4 (client limit orders) in respect of each other, but they must comply when they are executing orders on behalf of clients.

1.4 Appointed Representatives

Learning Objective 4.1.4

Know how the application of the FSA Conduct of Business Sourcebook applies to appointed representatives [COBS 1.1.1] including financial promotions and firms' responsibilities for appointed representatives [COBS 4.1]

The COBS rules also apply to firms in relation to the relevant activities carried on for them by their appointed representatives.

Appointed representatives are exempt; that is, they can carry out a range of regulated activity under the auspices of their principal firm, which has accepted responsibility for the activity. See Chapter 2 if you need to review the regulated activities that may or may not be conducted by appointed representatives.

In particular, firms must also ensure that their appointed representatives comply with the COBS rules when they communicate financial promotions. Particular mention is made of this in COBS because, technically, a financial promotion communicated by an appointed representative is an 'exempt promotion' and so does not need approval. Therefore, by making particular reference to this matter in COBS, the FSA reminds firms that they are responsible for the content of the financial promotions communicated by their appointed representatives.

1.5 Electronic Media

Learning Objective 4.1.5

Know the provisions of the FSA Conduct of Business Sourcebook regarding electronic media (Glossary definitions of 'Durable Medium' and 'Website Conditions')

Increasingly, firms and their customers communicate and transact business electronically. The FSA rules have adapted to reflect this. In particular, where the rules refer to information being transmitted or provided in a **durable medium**, this means:

- paper; or
- any instrument which lets the recipient store the information so that they can access it for future reference, for an appropriate time and on an unchanged basis. It includes storage on a PC but excludes internet sites, unless they meet the requirement for storage and retrieval. So, for example, information conveyed on a website page does not automatically meet the requirements for a durable medium.

With specific reference to website conditions, the FSA requires that:

- if information is provided by means of a website, that provision must be appropriate to the context in which the business between the firm and the client is (or is to be) carried on. That is, there must be evidence that the client has regular access to the internet. Such evidence could, for example, be by way of their providing their email address to carry on that business;
- the client must specifically consent to having information provided to them in that form;
- they must be notified electronically of the website address and the place on it where the information can be accessed;
- the information must be up-to-date; and
- it must be accessible continuously by way of that website for such a period of time as the client may reasonably need to inspect it.

1.6 Recording of Telephone Conversations and Electronic Communications

Learning Objective 4.1.6

Know the recording of voice conversations and electronic communications requirements [COBS 11.8]

Preventing, detecting and deterring market abuse is one of the FSA's key priorities. However, market abuse is one of the most difficult offences to investigate and prosecute. Good quality recordings of voice recordings and of electronic communications (taping) help firms and the FSA to detect and deter inappropriate behaviour.

This is the reason why the FSA developed rules requiring certain firms to record and retain telephone conversations and other electronic communications linked to taking client orders and dealing in financial instruments for a period of six months, and in a medium that allows storage of the information in a way accessible for future reference by the FSA. The rules apply with respect to a firm's activities carried on from an establishment maintained by the firm in the UK.

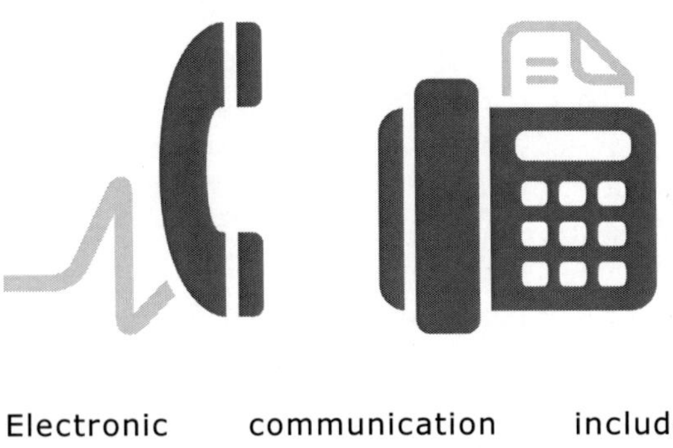

Electronic communication includes communication made by means of fax, email and instant messaging. The rules also cover telephone conversations made using firm-provided mobile phones but not personal mobile phones.

The rules on the recording of voice conversations and electronic communications apply to a firm which carries out any of the following activities:

- receiving client orders;
- executing client orders;
- arranging for client orders to be executed;
- carrying out transactions on behalf of the firm, or another person in the firm's group, and which are part of the firm's trading activities or of another person in the firm's group;
- executing orders that result from decisions by the firm to deal on behalf of its client;
- placing orders with other entities for execution that result from decisions by the firm to deal on behalf of its client.

The rules apply to the extent that the activities relate to:

- qualifying investments admitted to trading on a prescribed market;
- qualifying investments where a request for admission to trading on such a market has been made; and
- investments which are related to qualifying investments.

However, these rules do not apply to:

- activities carried out between operators, or between operators and depositories, of the same collective investment scheme (CIS);
- corporate finance business;
- corporate treasury functions;
- a discretionary investment manager, where the telephone call is made with a firm that they believe is subject to the recording obligations [COBS 11.8.5]. Discretionary managers may make a small proportion of calls, infrequently, without recording the call even where they are made to a firm that is not subject to the recording obligations.

For the purpose of the rules, a relevant conversation or communication is any one of the following:

- Between an employee or contractor of the firm with a client, or when acting on behalf of a client, with another person, which concludes an agreement by the firm to carry out the activities referred to above as principal or as agent.
- Between an employee or contractor of the firm with a professional or an eligible counterparty, or when acting on behalf of a

professional client or an eligible counterparty, with another person, which is carried on with a view to the conclusion of an agreement referred to above, and whether or not it is part of the same conversation or communication.

The rules do not include conversations or communications made by investment analysts, retail financial advisers or persons carrying on ba [illegible] general conver [illegible] ut market conditi [illegible]

A firm [illegible] o prevent an em [illegible] ving calls on pri [illegible] the firm cannot [illegible]

The re [illegible] least six months [illegible] ade in a medium [illegible]

- allow [illegible] access;
- allows for corrections/amendments to be identifiable;
- otherwise cannot be manipulated or altered.

2. Accepting Clients

2.1 Client Categorisation

Learning Objective 4.2.1

Understand client status [PRIN 1.2.1/2/3, Glossary, COBS 3]: the application of the rules on client categorisation [COBS 3.1]; definition of client [COBS 3.2]; retail client [COBS 3.4]; professional client [COBS 3.5] and eligible counterparty [COBS 3.6]

Learning Objective 4.2.2

Understand client status [PRIN 1.2.1/2/3, Glossary, COBS 3]: when a person is acting as agent for another person [COBS 2.4.1–3]; the rule on categorising elective professional clients [COBS 3.5.3–9]; the rule on elective eligible counterparties [COBS 3.6.4–6]; providing clients with a higher level of protection [COBS 3.7]; the requirement to provide notifications of client categorisation [COBS 3.3]

2.1.1 Application of the Client Categorisation Rules

A firm is required to categorise its clients if it is carrying on designated investment business.

MiFID laid down rules as to how client categorisation has to be carried out for MiFID business. For non-MiFID business, the FSA has used the same client categorisation terminology, but the rules on how the categories must be applied are modified in some cases.

If a firm provides a mix of MiFID and non-MiFID services, a firm must categorise clients in accordance with the MiFID requirements, unless the MiFID business is conducted separately from the non-MiFID business.

So, for example, if a firm were to advise a client on investing in a CIS (advice about which would fall within the scope of MiFID) and also about a life policy (which would not), it should use the MiFID client categorisation.

2.1.2 The Definition of a Client

COBS defines a client as someone to whom a firm provides, intends to provide, or has provided a service in the course of carrying on a regulated activity; and, in the case of MiFID or equivalent third country business, anything which is an 'ancillary service'. The term includes potential clients and people acting as agent for another person (see Section 2.1.4).

In addition, in relation to the financial promotion rules, it includes persons with whom the firm communicates, whether or not they are actually clients.

Clients of a firm's appointed representative or tied agent are regarded as clients of the firm.

2.1.3 The Client Categories

Under COBS, clients may be categorised as:

- a retail client;
- a professional client; or
- an eligible counterparty.

The classification determines the level of protection the client receives, with retail clients being afforded the most protection, and eligible counterparties the least.

A **retail client** is any client who is not a professional client or an eligible counterparty. (Note: the term 'customer' is an umbrella term covering both retail clients and professional clients.)

Professional clients may be either per se professional clients or elective professional clients (see below).

Per se professional clients are, generally, those which fall into any of the following categories – unless they are an eligible counterparty, or are categorised differently under other specific provisions.

The categories are:

- An entity required to be authorised or regulated to operate in the financial markets. This includes:
    - a credit institution;
    - an investment firm;
    - any other authorised or regulated financial institution;
    - an insurance company;
    - a CIS or the management company of such a scheme;
    - a pension fund or the management company of a pension fund;
    - a commodity or commodity derivatives dealer;
    - a local;
    - any other institutional investor.
- 'Large undertakings' – companies whose balance sheet, turnover or own funds meet certain levels. Specifically:
    - For MiFID and equivalent third country business, this means undertakings that meeting any two of the following size requirements on a company basis: a balance sheet total of €20 million; a net turnover of €40 million; or own funds of €2 million.
    - For other (non-MiFID) business, large undertakings are:
        - a company whose called up share capital or net assets is, or has at any time in the past two years been, at least £5 million, or currency equivalent (or any company whose holding companies/subsidiaries meet this test);
        - a company which meets (or of which the holding companies/subsidiaries meet) any two of the following criteria: a balance sheet total of €12.5 million; a net turnover of €25 million; an average of 250 employees during the year;
        - a partnership or unincorporated association whose net assets are, or have at any time in the past two years been, at least £5 million, or currency equivalent. In the case of limited partnerships, this should be calculated without deducting any loans owing to the partners;
        - a trustee of a trust (other than certain types of pension scheme dealt with in the next bullet point) which has, or has at any time in the past two years had, assets of at least £10 million;
        - a trustee of an occupational pension scheme or a small self-administered scheme, or the trustee/operator of a personal pension or stakeholder pension scheme, where the scheme has, or has at any time in the past two years had, at least 50 members, and assets under management of at least £10 million;
        - a local authority or public authority.

The list of per se professional clients also includes:

- governments, certain public bodies, central banks, international/supranational institutions and similar; and
- institutional investors whose main business is investment in financial instruments.

COBS contains a list with the types of client which can be classified as **eligible counterparties (ECPs)**.

Each of the following is a **per se eligible counterparty**, including an entity that is not from an EEA state that is equivalent to any of the following, unless and to the extent it is given a different categorisation under COBS 3:

[The list below is, to a certain extent, identical to the 'per se professional client' listed earlier in this section. However the ECP category is narrower as it does not include large undertakings].

- a credit institution;
- an investment firm;
- another financial institution authorised or regulated under EC legislation or the national law of an EEA state (that includes regulated institutions in the securities, banking and insurance sectors);
- an insurance company;
- a CIS authorised under the UCITS Directive or its management company;
- a pension fund or its management company;
- a national government or its corresponding office, including a public body that deals with the public debt;
- a supranational organisation;
- a central bank;
- an undertaking exempted from the application of MiFID under either Article 2(1)(k) (certain own account dealers in commodities or commodity derivatives) or Article 2(1)(l) (locals) of that directive;
- a supranational organisation.

A client can only be categorised as an ECP for the following types of business:

- executing orders; and/or
- dealing on own account; and/or
- receiving and transmitting orders;
- ancillary services relating to the above activities;
- arranging.

This means that if the same ECP wants to engage in other types of business, such as investment management or investment advice, for example, it will have to be classified as a per se professional client.

As explained earlier, many of the COBS rules do not apply when the client is an ECP; the result of this is that the ECP will not benefit from the protections afforded by these rules. Having said that, the majority of ECPs are large firms who are very familiar with the financial markets, or are themselves large players in the financial markets and do not need such protections anyway. Some ECPs, however, would rather have more protections by voluntarily asking to opt-down a client category and become a professional client (see Section 2.1.6).

2.1.4 Agents

If a firm knows that someone to whom it is providing services (A) is acting as the agent of another person (B), then the firm should regard A as its client.

The exception is when the firm has agreed in writing with A that it should treat B as its client instead.

There is a further exception if the involvement of A in the arrangement is mainly for the purpose of reducing the firm's duties to B: in this case, B should be treated as the client in any case.

2.1.5 Recategorising Clients and Providing Lower Levels of Protection

Elective Professional Clients

A retail client may be treated as an **elective professional client** when:

- the firm has assessed his (or its) expertise, experience and knowledge and believes he can make his own investment decisions and understands the risks involved (this is called the **qualitative test**); and – additionally – for MiFID business;
- any two of the following are true (this is called the **quantitative test**);

  - the client carried out, on average, ten significantly sized transactions on the relevant market in each of the past four quarters;
  - the size of the client's financial portfolio exceeds €500,000 (defined as including cash deposits and financial instruments);
  - the client works or has worked as a professional in the financial services sector for at least a year on a basis which would require knowledge of the transactions envisaged.

Assuming the client passes the qualitative and, for MiFID business, the quantitative test, the client must put in writing to the firm their wish to be reclassified and the specific services and/or products that this will apply to. The firm has to respond with a clear written warning of the investor protections that will be lost, and the client must state in writing, separately, that they are aware of the consequences of losing such protections.

It is up to the professional client to keep the firm up-to-date with their circumstances and notify the firm of anything that may affect their classification. If a firm becomes aware that a client no longer fulfils the conditions that made for categorisation as an elective professional client, the firm must take appropriate action. If the appropriate action involves recategorising the client as a retail client, the firm must notify that client of its new categorisation.

Elective Eligible Counterparties (ECPs)

A professional client may be treated as an elective ECP if it is a company and it is:

- a per se professional client (other than one which is only a professional client because it is an institutional investor); or
- it asks to be treated as such and is already an elective professional client (but only for the services for which it could be treated as a professional client); and
- it expressly agrees with the firm to be treated as an eligible counterparty.

2.1.6 Recategorising Clients and Providing Higher Levels of Protection

Firms must allow professional clients and eligible counterparties to request recategorisation, to retail client and professional client respectively, so as to benefit from the higher protections.

In addition, firms can, at their own initiative as well as at the client's request:

- treat per se professional clients as retail clients; and
- treat per se eligible counterparties as professional or retail clients.

Recategorisation may be carried out for a client:

- on a general basis; or
- on more specific terms, eg, in relation to a single transaction only.

A firm can classify a client under a different classification for different financial instruments that they may trade/undertake transactions in. However, this would mean complex internal arrangements for firms and this is why most firms will classify a client just once for all financial instruments that they may undertake transactions in.

2.1.7 Notifications of Client Classification

New clients must be notified of how the firm has classified them. They must also, before services are provided, be advised of their rights to request recategorisation and of any limits in their protections that would arise from this.

2.1.8 Policies, Procedures and Records

Firms must implement appropriate written internal policies and procedures to categorise its clients. Firms must make a record of the form or each notice provided and each agreement entered into. This record must be made at the time that standard form is first used and retained for the relevant period after the firm ceases to carry on business with clients who were provided with that form.

2.2 Client Agreements

Learning Objective 4.2.3

Know the requirement for firms to provide client agreements, when a client agreement is required to be signed and when it is acceptable to be provided to clients [COBS 8.1.1–8.1.3]

The requirement to enter into a client agreement applies to designated investment business for a retail client and, to MiFID business and ancillary services or equivalent third country business carried on for a professional client.

It does not apply to insurance firms issuing life policies as principal.

Firms must enter into a written basic agreement with the client, setting out the essential rights and obligations of the firm and the client. The agreement has to be on paper or other durable medium.

However, in good time **before** a retail client is bound by the agreement, or before the provision of investment services, (whichever is earlier) firms must provide the client with:

- the terms of any such agreement; and
- the information about the firm and its services relating to that agreement or those services required by COBS 6.1.4, including authorised communications, conflicts of interest and the firm's authorised status.

A firm may provide the agreement and the information immediately **after** the client is bound by any such agreement if the client requests the use of distance communications and the firm complies with rules on voice telephony communications.

Firms have to notify the client of any material change to terms in the client agreement – again, in good time before the change takes effect, and in a durable medium.

Client agreement records must be maintained for whichever is the longer of:

- five years;
- the duration of the relationship with the client; or
- in the case of a pension transfer, pension opt-outs or freestanding additional voluntary contributions indefinitely.

Firms should also consider other COBS rules, such as fair, clear and not misleading disclosure of information and distance communications, when considering its approach to client agreements.

2.3 Information Requirements

Learning Objective 4.2.4

Know the requirement to provide information to clients prior to providing services to clients including information relating to the nature and risk of the services and designated investments being offered [COBS 2.2, 6.1.1–16 & 14.3.1–10]

Learning Objective 4.2.5

Know the rules on the provision of information in connection with the service of managing investments [COBS 6.1.6]

Learning Objective 4.2.6

Know the rules on the provision of information concerning safeguarding of designated investments belonging to clients and client money [COBS 6.1.7]

2.3.1 Information about the Nature and Risks of Investments

COBS 2.2 sets out high level disclosure requirements. Firms carrying on MiFID business, or equivalent third country business, must provide clients with appropriate information in a comprehensible form about:

- the firm and its services;
- designated investments and proposed investment strategies, including appropriate guidance on, and warnings of, risks associated with investments in those designated investments or in respect of particular investment strategies;
- execution venues;
- costs and associated charges,

so that the client is reasonably able to understand the nature and risks of the service and of the specific type of designated investments that are being offered and to take investment decisions on an informed basis.

Firms carrying on non-MiFID business with or for a retail client in relation to derivatives, warrants or stock lending activity must also provide the information quoted above.

These high-level rules are expanded upon on COBS 6.1 in relation to information about the firm, and in COBS 14 in relation to information about products. In general terms, for non-MiFID business the disclosure requirements apply to retail clients and for MiFID business the disclosures must be made to professional clients also.

2.3.2 Information about the Firm

A firm must provide a retail client with the following general information, if relevant:

- The name and address of the firm and contact details necessary to enable the client to communicate effectively with the firm.
- In respect of MiFID business or equivalent third country business, the languages in which the client may communicate with the firm and receive documents and other information from the firm.
- The methods of communication to be used between the firm and the client, including those for the sending and reception of orders.
- A statement of the fact that the firm is authorised and the name and contact details of the competent authority that has authorised it.
- If the firm is acting through an appointed representative or, where applicable, a tied agent, a statement of this fact specifying in which EEA state the appointed representative or tied agent is registered.
- The nature, frequency and timing of the reports on the performance of the service to be provided by the firm to the client in accordance with the rules on reporting to clients on the provision of services [COBS 16].
- Information about the firm's conflict of interest policy – a summary of the firm's policy, including the manner in which the firm will ensure fair treatment of the client, and that further details are available on request.

2.3.3 Information Requirements Relating to Managing Investment

A firm that manages investments for a client must establish an appropriate method of evaluation and comparison, such as a meaningful benchmark, based on the investment objectives of the client and the types of investment included in the client's portfolio, to enable the client to assess the firm's performance.

The firm must provide the retail client with the following information, if applicable:

- Information on the method and frequency of valuation of the investments in the client's portfolio.
- Details of any delegation of the discretionary management of all or part of investments or funds in the client's portfolio.
- Specification of any benchmark against which performance of the portfolio will be compared.
- The types of investment that may be included and the types of transaction that may be carried out, including any limits.
- Objectives, the level of risk to be reflected in the manager's exercise of discretion and any specific constraints on that discretion.

2.3.4 Information on Safeguarding Investments/Money

Firms holding client money or investments for retail clients, subject to the MiFID custody/client money rules (as applicable), also have to provide the following information, as appropriate to the service being provided:

1. That the investments/money may be held by a third party on the firm's behalf.
2. What the firm's responsibility is for any acts/omissions of that third party.
3. What would happen if the third party were to become insolvent.
4. If the investments cannot be separately designated in the country in which they are held by a third party, what this means for

the client and what the risks are.

5. That the investments are subject to the laws of a non-EEA jurisdiction and what this means for their rights over them.
6. A summary of the steps the firm has taken to protect the client money/investments, including details of any relevant investor compensation scheme or deposit guarantee scheme.
7. If the money or investments are subject to any security interest, lien or right of set-off, this fact and the terms of it.
8. Full and clear information, in a durable medium, in good time before entering into securities financing transactions using the client's investments, about what the firm's obligations are with regard to those investments and what the risks might be.

Firms holding money or designated investments for **professional clients** must provide them with the information in 6 and 7 above.

2.4 Disclosure of Costs

Learning Objective 4.2.7

Know the rules on disclosure of costs and associated charges, timing of disclosure; medium of disclosure, changes to information provided to the client and compensation information [COBS 6.1.9–6.1.16]

Firms must provide their retail clients with information on the costs and charges to which they will be subject, including – where applicable – the following:

- the total price to be paid including all related fees, commissions, charges and expenses and any taxes payable via the firm;
- if these cannot be indicated at the time, the basis on which they will be calculated so that the client can verify them;
- the commissions charged by the firm, which must be itemised separately in every case;
- if the above are to be paid in foreign currency, what currency is involved and the conversion rates and costs;
- if other costs and taxes not paid or imposed by the firm could be applicable, the fact that this is so;
- how the above items are to be paid/levied;
- information about compensation schemes.

2.4.1 Timing and Medium of Disclosure

Information to clients should be provided in good time before the provision of services. Alternatively, the firm may instead provide the information immediately after the provision of services if:

a. at the request of the client, the agreement was concluded using a means of distance communication which prevented the firm from providing the information beforehand; and
b. the firm complies with the rule on voice telephone communications.

The disclosures must be made in a durable medium or, if the website conditions are satisfied, they can be made via the website.

2.4.2 Keeping the Client Up-to-Date

A firm must notify a client in good time about any material change to the information provided which is relevant to a service that the firm is providing to that client. This notification must be in a durable medium if the information to which it relates was given in a durable medium.

2.4.3 Existing Clients

A firm does not need to treat each of several transactions in respect of the same type of financial instrument as a new or different service. This means that it does not need to comply with the disclosure rules in relation to each transaction. The firm should, however, ensure that the client has received all relevant information in relation to a subsequent transaction, such as details of product charges that differ from those disclosed in respect of a previous transaction.

2.4.4 Compensation Information

A firm which carries on a MiFID business must make available to the client who has used or intends to use those services the information necessary for the identification of the compensation scheme or any other investor compensation scheme of which the firm is a member, or any alternative arrangement provided for in accordance with the investor compensation scheme. The information must include the amount and scope of the cover offered by the compensation scheme and any rules laid down by another EEA state, if relevant. If the client so requests, the firm must provide information concerning the conditions governing compensation and the formalities which must be completed to obtain compensation. This information must be provided in a durable medium or via a website if the website conditions are satisfied.

2.5 Disclosure in Respect of Packaged Products

Learning Objective 4.4.7

Know the application and purpose of the rules on advising on packaged products, including the scope and range of advising [COBS 6.2.1–6, 6.2.8–11]

Learning Objective 4.2.8

Know the rules on disclosure of information regarding packaged products [COBS 6.2.1/2/3/6/11, 6.3.1/2/3/7/8/14/17]

Until 31 December 2012 firms advising on packaged products must comply with certain disclosure rules, as summarised below.

Packaged products are defined by the FSA as any of the following:

a. a life policy;
b. a unit in a regulated CIS;
c. an interest in an investment trust savings scheme;
d. a stakeholder pension scheme; or
e. a personal pension scheme.

The rules on disclosures in respect of these products, where a firm makes a personal recommendation to a client to buy a packaged product, require that the firm takes reasonable steps to ensure that the retail client is provided with prescribed information on a packaged product. It must do this in good time before the client is bound by an agreement for a personal recommendation on the packaged product, or the firm conducts any preparatory work for the provision of the recommendation.

These rules do not apply if the firm is giving basic advice which is a restricted type of advisory service.

In all other cases, the disclosures must explain the scope of the firm's advice and the range of that advice. Scope of advice refers to the product providers whose products it sells, ie, whether the advice is:

- based on the whole of the market; or
- limited to several product providers; or
- limited to a single product provider.

Range of advice refers to which products, eg, pensions or investments.

A firm must accurately describe its scope and range of advice, and ensure that there are processes in place to prevent advisers acting out of scope/range.

A firm that holds itself out as independent or whole of market must make recommendations on packaged products from the whole of the market, or the whole of any sector of that market. Firms may not hold themselves out as whole of market in relation to pension schemes unless they advise on all types of pension scheme, including SIPPs.

The FSA has prepared disclosure statements called **key facts** documents, which firms may use to assist them in meeting most of the disclosure requirements for packaged products. Key facts are not mandatory for investment business, but if a firm wishes to use a key facts disclosure document it must follow the prescribed format in order to stay within the conditions for using the key facts logo, which is a registered trademark that the FSA allows firms to use under licence.

If a firm does not wish to use key facts, they can design their own disclosure documents, so long as they accurately describe the firm's arrangements. If any information that was given at the outset changes, the firm must provide updated information. Also, if commission is received that is in excess of that first disclosed, the firm must obtain the client's informed consent, in a durable medium, to the amended amount.

The RDR changes take effect on 31 December 2012. The new rules apply where a personal recommendation is made to a retail client, in respect of a retail investment product.

Retail investment products are a wider list than packaged products, namely:

- life policies (eg, investment bonds);
- units in regulated or unregulated CIS;
- stakeholder pension scheme/group stakeholder pension scheme;
- personal pension scheme (SIPP) and group personal pension scheme;
- interest in an investment trust savings scheme;
- security in an investment trust;
- structured capital at risk products;
- any other packaged investment product.

For a firm to be able to hold itself out as independent, it must have no restrictions on its service. That is, it must ensure that all its retail investment advisers are competent to advise on all retail investment products, and that the firm does not otherwise restrict its service.

In relation to advising on retail investment products, firms will agree their charges with clients (adviser charging) instead of being remunerated by commission paid by product providers. Commissions that are already in payment for previous advice (trail commissions) may continue so long as the firm provides an ongoing service for the receipt of the trail. Trail commission will cease when new advice is given that results in a change to the original contract. Exceptions are when the advice results in:

- a reduction in the amount invested, or in a regular contribution;
- a change in type of unit (eg, accumulation/ income);
- fund switches within a life policy.

Regardless of these changes, the principles of disclosure remain unchanged – that is, the firm must disclose to the client whether it offers an independent service, or whether it offers a restricted service, and the cost of the service it provides, in good time before providing the service or the client being bound by any agreement.

2.6 Reliance on Others

Learning Objective 4.2.9

Know the rules, guidance and evidential provisions regarding reliance on others [COBS 2.4.4/6/7]

If a firm carrying on MiFID business receives an instruction to provide investment or ancillary services for a client through another firm, and that other firm is a MiFID firm or is an investment firm authorised in another EEA state, and subject to equivalent regulations, then the firm can rely on:

- information relayed about the client to it by the third-party firm; and
- recommendations that have been provided by the third-party firm.

The third-party firm retains responsibility for the completeness and accuracy of information, and the appropriateness of recommendations.

The firm takes responsibility for concluding the services or transactions.

When a firm relies on information provided by a third party, this information should be given in writing.

For firms that are not MiFID investment firms, the FSA states that it will generally be reasonable for a firm to rely on information provided to it in writing by an unconnected authorised person, or a professional firm, unless it is aware, or ought reasonably to be aware, of anything that would give it reasonable grounds to question the accuracy of that information. The firm should take reasonable steps to establish that the other person is unconnected and competent to provide the information.

3. Communicating with Clients

3.1 The Application of the Rules on Communicating with Clients and the Financial Promotion Rules

Learning Objective 4.3.1

Know the application of the rules on communication to clients and on fair, clear and not misleading communications and financial promotions [COBS 4.1, 4.2.1–4]

Learning Objective *4.3.2*

Know the purpose of the financial promotion rules and the relationship with Principles for Businesses 6 and 7 [COBS 4.1]

Learning Objective 4.3.3

Know the rule on identifying promotions as such [COBS 4.3]

It is an offence under FSMA for a person to communicate a financial promotion unless:

- the person is an authorised firm;
- the financial promotion has been approved by an authorised firm.

The rules in COBS Chapter 4 apply to firms communicating with clients regarding their designated investment business and communicating or approving a financial promotion other than:

- for qualifying credit, a home purchase plan or a home reversion plan;
- a promotion for a non-investment insurance contract; or
- the promotion of an unregulated CIS which it is not permitted to approve.

They also apply to communications to authorised professional firms in accordance with COBS 18 (Specialist Regimes).

In general, these rules apply to a firm which carries on business with, or communicates a financial promotion to, a client in the UK (including where this is done from an establishment overseas), except that they do not apply to communications made to persons inside the UK by EEA firms. The majority of these rules do not apply when the client is an eligible counterparty.

3.1.1 The Purpose of the Rules

The purpose of the financial promotion rules is to ensure that such promotions are identified as such, and that they are fair, clear and not misleading.

The financial promotion rules are consistent with Principles 6 and 7 of the FSA's Principles for Businesses:

- **Principle 6** – a firm must pay due regard to the interests of its customers and treat them fairly.
- **Principle 7** – a firm must pay due regard to the information needs of its clients and

communicate information to them in a way which is clear, fair and not misleading.

Fair, Clear and Not Misleading

Firms must ensure that all communications relating to designated investment business, including financial promotions, are fair, clear and not misleading.

The way in which this is achieved should be appropriate and proportionate and take account of the means of communication and what information the communication is intended to convey. So, for example, communications aimed at professional clients may not need to include all the same information as those aimed at retail clients.

In connection with communications which are financial promotions, firms should ensure that:

- those which deal with products or services where a client's capital may be at risk make this clear;
- those quoting yields give a balanced impression of both the short-term and long-term prospects for the investment;
- if an investment product is, or service's charges are, complex, or if the firm may receive more than one element of remuneration, this is communicated fairly, clearly and in a manner which is not misleading and which takes into account the information needs of the recipients;
- if the FSA is named as the firm's regulator but the communication also includes matters not regulated by the FSA, that it is made clear that those matters are not regulated by the FSA (NB, a financial promotion **does not** have to include reference to the FSA);
- those relating to packaged or stakeholder products not produced by the firm itself, give a fair, clear and non-misleading impression of the producer or manager of the product.

FSA guidance advises that firms may wish to take account of the Code of Conduct for the Advertising of Interest-Bearing Accounts, produced by the British Bankers' Association (BBA) and the Building Societies Association (BSA), when they are drafting financial promotions for deposit accounts.

Identifying Promotions as Such

Firms must ensure that financial promotions which they communicate or approve, and which are addressed to clients, are clearly identifiable as such.

There are some exceptions, for example, if the financial promotion is made to a professional client or eligible counterparty.

3.2 Exceptions to the Financial Promotion Rules

Learning Objective 4.3.4

Know the main exceptions to the financial promotion rules in COBS [COBS 4.1, 4.8], the limitations in connection to MiFID business and the existence of the FPO

The financial promotion rules are disapplied in certain cases, notably for excluded communications. These are communications which:

- are exempt under the financial promotion order (FPO – this is a Treasury order which allows unauthorised persons to communicate specified types of promotion, or, in specified circumstances, without the communication having to be approved by an authorised firm); or
- originates outside the UK and cannot have an effect within the UK; or
- an overseas communication that meets criteria for exemption under the FPO; or
- are subject to (or exempted from) the Takeover Code or similar rules in another EEA state; or
- are personal quotes or illustration forms; or
- are one-off promotions that are not cold calls (subject to certain conditions); or
- are promotions about unregulated CIS that are permitted because they fall within one of the exemptions in the FSMA 2000 (Promotion of Collective Investment Schemes) (Exemption s) Order 2001.

However, the exemption for excluded communications will not generally apply in relation to MiFID business.

3.3 Types of Communication

Learning Objective 4.3.5

Know the types and methods of communication addressed by COBS 4

The methods of communication include:

- real time – such as face-to-face, telephone conversations, presentations or other interactive dialogue;
- unsolicited real time – 'cold calls';
- non-real time – such as emails, letters or website, typically where a record is made;
- direct offer financial promotions. These are promotions that make an offer to any person to enter into an agreement and include a form of response or specify the manner of responding.

3.4 The Rules on Prospectus Advertisements

Learning Objective 4.3.6

Know the rules on prospectus advertisements [PR 3.3]

The section of the COBS rules which deals with communications to clients – COBS 4 – does not apply where the Prospectus Rule PR 3.3 applies instead.

Prospectus Rule PR 3.3 applies to offers, or admission to trading, of transferable securities in respect of which:

- a prospectus is required under s.85 of the FSMA; or
- where an election to produce a prospectus has been made under s.87 of the FSMA.

A prospectus advertisement is any type of communication (eg, TV, press, email, letter, text, brochure) which specifically promotes the offer to subscribe or acquire securities.

An advertisement relating to such offers or admissions to trading must not be issued, unless:

1. it states that a prospectus has been (or will be) published, and where investors can obtain it;
2. it is clearly recognisable as an advertisement;
3. the information in it is not inaccurate, or misleading; and
4. it is consistent with the information that is, or is required to be, in the prospectus.

Any written advertisement falling under these rules must also contain a bold and prominent statement to the effect that it is not itself a prospectus, but an advertisement, and that investors should not subscribe for any transferable securities that it refers to, except on the basis of information in the prospectus.

3.5 Communicating with Retail Clients

Learning Objective 4.3.7

Know the general rule in connection with communicating with retail clients [COBS 4.5]

Firms must ensure that where they provide information about designated investment business, or issue/approve a financial promotion that is likely to be received by a retail client, they adhere to certain rules. These rules state that:

- the firm's name is included on the communication;
- the information is accurate and does not emphasise potential benefits without also giving fair and prominent indication of any relevant risks;
- the information is sufficient for, and presented in a way likely to be understood by, the average member of the group at whom it is directed or by whom it is likely to be received;
- the information does not disguise, diminish, or obscure important items, statements or warnings.

Where comparisons are made, they must be meaningful and presented in a fair and balanced way. For MiFID business, the data sources for the comparisons must be cited, as must any key facts and assumptions used.

Where tax treatment is mentioned, firms must explain that this depends on the individual circumstances of each client and that it may be subject to change.

Information included in financial promotions must be consistent with that given in the course of carrying on business.

These rules are disapplied for third-party prospectuses and image advertising. For non-MiFID businesses they are also disapplied for excluded communications.

3.6 Past, Simulated Past and Future Performance

Learning Objective 4.3.8

Know the rules on past, simulated past and future performance [COBS 4.6 excluding 4.6.4–4.6.4B]

3.6.1 Past Performance

Firms must ensure that information including indications of past performance is such that:

- the past performance indication is not the most prominent feature;
- it covers at least the immediately preceding five years (or the whole period that the investment has been offered/the financial index has been established/the service has been provided if this is less than five years); in any event, it must show complete 12-month periods;
- reference periods and sources are clearly shown;
- there is a clear and prominent warning that the data/figures refer to the past and that past performance is not a reliable indicator of future results;
- if the figures are in a currency other than that of the EEA state in which the client is resident, that the currency is stated and there is a warning about the possible effects of currency fluctuations;
- if the performance is cited 'gross', that the effect of commissions, fees and other charges is disclosed.

3.6.2 Simulated Past Performance

When firms give figures based on simulated (ie, notional, not having taken place in reality) past performance because the product or service does not have a track record, a firm must ensure that the simulated past performance figures:

- relate to an investment or financial index;
- are based on the actual past performance of one or more investments/indices which are the same as, or underlie, the investments being simulated;
- meet the rules set out above on past performance (except for the statement that they relate to that investment's past performance, since they do not);
- contain a prominent warning that they relate to simulated past performance and that past performance is not a reliable indicator of future performance.

3.6.3 Future Performance

Firms must ensure that information containing an indication of the possible future performance of relevant business, a relevant investment, a structured deposit or a financial index:

- is not based on, and does not refer to, simulated past performance;
- is based on reasonable assumptions supported by objective data;
- where it is based on gross performance, discloses the effects of commissions, fees or other charges; and
- contains a prominent warning that such forecasts are not reliable indicators of future performance.

3.7 Direct Offers or Invitations

Learning Objective 4.3.9

Know the rule on financial promotions containing offers or invitations [COBS 4.7.1–4]

Direct offer promotions – those making a direct offer or invitation, such as in a newspaper, trade magazine or mailed directly – likely to be received by a retail client must contain:

- prescribed information about the firm and its services;
- where relevant, prescribed information about the management of the client's investments;
- prescribed information about the safekeeping of client investments and money;
- prescribed information about costs and charges;
- prescribed information about the nature and risks of any relevant designated investments, including information about taxation, where relevant;
- where an investment is the subject of a public offer, where any prospectus published in accordance with the Prospectus Directive is available;
- where a designated investment combines two or more investments or services, so as to result in greater risk than the risks associated with the components singly, an adequate description of those components and how that increase in risk arises;
- where a designated investment incorporates a third-party guarantee, enough detail for the client to make a fair assessment of it.

The above need not be included, however, if the client would have to refer to another document

containing that information in order to respond to the offer.

The offer should include a statement that the recipient should seek a personal recommendation if they are unsure about the suitability of the investment or service being promoted.

3.8 Unwritten Promotions and Cold Calling

Learning Objective 4.3.10

Know the rules on unwritten promotions [COBS 4.8.3] and the restriction on cold calling [COBS 4.8.2]

3.8.1 Unwritten Promotions

A firm must not initiate an unwritten promotion to a particular person outside its premises, unless the individual doing so:

- does so at an appropriate time of day;
- identifies himself and his firm at the outset and makes the reason for the contact clear;
- gets clarification of whether the client would like to continue with the communication or terminate it (and does so if requested); and
- gives the client a contact point, if he arranges an appointment with him.

3.8.2 Cold Calling

Cold calling is the practice of authorised persons or exempt persons contacting people without a prior appointment with a view to communicating a financial promotion to them.

Firms must not cold call unless:

- the recipient has an existing client relationship with the firm and would envisage receiving such a call; or
- the call relates to a generally marketable packaged product which is neither a higher-volatility fund, nor a life policy linked to such a fund; or
- it relates to a controlled activity relating to a limited range of investments, including

deposits and readily realisable investments other than warrants or generally marketable non-geared packaged products.

3.9 Overseas Persons

Learning Objective 4.3.11

Know the rule on financial promotions for overseas persons [COBS 4.9.3]

Firms are not permitted to communicate or approve financial promotions for overseas firms, unless the promotion sets out which firm has approved/communicated it, and (if relevant) explains:

- that the rules for the protection of investors will not apply;
- the extent that the UK compensation scheme arrangements will be available (and if they will not, that fact); and
- if the communicator wishes to do so, the details of any overseas compensation/deposit protection scheme applicable.

The firm must not communicate/approve the promotion unless it has no doubt that the overseas firm will deal with its UK retail clients honestly and reliably.

3.10 Approval of Financial Promotions

Learning Objective 4.3.12

Know the requirement for approving financial promotions and the circumstances of relying on another firm's confirmation of compliance [COBS 4.10, SYSC 3 & 4]

As mentioned above, it is an offence for an unauthorised person to communicate a financial promotion, unless the promotion is exempt (by virtue of the financial promotion order) or it has been approved by an authorised firm.

Approving a financial promotion is a formal process set out in the FSMA and reflected in COBS 4.10 rules.

The COBS rules on approval of financial promotions complement requirements under the FSA's Senior Management Arrangements, Systems and Controls Sourcebook (SYSC). SYSC 3 and SYSC 4 require that a firm which:

- communicates with a client, in relation to designated investment business; or
- communicates or approves a financial promotion,

puts in place systems and controls or policies and procedures in order to comply with the rules on financial promotions.

3.10.1 Approving a Financial Promotion

COBS states that, before an authorised firm approves a financial promotion for communication by an unauthorised person, it must confirm that it complies with the financial promotion rules. If, later, it becomes aware that the financial promotion no longer complies, it must withdraw its approval and notify anyone it knows to be relying on that approval as soon as is reasonably practicable. The rules for approving a financial promotion apply in the same way as though the firm was communicating the financial promotion itself.

Firms may not approve real-time financial promotions, that is, financial promotions to be made in the course of personal visits, telephone conversations or other interactive dialogue.

Authorised firms are restricted in the promotion of unregulated collective schemes, and so they may not approve a financial promotion relating to such a scheme unless they would have been able to legitimately promote it for themselves, namely, by way of an exemption or in compliance with certain FSA rules made for this purpose.

If a firm approves a financial promotion for which any of the financial promotion rules are disapplied, it must do so on the terms that its approval is limited to those circumstances. For example, if the approval is for communication to a professional client or ECP, the approval must state this limitation. If an unauthorised person then communicates the promotion outside of the limited approval, they are committing an offence.

3.10.2 Firms Relying on Promotions Approved by Another Party

In relation to non-MiFID business only, a firm is not in breach of the rules if it communicates a financial promotion that has been produced by another party and:

- takes reasonable care to establish that another authorised firm has confirmed that the promotion complies with the rules;
- takes reasonable care that it communicates it only to the type of recipient it was intended for at the time of the confirmation;
- as far as it is (or should be) aware, the promotion is still fair, clear and not misleading, and has not been withdrawn by the other party.

4. Advising and Selling

4.1 Application of the Rules on Suitability

Learning Objective 4.4.1

Understand the application of the rules on identifying client needs and advising [COBS 9.1.1–9.1.4] and the rules on churning and switching [COBS 9.3.2]

The COBS rules on the suitability requirements apply when firms:

- make personal recommendations relating to designated investments;
- manage investments.

There are specific rules relating to the provision of basic advice (personal recommendations on stakeholder products); firms may, if they choose, apply those rules instead of the more general rules on suitability when advising on stakeholder products.

For non-MiFID business, the rules only apply to:

- retail clients; or
- where the firm is managing the assets of an occupational, stakeholder or personal pension scheme.

4.1.1 Churning and Switching

Churning is the activity of over dealing/ trading more frequently for a client in order to generate additional fees/commissions for the firm. It is relevant where, for example, a firm manages a client's portfolio on a discretionary basis. Switching is the activity of selling one investment and replacing it with another.

The FSA's guidance on churning and switching is contained in the COBS rules on suitability. It states that, in the context of assessing suitability, a series of transactions that look suitable in isolation may not be so if the recommendations/trading decisions to make them are so frequent as to be detrimental to the client.

It states also that firms should bear the client's investment strategy in mind when determining how frequently to deal for them, including determining whether or not it is suitable to switch between packaged products.

4.2 Suitability Assessment

4.2.1 The Requirement to Assess Suitability

Learning Objective 4.4.2

Understand the purpose of the suitability rules and the requirement for assessing suitability [COBS 9.2.1–3]

The suitability rules exist to ensure that firms take reasonable steps to ensure that personal recommendations (or decisions to trade) are suitable for their clients' needs.

When a firm makes a personal recommendation or is managing a client's investments, they should obtain the necessary information regarding the client's:

- knowledge and experience in the investment field relevant to the specific type of designated investment business;
- financial situation; and
- investment objectives.

This enables the firm to make the recommendations, or take the decisions, which are suitable for the client.

It is a matter of ongoing concern for the FSA, that, despite the rules, there are persistent failings within firms to ensure that personal recommendations, or decisions to trade, are suitable for their clients. The concerns centre on the failure to properly assess the risk a client is prepared to take, and inappropriate use of risk profiling and asset allocation tools that may not be fit for purpose.

The FSA requires firms to ensure that:

- they have a robust process for assessing the risk a customer is willing and able to take, including:
    - assessing a customer's capacity for loss;
    - identifying customers that are best suited to placing their money in cash deposits because they are unwilling or unable to accept the risk of loss of capital;
    - appropriately interpreting customer responses to questions and not attributing inappropriate weight to certain answers;
- tools, where used, are fit for purpose and any limitations recognised and mitigated;
- any questions and answers that are used to establish the risk a customer is willing and able to take, and descriptions used to check this, are fair, clear and not misleading;
- they have a robust and flexible process for ensuring investment selections are suitable given a customer's investment objectives and financial situation (including the risk they are willing and able to take) as well as their knowledge and experience;
- they understand the nature and risks of products or assets selected for customers; and
- they engage customers in a suitability assessment process (including risk-profiling) which acts in the best interests of those customers.

4.2.2 The Suitability Report

Learning Objective 4.4.5

Understand the obligation to provide a retail client with a suitability report [COBS 9.4.1–3]

Learning Objective 4.4.6

Know the timing and contents of a suitability report [COBS 9.4]

A firm must provide a retail client with a suitability report if it makes a personal recommendation to the client, where the client:

- acquires a holding in, or sells all or part of a holding in:
    - a regulated CIS;
    - an investment trust, where the shares have been or are to be acquired through an investment trust savings scheme;
    - an investment trust where the shares are to be held in an ISA which has been promoted as the means for investing in one or more specific investment trusts; or
- buys, sells, surrenders, converts or cancels rights under, or suspends contributions to, a personal pension scheme or a stakeholder pension scheme; or
- elects to make income withdrawals or purchase a short-term annuity; or
- enters into a pension transfer or pension opt-out.

A firm must also provide a suitability report if it makes a personal recommendation in connection with a life assurance policy.

There are some exceptions to the requirement to provide a suitability report:

- if a firm, acting as investment manager for a retail client, makes a personal recommendation in connection with a regulated CIS;
- if the client is habitually resident outside the EEA and is not present in the UK at the time of acknowledging consent to the proposal

form to which the personal recommendation relates;
- if the personal recommendation is made by a friendly society in connection with a small life policy sold by it, with a premium not exceeding £50 a year or (if payable weekly) £1 a week;
- if the personal recommendation is to increase a regular premium to an existing contract; or
- if it is to invest additional single premiums or single contributions to an existing packaged product, to which a single premium or single contribution has previously been paid.

In terms of timing, a suitability report must be provided:

- in connection with a life policy, before the contract is concluded – unless the necessary information is provided orally, or cover is required immediately (in which case the report must be provided in a durable medium immediately after the contract is concluded); or
- in connection with a personal pension scheme or a stakeholder pension, where the cancellation rules apply, within 14 days of concluding the contract; or
- in any other case, when or as soon as possible after the transaction is effected or executed.

The suitability report must, at least, specify the client's demands and needs, explain any possible disadvantages of the transaction for the client and why the firm has concluded that the recommended transaction is suitable for the client – having due regard to the information provided by the client.

If the transaction is the sale of a life policy by telephone, and the only contact between the firm and client before the contract is concluded is by telephone, then the suitability report must:

- comply with the Distance Marketing Directive (DMD) rules;
- be provided immediately after conclusion of the contract; and
- be in a durable medium.

4.2.3 Information Required to Make a Suitability Assessment

Learning Objective 4.4.3

Understand the information which a firm must obtain from a client in order to make a suitability assessment [COBS 9.2.1–7]; and the guidance on assessing suitability [COBS 9.3.1]

In order to make a suitability assessment, a firm should establish, and take account of, the client's:

- knowledge and experience in the investment relevant to the specific type of designated investment or service;
- level of investment risk that they can bear financially and that is consistent with their investment objectives; and
- investment objectives.

In order to do so, a firm should gather enough information from its client to understand the essential facts about them. It must have a reasonable basis to believe that (bearing in mind its nature) the service or transaction:

- meets their investment objectives;
- carries a level of investment risk that they can bear financially; and
- carries risks that the client has the experience and knowledge to understand.

In terms of assessing the client's knowledge and experience, the firm should gather information on:

- the types of service/transaction/investment with which they are familiar;
- the nature, volume, frequency and period of their involvement in such transactions/ investments; and
- their level of education, profession or relevant former profession.

Firms must not discourage clients from providing this information (eg, because it would rule a particular transaction out and result in a loss of business to the firm). They are entitled to rely on the information the client provides, unless it is manifestly out of date, inaccurate or incomplete.

If a firm does not obtain the information it needs to assess suitability in this way, it must not make a personal recommendation to the client or take a decision to trade for them.

4.2.4 Assessing Suitability – Professional Clients

Learning Objective 4.4.4

Know the application of the assessing suitability rules for professional clients [COBS 9.2.8]

A firm is entitled to assume that a client classified as a professional client in respect of MiFID or equivalent third country business, for certain products, transactions or services, has the necessary experience and knowledge in that area and that the client is able financially to bear any related investments risks consistent with their investment objectives.

4.3 The Application of the Rules on Appropriateness (Non-Advised Sales)

Learning Objective 4.4.8

Understand the application and purpose of the rules on non-advised sales [COBS 10.1]

Learning Objective 4.4.9

Understand the obligations for assessing appropriateness [COBS 10.2]

Learning Objective 4.4.10

Know the circumstances in which it is not necessary to assess appropriateness [COBS 10.4–10.6]

The rules on non-advised sales apply to a range of MiFID (and some non-MiFID) investment services which do not involve advice or discretionary portfolio management. Specifically, they apply to:

- firms providing MiFID investment services other than the provision of personal recommendations or the managing of investments (because these services are covered by suitability rules);
- firms arranging deals, or dealing, in warrants and derivatives for retail clients, where the firm is, or should be, aware that the client's application or order is in response to a direct offer financial promotion;
- firms which assess appropriateness on behalf of other MiFID firms.

The purpose of the appropriateness test is to provide a degree of protection for non-advised transactions.

4.3.1 The Obligation to Assess Appropriateness (Non-Advised Sales)

When a firm provides one of the above services, it must ask the client for information about their knowledge and experience in the investment field of the specific type of product or service offered or demanded so that it can assess whether the product/service is appropriate.

In assessing appropriateness, the firm:

- must determine whether the client has the experience and knowledge to understand the risks involved;
- may assume that a client classified as a professional client for certain services/ products has the necessary knowledge and experience in that field for which it is classified as a professional client.

In terms of a client's knowledge and experience, a firm should obtain information (to the extent appropriate to the circumstances) on:

- the types of service/transaction/investment with which they are familiar;
- the nature, volume, frequency and period of their involvement in such transactions/ investments;
- the level of education, profession or relevant former profession.

The firm must not discourage a client from providing this information.

A firm is entitled to rely on information provided by a client unless it is aware that the information is out of date, inaccurate or incomplete. A firm can use information it already has in its possession. A firm may satisfy itself that a client's knowledge alone is sufficient for them to understand the risk involved in a product or service. Where reasonable, a firm may infer knowledge from experience.

4.3.2 The Obligation to Warn Clients

If a firm believes, based on the above assessment, that the product or service contemplated is not appropriate for the client, it must warn them of that fact. It may do so in a standardised format.

Further, if the client declines to provide the information the firm needs to assess appropriateness, the firm must warn them that it will then be unable to assess the product/ service's appropriateness for them (and again it may do so in standard format). If the client then asks the firm to proceed regardless, it is up to the firm to decide whether to do so based on the circumstances.

4.3.3 Circumstances when Assessment is Unnecessary

Firms are not required to ask clients to provide information or assess appropriateness if:

- the service is execution-only, or for the receipt and transmission of client orders, in relation to particular financial instruments and is at the client's initiative; and
- the client has been clearly informed that the firm is not required to do so in this particular case and that they will therefore not get the benefit of the protection under the rules on assessing and suitability; and
- the firm complies with its obligations regarding conflicts of interest. (You should remember as well that Principle 8 of the Principles for Businesses states that *"a firm must manage conflicts of interest fairly, both between itself and its customers and between a customer and another client"*.)

The particular financial instruments are:

- shares listed on a regulated market or an equivalent third-country market;
- money market instruments, bonds or other forms of securitised debt (provided they do not have embedded derivatives);
- holdings in UCITS funds;
- other investments meeting a definition of 'non-complex' investments.

A financial instrument is non-complex if:

- it is not a derivative;
- there is sufficient liquidity in it;
- it does not involve liability for the client that exceeds the cost of acquiring the investment; and
- it is publicly available and comprehensive information is available on it.

Firms do not need to reassess appropriateness each time if a client is engaged in a series of similar transactions or services, but they must do so before beginning to provide a new service. If a client was engaged in a course of dealings of this type before 1 November 2007, the firm may assume that he has the necessary experience and knowledge to understand the risks. (Note this does not mean, however, that the other criteria may necessarily be deemed to have been met.)

5. Product Disclosure

5.1 The Purpose and Nature of the Rules

Learning Objective 4.5.1

Know the purpose of the rule on the sale of packaged products to retail clients, the rule requiring the provision of key features to retail clients and the main features to be explained in the key features [COBS 13.1.1/3/4, 13.2.1/2/4, 13.3.1/2 (excluding Annex 1R) & 14.1.1, 14.3.1/2]

The rules on product disclosure require that a firm prepares a key features document (KFD) in good time before it needs to provide it to clients, for each:

- packaged product;
- cash deposit ISA; and
- cash deposit child trust fund (CTF0.

The exceptions are:

- if another firm has agreed to prepare such a document;
- KFDs are not needed for certain types of schemes, or in some cases where the information is already provided in enough detail in another document such as a prospectus;
- there are some specific rules for reinsurance and pure protection insurance contracts.

The form and content of KFDs is prescribed, namely:

- the document must be of the same quality and standard as other marketing material relating to the product;
- the firm's brand must be displayed as prominently as any other;
- it must include the Key Facts logo (see Section 2.5) in a prominent position at the top of the document;
- it must include a prescribed statement about the FSA and the purpose of the KFD.

The intention is to make sure that a client is not misled about the identity of the product provider. Concerning the product, it must set out:

- enough information about how it works, its benefits and its risks to enable a retail client to make an informed decision;
- information on its arrangements for handling complaints;
- information about compensation from the FSCS;
- whether or not a right to cancel or withdraw exists and, if so, how to exercise this right and the consequences of doing so;
- availability of CTFs (if relevant);
- a statement of the availability of comparable stakeholder pension schemes (if the KFD is for a pension scheme);
- additional prescribed content for packaged products: 'Its Aims'; 'Your Commitment' or 'Your Investment'; 'Risks' and 'Questions and Answers'.

A Key Features Illustration (KFI) must be produced for the sale of a packaged product.

It is fine to have a single document describing different schemes in a fund supermarket, so long as the document clearly describes the differences between the schemes.

Firms must provide particular information on the nature and risks of designated investments to all clients for whom they undertake MiFID business; they must also do so for retail clients in relation to certain other business. In the context of product information, 'retail client' also includes trustees or operators of pension schemes.

There are additional rules about providing information on designated investments generally, when the firm is managing investments, advising, arranging or engaging in stock lending activity. The firm must provide the client with a description of the investment in sufficient detail to allow the client to make an informed decision, specifically:

- the risks associated with the investment, including an explanation of leverage and its effects and the risk of losing the entire investment;
- the volatility of the price of the investment and any limitations on the available markets;
- whether the investor may assume additional commitments, obligations or contingent liabilities over and above the cost of acquiring the investment;
- any margin requirements or similar obligations.

5.2 Cancellation and the Right to Withdraw

Learning Objective 4.5.2

Know the purpose and requirements of the cancellation and withdrawal rights [COBS 15.1.1, 15.2.1, 15.2.3, 15.2.5, 15.3.1, 15.3.2]

The rules on cancellation apply to:

- most firms providing retail financial products based on designated investments or deposits; and
- firms entering into distance contracts with consumers, relating to deposits or designated investments.

They are intended to ensure that clients entering into the relevant range of transactions have the opportunity to reconsider, within a certain period of time, and to cancel the transaction. When a consumer does so, the effect is that the contract is terminated.

In summary, the **cancellation periods** are as follows:

- life and pension products – 30 calendar days;
- cash deposit ISAs – 14 calendar days;
- non-life and pensions products (advised, non-distance contracts) – 14 calendar days;
- non-life and pensions products (distance contracts) – 14 calendar days.

For example, should a client who receives a cancellation notice in respect of an advised purchase of an authorised unit trust or OEIC wish to exercise his right to cancel, he must do so within 14 days.

The cancellation period starts either from the day the contract concludes, or from the day the client receives contractual information, if later.

Where cancellation rights apply, firms must tell consumers of their rights in good time before (or where that is not possible, immediately after) the consumer is bound by the contract; and they must do so in a durable medium. They must tell the consumer of:

- the existence of the cancellation/withdrawal right;
- its duration;
- the conditions for exercising it (including information on any amount the consumer may have to pay);
- what happens if he does not exercise it; and
- practical details of how to exercise it, including the address to which he must send any notification.

A firm need not do this if the consumer is already receiving similar information from it, or another person, under the COBS rules (distance marketing disclosures rules and providing product information).

If a consumer exercises the right to cancel, they must notify the firm; the notification is deemed to have been observed if it is despatched before the deadline expires. The consumer does not need to give any reason for cancelling.

The record-keeping retention period is:

- indefinitely for pension transfers, pension opt-outs or free-standing additional voluntary contributions (FSAVCs);
- at least five years in relation to a life policy, pension contract, personal pension scheme or stakeholder pension scheme;
- at least three years in any other case.

6. Dealing and Managing

6.1 The Application of the Rules on Dealing and Managing

Learning Objective 4.6.1

Know the application of the rules on dealing and managing [COBS 11.1]

The COBS rules on dealing and managing are:

- Best execution (COBS 11.2).
- Client order handling (COBS 11.3).
- Client limit orders (COBS 11.4).
- Record keeping, client orders and transactions (COBS 11.5).
- Use of dealing commission (COBS 11.6) (see Section 5.5).
- Personal account dealing (COBS 11.7).
- Recording telephone conversations and electronic communications (COBS 11.8).

The rules on dealing and managing (aside from those on personal account dealing) apply generally to authorised firms; there are some variations in application, depending on the nature of business and location of the firm.

- Certain provisions (those marked in the FSA Handbook with an 'EU') apply to non-MiFID firms as if they were rules.
- The rules on the use of dealing commissions (see Section 6.3) apply to a firm that acts as an investment manager.
- The rules on personal account dealing (see Section 6.8) apply to the designated investment business of an authorised firm, in relation to the activities it carries on from an establishment in the UK. These rules:
  - also apply to passported activities carried on by a UK MiFID investment firm from a branch in another EEA state;
  - do not apply to the UK branch of an EEA MiFID firm in relation to its MiFID business.

6.2 Conflicts of Interest

6.2.1 The Principles and Rules on Conflicts of Interest

Learning Objective 4.6.2

Understand the application and purpose of the principles and rules on conflict of interest; the rules on identifying conflicts and types of conflicts; the rules on recording and disclosure of conflicts [PRIN 2.1.1 Principle 8, SYSC 10.1.1–6 + 10.1.8/9]

Learning Objective 4.6.4

Understand the rules on managing conflicts of interest [SYSC 10.1.7] and how to manage conflicts of interest to ensure the fair treatment of clients [SYSC 10.2] including: information barriers such as 'Chinese walls'; reporting lines' remuneration structures; segregation of duties; policy of independence

The rules on conflicts of interest are contained in SYSC. They apply to both common platform firms in respect of regulated business and of ancillary services which constitute MiFID business, as well as to non-MiFID firms and business.

They require that firms take all reasonable steps to identify conflicts of interest between:

- the firm, including its managers, employees, appointed representatives/tied agents and parties connected by way of control and a client of the firm; and
- one client of the firm and another.

The types of conflicts of interests that may arise include:

- realising a financial gain, or avoiding a financial loss, at the expense of a client;
- having an interest in the outcome of a service or transaction that is distinct from the client's interest;
- having an incentive to favour one client over others;
- carrying on the same business as the client;
- receiving inducements from someone other than the client, that are over and above the standard commission or fee.

Firms under these obligations should:

- maintain and operate effective organisational and administrative arrangements, designed to prevent conflicts of interest from adversely affecting the interests of their clients;
- for those producing externally facing investment research, have appropriate information controls and barriers to stop information from these research activities from flowing to the rest of the firm's business;
- if a conflict arises the firm must disclose the interest to the client before undertaking business for the client – the disclosure must be in a durable medium and be in sufficient detail to allow the client to make an informed decision as to the provision of the service. (note that disclosure alone is insufficient to meet the rules; the firm's arrangements should be designed to prevent conflicts arising in the first place);
- prepare, maintain and implement an effective conflicts policy – see Section 6.2.2;
- provide retail clients and potential retail clients with a description of that policy; and
- keep records of those of its activities where a conflict has arisen.

One type of organisational arrangement for controlling information is to establish **'Chinese walls'**. This is the term given to arrangements whereby information held by an employee in one part of the business must be withheld from (or, if this is not possible, at least not used by) the people with or for whom he acts in another part of the business.

If a firm establishes and maintains a Chinese wall, it must:

- withhold or not use the information held; and
- for that purpose, permit its employees in one part of the business to withhold the information from those employed in another part of the business;
- but only to the extent that at least one of those parts of the business is carrying on regulated activities, or another activity carried on in connection with a regulated activity.

The requirement to maintain Chinese walls includes taking reasonable steps to ensure that these arrangements remain effective and are adequately monitored.

Example of a Chinese Wall

When a firm establishes and maintains a Chinese wall, it allows the persons on one side of the wall, eg, corporate finance, to withhold information from persons on the other side of the wall, eg, equity research/market-making arm.

The effect of the Chinese wall rule is that the corporate finance department may have plans for a company that will change the valuation of that company's shares. The equity research/market-making arm on the other side of the 'wall' should have no knowledge of these plans; consequently the inability to pass this knowledge on to clients is not seen as a failure of duty to their clients.

A firm will therefore not be guilty of the offences of Market Manipulation (s.397 FSMA), Market Abuse (s.118 FSMA) or be liable to a lawsuit under s.150 FSMA when the failure arises from the operation of a Chinese wall.

6.2.2 Conflicts of Interest Policies

Learning Objective 4.6.3

Know the rule requiring a conflicts policy and the contents of the policy [SYSC 10.1.10–10.1.15]

As noted above, affected firms are required to have in place effective arrangements for preventing and managing conflicts of interest. Specifically, the rules require firms to have a written conflicts of interest policy, that is appropriate to the scale and nature of the firm's activity.

If a firm is a member of a group, the policy should take into account any potential conflicts arising from the structure/business activities of other members of that group.

Firstly, the policy needs to set out the circumstances that may give rise to a conflict, paying particular attention to circumstances where a person performs two or more roles in relation to (for example) investment research and advice, proprietary trading, portfolio management and corporate finance business.

Secondly, the policy needs to state the procedures for managing such conflicts. These procedures should cover:

- control of information to prevent the exchange of information that may harm the interest of one or more clients;
- separate supervision of persons who are engaged in activities for different clients whose interests may conflict with each other or those of the firm;
- removal of any direct link between remuneration of individuals whose activities may give rise to conflicts;
- measures to prevent or limit one person exercising inappropriate influence over another;
- measures to control an individual's involvement in a series of activities that may give rise to a conflict.

For corporate finance firms who are managing an offering of securities, the policy needs to have particular regard to the offering process (for example, whether the firm might place securities with its investment clients or with its own proprietary book); and it should include specific detail on arrangements for allocation and pricing.

6.2.3 Investment Research and Research Recommendations

Learning Objective 4.6.5

Know the rules on managing conflict in connection with investment research and research recommendations [COBS 12.2.1/3/5/10, 12.3.1/2/3/4, 12.4.4/4/5/6/7/9/10/15/16/17]

There are particular conduct of business rules for managing conflicts of interest, when a firm produces **investment research**. Investment research is information recommending or suggesting an investment strategy, including opinion as to the present or future value/ price of the investments, and intended for distribution to the public as opposed to just for use within the firm or the firm's group.

It has to be clearly labelled as investment research and presented as an objective or independent explanation of the matters that are the subject of the research. It must not be presented in such a way that it would constitute a personal recommendation to a client of an investment firm.

Measures and Arrangements

If a firm produces investment research, it must implement all the measures for managing conflicts of interest set out in SYSC 10.1.11R in relation to the financial analysts involved in producing research, and other relevant persons, if their interests may conflict with those to whom it is disseminated. The arrangements must be such as to prevent dealing ahead, by ensuring that:

- Financial analysts and other relevant persons who know the likely timing/content of investment research which is not yet publicly available or available to clients and which cannot be inferred from information that is available do not undertake personal

transactions, or trade for others, until the recipient of the investment research has had a reasonable opportunity to act on it. There are certain exceptions, such as the receipt of an instruction from an execution-only client or a market maker acting in good faith.
- In any event, they do not undertake personal account transactions in the investments to which the research relates without prior approval from the firm's compliance or legal department and then only in exceptional circumstances.
- The firm and any person involved in the production of research do not accept inducements from those with a material interest in the subject matter of the research.
- They do not promise issuers favourable research coverage.
- If draft investment research includes a recommendation or target price, no-one other than financial analysts may review the draft, other than for the purpose of verifying compliance with the firm's legal obligations.

The firm does not have to comply with the rules on conflict of interest, or with the above arrangements, if it is disseminating investment research on behalf of another person. That is, so long as the following conditions are met:

- that person is not in the same group as the firm;
- the firm does not substantially amend the research;
- the firm does not hold itself out as having produced the research; and
- the firm verifies that the person who has produced the research is subject to the conflicts of interest requirements and the rules on the above arrangements, or has established a policy covering these requirements.

The rules are different if a firm produces **non-independent research**. That is, in summary, research that includes a **research recommendation**; this being a recommended strategy or a particular investment recommendation and the research does not otherwise comply with the conditions to ensure the independence of the research.

In this case, research is treated as a financial promotion and the rules of COBS 4 apply. Additionally, the research must include the following aspects:

- it is clearly identified as a marketing communication; and
- it contains a clear and prominent statement that it has not been prepared in accordance with the requirements for the independence of investment research, and that it is not subject to the prohibitions on dealing ahead that apply to investment research.

There is a high-level requirement to take reasonable steps to identify and manage conflicts of interest that may arise from the production of non-independent research, for example, research that is intended firstly for internal use by the firm and then later publication to clients.

Firms that prepare or disseminate **research recommendations** have to comply with detailed standards for presentation and disclosure of certain information. In summary, these are to:

- ensure that a research recommendation is fairly presented;
- disclose the firm's interests in, or any conflicts of interest concerning, the investments that are the subject of the research recommendation;
- give the name of the firm and its regulator;
- give the identity and job title of the person who prepared the research recommendation;
- ensure that facts are clearly distinguished from interpretation, estimates and opinion;
- ensure that sources are reliable or, if there is any doubt, this should be indicated;
- ensure that projections, forecasts and price targets are clearly labelled and include the main assumptions;
- ensure that the research recommendation can be substantiated as reasonable, if so requested by the FSA.

Fair presentation requires that:

- material sources are indicated, including the issuer (where relevant) and whether the recommendation has been disclosed to the issuer and amended prior to dissemination;

- basis of valuation for setting price targets are adequately summarised;
- the meaning of 'buy', 'sell', or 'hold', including time horizons, should be adequately explained, and include risk warnings and sensitivity analysis of the relevant assumptions;
- reference is made to planned frequency of updates to the research recommendation (if any) or any changes to coverage policy previously announced;
- the date of first release of the research recommendation, and the date and time of any prices, are given;
- any substantive difference between this and a research recommendation issued during the previous 12 months has to be clearly indicated, specifying the change and the date of the change.

The standards for **disclosure of interests and conflicts of interest** are:

- all relationships of the firm or affiliated company that may impair the objectivity of the research recommendation, including relationships with, or conflicts of interests with, issuers;
- relationships of legal and natural persons within the firm who were involved in the preparation of the research recommendation, including whether their remuneration is linked to investment banking transactions by the firm or affiliated company;
- any interests that may be accessible, prior to dissemination, by persons producing the research recommendation, or by any other person who could reasonably have had access to the information (other than those responsible for compliance);
- disclosures concerning a firm's (or affiliated company's) shareholdings in excess of 5% in an issuer, and any other financial interests;
- statements indicating (where relevant) that the firm is a market maker, liquidity provider, lead manager; or concerning any investment banking services, or research recommendation services, provided for the issuer;
- disclosure of the firm's arrangements for preventing conflicts of interest, including information barriers;
- if shares are acquired by a person involved in the research recommendation, the price and date of acquisition.

If compliance with the disclosure standards would be disproportionate to the length of the research presentation, the firm can indicate where the information may be found, eg, on a website page.

The following information has to be published **quarterly**, and also disclosed in research recommendations:

- the proportion of research recommendations published during the quarter that are 'buy' 'hold' and 'sell';
- the proportion of investments, in each category, issued by issuers to which the firm supplied material investment banking services during the previous 12 months.

If the firm disseminates research recommendations produced by a **third party**, it must:

- state the identity of the firm and its regulator;
- ensure that any summaries of third party recommendations are fair, clear and not misleading;
- identify the source research recommendation and identify where the third party's disclosures are accessible;
- ensure that the detailed disclosures above are made as though it had produced the recommendation itself.

If the firm materially **amends a third party recommendation** prior to dissemination, it has to:

- give a description of any alterations made by the firm prior to dissemination if there is a change of direction (eg, buy to sell) or comply with the disclosure rules concerning time horizons as though it had produced the research recommendation;
- maintain a written policy providing for recipients of the information to be directed to where they can access the third party producer, the original recommendation and the third party's disclosures.

6.3 Inducements and the Use of Dealing Commissions

Learning Objective 4.6.6

Know the application of the inducements rules [COBS 2.3.1–2 & 2.3.10–16] and the use of dealing commission, including what benefits can be supplied/obtained under such agreements [COBS 11.6]

6.3.1 Inducements

The inducements rules should be seen as 'payments rules' as they prohibit any payment unless expressly permitted. The rules on inducements apply to firms carrying on designated investment business which is MiFID business as well non-MiFID business. The rules only apply to professional clients and retail clients, therefore, investment firms undertaking eligible counterparty business will not be subject to the detailed inducement provisions.

In relation to MiFID business, firms are prohibited from paying or accepting any fees or commissions, or providing or receiving non-money benefits, other than:

- fees, commissions or non-monetary benefits paid to or by the client, or someone on his behalf (such as management fees); or
- proper fees which are necessary for the provision of the service (eg, custody costs, legal fees, settlement fees) and which cannot by their nature give rise to conflicts;
- fees, commissions or non-monetary benefits paid to/by a third party (or someone on their behalf). These are permissible only if;
  - they do not impair compliance with the firm's duty to act in the client's best interests;
  - they are designed to enhance the quality of the service to the client; and
  - they are disclosed in accordance with set standards prior to the provisions of the service to the client.

Packaged product providers must not pay commissions on terms that are linked to the volume of business transacted, or if the recipient has a financial interest in the commission being repaid.

Reasonable non-monetary benefits that may be provided include:

- gifts, hospitality and promotional competition prizes of reasonable value;
- assistance with financial promotion;
- joint marketing exercises – the provision of product literature, Freepost envelopes, articles and news for publication;
- training, seminars and conferences;
- travel and accommodation expenses incurred in training, seminars, conferences
- technical services and information technology.

In all cases, it is a requirement that the benefit enhances the service for the client, that such benefits are not made available to one firm and not another, and that the value of benefits is reasonable.

Firms can satisfy their disclosure obligations under these rules if they:

- disclose the essential arrangements for such payments/benefits in summary form;
- undertake to their client that further details will be disclosed on request; and
- do, in fact, give such details on request.

Firms must also keep full records of such payments/benefits made to other firms, for all MiFID business.

From 31 December 2012, providers of retail investment products, and their associated firms, must not have any shareholdings or voting power in advisory firms and must not provide credit to such firms, other than in accordance with specified conditions to prevent conflicts of interest and bias (such as the channelling of business).

6.3.2 The Use of Dealing Commissions

In addition to the general rules on inducements, there are specific rules concerning the use of dealing commission.

When an investment manager executes customer orders that relate to certain designated investments (shares, warrants, certificates representing certain securities, options and rights to, or interests in, investments of shares), then it is not permitted to use client-dealing commissions generated from dealing on behalf of its clients to purchase goods or services, unless these goods or services relate to **execution services** or the **provision of research**.

These commission agreements are allowed only for goods or services that assist the recipient firm in providing a better service to its customers.

The rules state that an investment manager must not execute its customer orders through a broker or another person and pass the charges on to its customers, unless the investment manager has reasonable grounds to be satisfied that the goods and services in return for the charges are:

1. related to the **execution of trades** on behalf of the investment manager's customers;
2. comprise the **provision of research**; and
3. will reasonably assist the investment manager in providing services to its customers and do not (or are not likely to) impact the investment manager's duty to act in the best interests of its customers.

When the goods or services relate to the **execution of trades**, an investment manager has reasonable grounds to be satisfied that the requirements are met if the goods or services are:

1. linked to the arranging and conclusion of a specific investment transaction, or series of related transactions; and
2. provided between the point at which the investment manager makes an investment or trading decision and the point at which the investment transaction, or series of transactions, is concluded.

When the goods or services relate to the **provision of research**, an investment manager has reasonable grounds to be satisfied that the requirements are met if the research:

1. is capable of adding value to the investment or trading decisions by providing new insight that informs the investment manager when making such decisions;
2. whatever form its output takes, represents original thought, in the critical and careful consideration and assessment of new and existing facts, and does not merely repeat or repackage what has been presented before;
3. has intellectual rigour and does not merely state what is commonplace or self-evident; and
4. involves analysis or manipulation of data to reach meaningful conclusions.

The FSA indicates that the following goods and services do not meet the requirements:

- valuation or portfolio measurement services;
- computer hardware;
- connectivity services, such as electronic networks and dedicated telephone lines;
- seminar fees;
- subscription for publications;
- travel, accommodation or entertainment costs;
- order and execution management systems;
- office administration software, such as word processing or accounting programmes;
- membership fees to professional associations;
- the purchase or rental of standard office equipment or ancillary facilities;
- employee salaries;
- direct money payments;
- publicly available information; and
- custody services (other than incidental to the execution of trades).

Furthermore, the investment manager should not enter into any arrangements that could compromise its ability to comply with its best execution obligations.

An investment manager that enters into arrangements concerning the receipt of goods or services that relate to the execution of trades or the provision of research must make adequate prior disclosure to customers. This must include the firm's policy, why it feels the need to use dealing commission to purchase goods and services and a description of those received for execution and those for research.

Additionally, investment managers must make the above disclosures periodically, eg, annually, and keep records of all prior and periodic disclosures made. The record needs to be kept for five years.

6.4 Best Execution

6.4.1 The Requirement for Best Execution

Learning Objective 4.6.7

Understand the requirements of providing best execution [COBS 11.2.1–13]

The rules on best execution apply to MiFID and non-MiFID firms and business; however, there is an exemption from the requirements for firms acting in the capacity of an operator of a regulated collective scheme when purchasing or selling units/shares in that scheme.

The **best execution** rules under COBS require firms to execute orders on the terms that are most favourable to their client. Broadly, they apply where a firm owes contractual or agency obligations to its client and is acting on behalf of that client.

Specifically, they require that firms take all reasonable steps to obtain, when executing orders, the best possible result for their clients, taking into account the **execution factors**. These factors are price, costs, speed, likelihood of execution and settlement, size, nature or any other consideration relevant to the execution of an order. The relative importance of each factor will depend on the following criteria and characteristics:

- the client, including how they are categorised;
- the client order;
- the financial instruments involved; and
- the execution venues to which that order can be directed.

Best execution is not merely how to achieve the best price. Any of the other factors mentioned above should be considered and, depending on the criteria or characteristics, could be given precedence. For some transactions, for example, the likelihood of execution could be given precedence over the speed of execution. In other transactions, the direct and/or implicit execution costs of a particular venue could be so high, as to be given precedence over the price of the instrument of this venue.

The obligation to take all reasonable steps to obtain the best possible results for its clients applies to a firm which owes contractual or agency obligations to the client. The obligation to deliver the best possible result when executing client orders applies in relation to all types of financial instruments. However, given the differences in market structures or the structure of financial instruments, it may be difficult to identify and apply a uniform standard of and procedure for best execution that is effective and appropriate for all classes of instrument. Therefore, best execution obligations should be applied in a manner that takes into account all the different circumstances associated with the execution of orders related to particular types of financial instruments.

The Role of Price

For retail clients, firms must take account of the total consideration for the transaction, ie, the price of the financial instrument and the costs relating to execution, including all expenses directly related to it, such as execution venue fees, clearing and settlement fees, and any fees paid to third parties.

Best Execution Where There Are Competing Execution Venues

If a firm can execute the client's order on more than one execution venue, the firm must take into account both its own costs and the costs of the relevant venues in assessing which will give the best outcome. Its own commissions should not allow it to discriminate unfairly between execution venues, and a firm should not charge a different commission or spread to clients for execution in different venues if that difference does not reflect actual differences in the cost to the firm of executing on those venues.

6.4.2 Order Execution Policies

Learning Objective 4.6.8

Understand the requirements for an order execution policy, its disclosure, the requirements for consent and review [COBS 11.2.14–18, 11.2.22–26 & 11.2.28]

Learning Objective 4.6.10

4.6.10 Understand the rules on monitoring the effectiveness of execution arrangements and policy; demonstrating compliance with the execution policy; and the duties of portfolio managers and receivers and transmitters to act in a client's best interest [COBS 11.2.27, 11.2.29–34]

Firms are required to establish an order execution policy to enable them to obtain the best possible results for their clients. This must include, for each class of financial instrument in which the firm deals, information about the different execution venues where the firm executes its client orders, and the factors that will affect the choice of venue used.

The policy must include those venues that enable the firm to obtain the best possible result for its clients consistently.

Firms must give their clients appropriate information about their execution policies; this needs to be more detailed for retail clients. Firms must obtain their clients' prior consent to their order execution policies (although this may be tacit).

Firms must review their order execution policies whenever a material event occurs, but at least annually. Firms must notify clients of any material changes to their order execution arrangements or execution policy. However, the FSA does not define the term 'material change'.

Compliance with Policies, and the Obligations on Portfolio Managers and Firms Receiving/Transmitting Orders

Firms must monitor the effectiveness of their execution arrangements and policies, to identify and (if need be) correct any deficiencies. In addition they must be able to demonstrate to their clients, on request, that they have executed their orders in accordance with their execution policy.

Portfolio managers must act in their clients' best interests when placing orders for them, on the basis of the firm's investment decisions.

Firms receiving and transmitting orders for clients must also act in their clients' best interests when transmitting those orders to other parties (eg, brokers) to execute. This means taking account of the execution factors listed in Section 6.4.1 (unless the client has given specific instructions, in which case these must be followed).

Portfolio managers, and receivers/transmitters of orders, must also maintain order execution policies, but need not get client consent to them.

The policy must identify, in respect of each class of instruments, the entities with which the orders are placed or to which they transmit orders for execution. The entities must have execution arrangements that enable the firm to comply with its obligations under the best execution requirements when it places an order with or transmits an order to that entity for execution.

6.4.3 Specific Client Instructions

Learning Objective 4.6.9

Understand the rules on following specific instructions from a client [COBS 11.2.19–21]

Wherever a firm receives a specific instruction from a client, it must execute the order as instructed. It will be deemed to have satisfied its obligation to obtain the **best possible result** if it follows such specific instructions (even if an alternative means of executing the order would have given a better result).

Firms should not induce clients to instruct an order in a particular way, by expressly indicating or implicitly suggesting the content of the instruction to the client, where they know that any instruction to the client will have the likely effect of preventing them from obtaining the best possible result for the client.

6.5 Client Order Handling

Learning Objective 4.6.11

Understand the rule on client order handling [COBS 11.3.1] and the conditions to be satisfied when carrying out client orders [COBS 11.3.2–6]

Firms must apply procedures and arrangements which provide for the prompt, fair and expeditious execution of client orders, relative to the other orders or trading interests of the firm. (Note, you should see that this rule is also consistent with the need for firms to avoid conflicts of interest, where possible.)

In particular, these should allow comparable client orders to be executed in the order in which they are received.

Firms should ensure that:

- executed client orders are promptly and accurately recorded and allocated;
- comparable orders are executed sequentially and promptly, unless this is impracticable or client interests require otherwise;
- retail clients are informed of any material difficulty in the prompt execution of their order, promptly on the firm becoming aware of this;
- if the firm is responsible for overseeing or arranging settlement, that the assets or money are delivered promptly and correctly.

Firms must not misuse information relating to client orders and must also take steps to prevent its abuse (eg, in order to profit by dealing on its own account).

6.6 Aggregation and Allocation

Learning Objective 4.6.12

Understand the rules on aggregation and allocation of orders [COBS 11.3.7–8]; and the rules on aggregation and allocation of transactions for own account [COBS 11.3.9–13]

Firms must only aggregate their own-account deals with those of a client, or aggregate two or more clients' deals, if:

- this is unlikely to disadvantage any of the aggregated clients;
- the fact that aggregation may work to their disadvantage is disclosed to the clients; and
- an order allocation policy has been established which provides (in sufficiently precise terms) for the fair allocation of transactions. This must cover how volume and price of orders will affect allocation; it must also cover how partial allocations will be dealt with.

If an aggregated order is only partly executed, the firm must then allocate the various trades in order with this allocation policy.

If a firm has own-account deals in an aggregated order along with those of clients, it must not allocate them in a way which is detrimental to the clients. In particular, it must allocate the client orders in priority over its own, unless it can show that, without the inclusion of its own order, less favourable terms would have been obtained; in these circumstances, it may allocate the deals proportionately.

The firm's order allocation policy must incorporate procedures preventing the reallocation of own-account orders aggregated with client orders in a way detrimental to a client.

6.7 Client Limit Orders

Learning Objective 4.6.13

Know the rules on client limit orders – the obligation to make unexecuted client limit orders public [COBS 11.4]

Unless the client instructs otherwise, a firm which receives a client limit order for shares listed on a regulated market and which cannot immediately execute it under the prevailing market conditions must make the limit order public (in a manner easily accessible to other market participants) immediately so that it can be executed as soon as possible. (It need not do so, however, for orders over normal market size.) It may do this by:

- transmitting the order to a regulated market or MTF operating an order book trading system; or
- ensuring the order is made public and can be easily executed as soon as market conditions allow.

6.8 Personal Account Dealing

Learning Objective 4.6.14

Understand the purpose and application of the personal account dealing rule and the restrictions on personal account dealing [COBS 11.7.1–3]

Learning Objective 4.6.15

Know the arrangements required to comply with the personal account dealing rules including the notification requirements; and exceptions regarding personal account dealing [COBS 11.7.4–7]

6.8.1 The Application and Purpose of the Personal Account Dealing Rules

Firms must have arrangements in place to prevent their employees who are relevant persons (directors, partners of the firm or its appointed representatives, and other personnel involved in regulated activities either directly or via an outsourcing arrangement) from:

1. entering into a personal transaction that is contrary to the Market Abuse Directive (MAD); involves misuse or improper disclosure of confidential information; or conflicts with the firm's duties to a customer;
2. improperly advising or procuring that anyone else enters into a transaction that (if it had been done by the employee himself) would have fallen foul of 1. above or of a relevant provision; or
3. improperly disclosing information or opinion, if he knows or should know that the person to whom he has disclosed it is likely to enter into a transaction that (if it had been done by the employee himself) would have fallen foul of 1. above or of a relevant provision, or encouraging someone else to do so.

The relevant provisions are:

- the rules on personal account transactions undertaken by financial analysts contained elsewhere in COBS. These rules were explained in Section 6.2.3;
- the rules on the misuse of information relating to pending client orders (which were explained in Section 6.5).

Firms must keep records of all personal transactions notified to them, and of any authorisation or prohibition made in connection with them.

6.8.2 Compliance with, and Exceptions to, the Personal Account Dealing Rules

The arrangements must ensure that the affected employees are aware of the restrictions on personal transactions, and of the firm's procedures in this regard. They must be such that the firm is informed promptly of any such personal transaction, either by notification of it or some other procedure enabling the firm to identify it.

If outsourcing takes place, the arrangements must be such that the outsource maintains a record of personal transactions undertaken by any relevant person and provides it to the firm promptly on request.

The rules on personal account dealing do not apply to:

- deals under a discretionary management service, if there is no prior communication between the portfolio manager and the relevant person (or any other person for whose account the transaction is being executed) about the deal;
- deals in units/shares in certain classes of fund, where the relevant person (and any other person for whom the deals are effected) is not involved in the management of the fund;
- personal transactions in life policies.

Personnel (other than directors or partners of a firm or its appointed representatives) are only subject to the personal account dealing rules to the extent that they are involved in the provision of the firm's investment or portfolio management services.

The restrictions do not apply separately to each transaction in a succession that are being carried out in accordance with a prior instruction, unless the instruction is changed or a new instruction is issued. Nor do they apply if the instruction is withdrawn, so long as the investments that had been acquired are not disposed of at the same time as the instruction is withdrawn.

7. Reporting to Clients

7.1 Confirmation of Transactions and Periodic Statements

Learning Objective 4.7.1

Know general client reporting and occasional reporting requirements (COBS 16.1–16.2)

Learning Objective 4.7.2

Know the rules on periodic reporting to retail and professional clients, the exceptions to the requirements and the record keeping requirements [COBS 16.3]

7.1.1 Transaction Reporting

Firms are required to ensure that clients receive adequate reports on the services they provide to them. These must include any associated costs.

If a firm (other than one managing investments – see Section 7.1.2 below) carries out an order for a client it must:

- provide the essential information on the execution of the order, promptly and in a durable medium;
- for retail clients only, send the **trade confirmation information** as soon as possible (but no later than on the next business day); if the confirmation is received from a third party, the firm must pass the details on no later than the business day following receipt;
- provide clients with information about the status of their orders on request.

It need not do this if the same details are already being sent to the client by another person.

There are also some exceptions to the above rules eg, for a series of orders executed in funds, where the firm may report all the trades once every six months. Also, for non-MiFID business, eg, if the client has confirmed that confirmations need not be sent, or for transactions in life policies or personal pensions, or if the investment is held within a CTF.

Trade confirmation information includes:

- the firm's identification;
- name/designation of the client;
- trading day and time;
- type of order;
- venue and instrument identification;
- buy/sell indicator or the nature of the order if not buy/sell;
- quantity, price and total consideration;
- total commission and expenses, including mark-up or mark-down (if relevant);
- rate of exchange (if relevant);
- client's responsibilities for settlement;
- statement that the firm was the client's counterparty (if relevant).

Firms must keep copies of all confirmations sent to clients:

- for MiFID business, for at least five years from the date of despatch;
- for other business, for at least three years from the date of despatch.

For the purpose of calculating the unit price in the trade confirmation information, when the order is executed in tranches, firms may supply clients with the information about the price of each tranche or the average price.

7.1.2 Periodic Reporting

The reporting rules for firms providing investment management services are addressed in the FSA's **periodic reporting** rules. Investment managers must provide retail and professional clients with periodic statements, unless these are provided by another party.

For retail clients only, the statement must contain prescribed information ('periodic information'), being:

- the name of the firm;
- the name/designation of the retail client's account;
- the contents and valuation of the portfolio, including each investment and its value, cash balance at the beginning and end of the period, and performance;
- total amount of charges, itemised to show management fees and execution costs, together with a note that a more detailed breakdown can be provided on request;
- a comparison of the firm's performance against the relevant benchmark(s);
- total amount of dividends, interest and other payments received;
- information about corporate actions.

Periodic statements must be sent to the retail client at least six-monthly, with the following exceptions:

- the retail client may request statements three-monthly instead (the firm must advise the client of this right);
- if the client receives deal-by-deal confirmations, and certain higher-risk investments are excluded, the statement may be sent every 12 months;
- if the client has authorised that their portfolio be leveraged, the statement must be provided monthly.

If a retail client elects to received deal-by-deal confirmation, the investment manager must comply with the transaction reporting rules above for prescribed content and timing of the report.

For professional clients, the firm must promptly provide essential information relating to each deal.

A firm must make and retain a copy of any periodic statement:

- for MiFID business, for a period of at least five years;
- for other business, for a period of at least three years.

There are also exceptions for certain overseas customers and in respect of CTFs.

If firms manage investments for retail clients, or operate certain types of account for them which include uncovered open positions, they must report any losses over a pre-agreed limit to the client. They must do so by the end of the business day on which the limit is breached; if this happens on a non-business day, by the end of the next business day.

8. Client Assets

8.1 The Purpose of the Client Money and Custody Rules

Learning Objective 4.8.1

Understand the purpose of the client money and custody rules in CASS including the requirement for segregation and that it is held in trust [CASS 6.2.1–3, 7.3.1–2, 7.4.11, 7.7.1–2]

The rules relating to the custody and safeguarding of client money and client assets are contained in the Client Assets Sourcebook (CASS). They exist to ensure that firms take adequate steps to protect those client assets for which they are responsible.

CASS, in general, applies to every firm, with some specific exemptions (see the end of this section). CASS applies directly in respect of activities conducted with or for all categories of client, ie, retail clients, professional clients and eligible counterparties.

CASS 6 contains the custody rules that apply when a firm holds financial instruments of a client in the course of MiFID business and when it is safeguarding and administering investments in the course of non-MiFID business.

CASS 7 (Client Money and Distribution Rules) applies to a MiFID investment firm either:

- when it holds client money in the course of its MiFID business or in respect of any investment agreement entered into, or to be entered into, with or for a client; or
- when, in the course of non-MiFID business, it opts to comply with the MiFID client money rules.

Firms must, when holding safe custody assets belonging to clients, make adequate arrangements so as to safeguard clients' ownership rights, especially in the event of the firm's insolvency and to prevent the use of safe custody assets belonging to a client on the firm's own account, except with the client's express consent. Firms must also introduce adequate organisational arrangements to minimise the risk of loss or diminution of client's safe custody assets.

The firm must effect correct registration of legal title to the assets in the name of the client, nominee or other authorised person as appropriate to the nature of the service being provided. If a firm owns a nominee, it must accept the same level of responsibility for the nominee as though the assets were held by the firm.

The firm must have robust organisational arrangements to prevent the misuse or loss of client money.

Within CASS, there is a requirement to segregate client money from any other money held by the firm. This is aimed at ensuring that, if the firm fails, money will not be used to repay its creditors. Usually, this is done by ensuring that it is placed promptly in a separately designated client money account with a bank and ensuring that the bank treats it as separate from the firm's own. This is achieved by the firm holding the client money in trust. The trust is a statutory trust, created by CASS 7.7.2R.

When a client bank account is opened, the firm must send a notice to the bank about the trust, and state that the bank may not combine money in the client account with any other accounts held in the name of the firm. The title of the client account must distinguish it from any other account held by the firm. The bank must acknowledge this arrangement within 20 days, otherwise the firm must withdraw the money and deposit it with another bank as soon as possible.

There are a number of circumstances when the client money rules will not apply, for example where money is held in connection with a delivery versus payment (DvP) transaction (unless the DvP does not occur by the close of business on the third business day following the date of payment of a delivery obligation) or where it becomes due and payable to the firm.

8.2 The Requirement to Reconcile

Learning Objective 4.8.2

Know the requirements for reconciling client assets and client money including the timing and identification of discrepancies [CASS 6.5.4–13, 7.6.9–16, 7.7.1]

8.2.1 Reconciliation of Client Assets

Firms must keep such records and accounts as necessary to enable it at any time and without delay to distinguish safe custody assets held for one client from safe custody assets held for any other client, and from the firm's own assets.

CASS 6.5 sets out the obligations of firms to perform internal and external reconciliations on client assets.

Broadly, reconciliations should be made as often as necessary to ensure the accuracy of a firm's records and accounts, between its internal accounts and records and those of any third parties by whom those safe custody assets are held. If possible, they should be done by someone who has not been involved in the production or maintenance of the records being reconciled.

If the reconciliation shows a discrepancy, the firm must make good (or provide the equivalent of) any shortfall for which it is responsible. If another person is responsible, the firm should take reasonable steps to resolve the position with that person.

Firms must inform the FSA without delay of any failure to comply with the reconciliation requirements, including reconciliation discrepancies and making good any such differences.

Firms that hold client assets and money are required to have an external audit and report on the systems and controls. The firm's auditor must conduct this report at least annually and send it to the FSA within four months of the date of the audit.

8.2.2 Reconciliation of Client Money

Firms must keep such records and accounts as necessary to enable them at any time and without delay to distinguish client money held for one client from client money held for any other client, and from their own money.

CASS 7.6 sets out the obligations of firms to perform internal and external reconciliations on client money.

Internal Client Money Reconciliations

As explained in CASS 7.6.6 G, in complying with its obligations under CASS 7.6.2 R (Records and accounts), and where relevant SYSC 4.1.1 R (General organisational requirements) and SYSC 6.1.1 R (Compliance), firms should carry out internal reconciliations of records and accounts of client money the firm holds in client bank accounts and client transaction accounts. The FSA considers the following method of reconciliation to be appropriate for these purposes (the standard method of internal client money reconciliation).

- Each business day, a firm that adopts the **normal approach** should check whether its client money resource, being the aggregate balance on the firm's client bank accounts, as at the close of business on the previous business day, was at least equal to the client money requirement as at the close of business on that day.
- Each business day, a firm that adopts the **alternative approach** should ensure that its client money resource, being the aggregate balance on the firm's client bank accounts, as at the close of business on that business day is at least equal to the client money requirement as at the close of business on the previous business day. No excess or shortfall should arise when adopting the alternative approach.

For the purposes of performing its reconciliations of records and accounts, a firm should use the values contained in its accounting records, for example its cash book, rather than values contained in statements received.

If a reconciliation shows a discrepancy, the firm must investigate to identify the reason for the discrepancy and ensure that either any shortfall is paid into the client bank account or any excess is withdrawn from the client bank account by close of business on the day the reconciliation is performed.

A remittance made up of client money and money intended to pay the firm's fees is classified as client money. The FSA has set a method of reconciliation of client money balances called the **standard method of client reconciliation**.

External Reconciliations

This means cross-checking the internal client money accounts against the records of third parties (for example, banks) with whom client money is held. Firms must perform external reconciliations as often as is necessary and as soon as reasonably practicable after the date to which the reconciliation relates.

If there is a discrepancy, the firm must investigate and correct it as soon as possible. If it cannot do so and the firm should be holding a greater amount of client money, it must pay its own money into the client bank account pending resolution of the discrepancy, which it must correct as soon as possible.

If a firm has not complied with these requirements, or is for some reason unable to comply in a material aspect with a particular requirement, it must inform the FSA in writing.

The FSA believes that an adequate method of reconciling client money balances with external records is as follows:

- A reconciliation of a client bank account as recorded by the firm with the statement issued by the bank (or other form of confirmation issued by the bank).
- A reconciliation of the balance on each client transaction account as recorded by the firm, with the balance of that account as set out in the statement (or other form of confirmation) issued by the person with whom the account is held.

8.3 The Exemptions from CASS

Learning Objective 4.8.3

Know the exemptions from the requirements of the CASS rules [CASS 1.2.3/4, 6.1.1–6, 7.1.1–12]

CASS does not apply to:

- ICVCs;
- incoming EEA firms other than insurers, for their passported activities;
- UCITS-qualifying schemes;
- a credit institution (eg, a bank) under the Banking Consolidation Directive, in relation to deposits held;
- coins held for the value of their metal;
- money transferred under 'title transfer collateral arrangements';
- money held in connection with a DvP transaction (unless payment does not occur after three business days);
- money due and payable to the firm;
- if a firm carries on business in its name but on behalf of the client where that is required by the very nature of the transaction and the client is in agreement;
- the custody rules [CASS 6] do not apply if a client transfers full ownership of a safe custody asset to a firm for the purpose of securing or otherwise covering present or future, actual contingent or prospective obligations.

Specific rules within CASS may be disapplied depending on the nature of a firm's activities; the details are set out within the individual rules.

8.4 Enhancing the Client Money and Assets (CASS) Regime

The FSA has introduced several changes to its CASS regime designed to enhance consumer protection by improving governance and oversight in the holding of client money and assets.

- **Prime brokerage – increased rehypothecation disclosure and transparency** – Each prime brokerage agreement must include a disclosure annex that summarises contractual re-hypothecation provisions. Prime brokers must also offer clients daily reporting.
- **Restricting the placement of client money deposits within a group** – the FSA have imposed a 20% limit on the amount of client money which can be deposited intra-group.
- **Prohibiting the use of general liens in custodian agreements** – the FSA has introduced a prohibition on general or omnibus liens, the only exceptions being liens relating to charges and liabilities properly incurred as a result of the provision of custody services: intra-day payments, contractual settlement and standing credit lines.
- **CASS classification –** CASS firms are classified according to the amount of client money and assets held. Large CASS firms are firms holding than £1 billion of client money or more than £100 billion of client assets; medium CASS firms are those holding between £1 million and £1 billion of client money or between £10 million and £100 billion of client assets; and small. CASS firms are those holding less than £1 million of client money or less than £10 million of client assets.
- **Client money and assets return (CMAR)** - submitted monthly by large and medium CASS firms. The return includes detailed information on a firm's holding of client money and client assets such as:
  - balances of client money and assets;
  - institutions where the client money and assets are held and amounts;
  - information on internal and external reconciliations;
  - information on outsourcing arrangements;
  - CASS breaches.
- **CASS operational oversight controlled function (CF10A)** – a new significant influence function has been established for large and medium CASS firms. This is a required function that can only be held by one person with the firm. This requirement is modified for small CASS firms (see above) and these firms can allocate this responsibility to their existing holder of the CF10 function or any significant influence function holder, providing they make a record of this decision.

A specialist unit within the FSA – the Client Assets Unit (CASS Unit) – has been created with specific responsibility for the supervision of the client assets regime.

End of Chapter Questions

Think of an answer for each question and refer to the appropriate section for confirmation.

1. What is the impact of location on the application of the COBS rules?

   Answer Reference: Section 1.2

   ....

   ....

   ....

2. Which COBS rules are disapplied for firms undertaking eligible counterparties business?

   Answer Reference: Section 1.3

   ....

   ....

   ....

3. What activities are subject to the FSA COBS rules?

   Answer Reference: Section 1.3

   ....

   ....

   ....

4. Do appointed representatives have to comply with the COBS rules?

   Answer Reference: Section 1.4

   ....

   ....

   ....

5. What types of conversations must be recorded?

   Answer Reference: Section 1.6

   ....

   ....

   ....

6. How will a MiFID firm classify its client in relation to non-MiFID business?

   Answer Reference: Section 2.1.1

   ....

   ....

   ....

7. What are the three client categories?

   Answer Reference: Section 2.1.3

   ....

   ....

   ....

8. What are the criteria for reclassifying a retail client as an elective professional client?

   Answer Reference: Section 2.1.5

   ....

   ....

   ....

9. Who are elective eligible counterparties?

   Answer Reference: Section 2.1.5

   ....

   ....

   ....

10. What are the notification requirements to clients on their client categorisation?

    Answer Reference: Section 2.1.7

    ....

    ....

    ....

11. When is a firm required to provide a client agreement?

    Answer Reference: Section 2.2

    ....

    ....

    ....

12. What information must be disclosed prior to providing services?

    Answer Reference: Section 2.3.1

    ....

    ....

    ....

13. What is a retail investment product?

    Answer Reference: Section 2.5

    ....

    ....

    ....

14. Which two of the Principles for Businesses are amplified by the financial promotion rules?

    Answer Reference: Section 3.1.1

    ....

    ....

    ....

15. What is the purpose of the financial promotion rules?

Answer Reference: Section 3.1.1

....

....

....

16. What types of communication are subject to the fair, clear and not misleading communication rule?

Answer Reference: Section 3.1.1

....

....

....

17. List the main exceptions to the financial promotion rules

Answer Reference: Section 3.2

....

....

....

18. When do the prospectus advertisements rules apply?

Answer Reference: Section 3.4

....

....

....

19. When is a firm permitted to cold call retail clients?

Answer Reference: Section 3.8

....

....

....

20. What are the rules on churning and who they do they apply to?

    Answer Reference: Section 4.1.1

    ....

    ....

    ....

21. What is the purpose of the suitability rules for retail clients?

    Answer Reference: Section 4.2.1

    ....

    ....

    ....

22. What is the appropriateness test?

    Answer Reference: Section 4.3.1

    ....

    ....

    ....

23. What is the purpose of the cancellation rules?

    Answer Reference: Section 5.2

    ....

    ....

    ....

24. State four steps a firm could take to manage conflicts of interest?

    Answer Reference: Section 6.2

    ....

    ....

    ....

25. What is the difference between investment research and research recommendations?

Answer Reference: Section 6.2.3

....

....

....

26. What payments are permitted under the inducements rules?

Answer Reference: Section 6.3.1

....

....

....

27. What is the purpose of the best execution requirements?

Answer Reference: Section 6.4.1

....

....

....

28. What is an order execution policy?

Answer Reference: Section 6.4.2

....

....

....

29. What is the purpose of the personal account dealing?

Answer Reference: Section 6.8

....

....

....

30. What is trade confirmation information?

    Answer Reference: Section 7.1.1

    ....

    ....

    ....

31. How frequently must a periodic statement be sent to a retail client?

    Answer Reference: Section 7.1.2

    ....

    ....

    ....

32. What is the purpose of the segregation and trust rules?

    Answer Reference: Section 8.1

    ....

    ....

    ....

33. What are the reconciliation requirements for safe custody investments and client money?

    Answer Reference: Section 8.2

    ....

    ....

    ....

34. What is CF10A?

    Answer Reference: Section 8.4

    ....

    ....

    ....

5

Complaints and Redress

This syllabus area will provide approximately 2 of the 50 examination questions

CISI CHARTERED INSTITUTE FOR SECURITIES & INVESTMENT

Complaints and Redress

1. Complaints

1.1 The Purpose of the Rules

It is almost inevitable that customers will raise complaints against a firm; sometimes these complaints will be valid and sometimes they will not. The FSA requires authorised firms to deal with all complaints promptly and fairly, and there are additional requirements for handling complaints from persons who are eligible to subsequently take their grievance to the Financial Ombudsman Service (FOS).

1.2 Procedures

Learning Objective 5.1.1

Know the procedures a firm must implement and follow to handle customer complaints [DISP 1.2.1/3, 1.3.3, 1.4.1, 1.6.1/2/5, 1.9.1, 1.10.1]

The FSA requires firms to have appropriate written procedures for handling expressions of dissatisfaction from **eligible complainants** (see Section 1.3). However, a firm is able to apply these procedures to other complainants as well, if it chooses to. These procedures should be followed regardless of whether the complaint is oral or written, and whether the complaint is justified or not, as long as it relates to the firm's provision of (or failure to provide) a financial service.

These internal complaints-handling procedures should provide for:

- the receiving of complaints;
- responding to complaints;
- appropriately investigating complaints; and
- notifying eligible complainants of their right to go to the FOS where relevant. You should remember that we looked at the FOS, and its relationship with the FSA, in Chapter 1.

The complaints-handling rules are contained in the **Disputes Resolution: Complaints Sourcebook (DISP 1)** which is entitled: **'Treating Complainants Fairly'**. This chapter of DISP contains rules and guidance on how respondants should deal promptly and fairly with complaints in respect of business carried on from establishments in the UK or by branches of UK firms in other EEA states.

In order to aid consumer awareness of the protections offered by the regulatory system, firms must:

- publish appropriate summary details of their internal process for resolving complaints and of the right of eligible complainants to take unresolved complaints to the FOS;
- refer eligible complainants in writing to the availability of these summary details at, or immediately after, the point of sale; and
- provide such summary details in writing on request and when acknowledging a complaint.

These provisions are the **Consumer Awareness Rules (DISP 1.2)**.

The **Complaints-Handling Rules** are set out in **DISP 1.3** and require firms to have effective and transparent procedures for the reasonable and prompt handling of all complaints, without charge to a complainant. These procedures should allow complaints to be made by any reasonable means, and recognise the need for resolution. Firms must put in place appropriate management controls and take reasonable steps to ensure that when handling complaints they identify and remedy any recurring of systemic problems, for example, by establishing formal processes for:

- identifying the root causes of complaints and common root causes of complaints about particular products or services;
- analysing how many complaints are resolved within one business day of receipt;
- considering whether root causes may also affect other processes or products, including those not directly complained of: and
- correcting, where reasonable to do so, such root causes and prioritising how they are dealt with;
- providing regular reports to senior personnel on recurring or systemic problems;
- keeping records of analysis, and of senior personnel response to management information on root causes of complaints.

The **Complaints Resolution Rules (DISP 1.4)** state that, once a firm has received a complaint, it must investigate the complaint competently, diligently and impartially, obtaining additional information as necessary. It must assess fairly, consistently and promptly:

- the subject matter of the complaint;
- whether the complaint should be upheld;
- what remedial action or redress (or both) may be appropriate; and
- if appropriate, whether it has reasonable grounds to be satisfied that another firm may be solely or jointly responsible for the matter alleged in the complaint.

The following factors may be relevant when assessing a complaint: all the evidence available and the particular circumstances of the complaint; similarities with other complaints received by the firm; relevant guidance published by the FSA, other relevant regulators or the FOS and analysis of FOS decisions.

The firm must offer redress or remedial action when it decides this is appropriate and explain to the complainant promptly and in a way that is fair, clear and not misleading its assessment of the complaint, its decision on it and any offer of remedial action or redress. Finally, it should comply promptly with any offer of remedial action or redress accepted by the complainant.

1.3 Eligible Complainants

Learning Objectives 5.1.3

Know the criteria for a complainant to be eligible to lodge a complaint [DISP 2.2]

Learning Objectives 5.1.1

Know the procedures a firm must implement and follow to handle customer complaints [DISP 1.2.1/3, 1.3.3, 1.4.1, 1.6.1/2/5, 1.9.1, 1.10.1]

Not all complainants will have the right to subsequently take their grievance to the FOS. Access to the FOS depends on whether the circumstances fall within the FOS jurisdiction (see below) and whether the complainant is an 'eligible complainant'.

Eligible complainants are:

- **consumers** – any person using or contemplating using the services of an authorised firm or an appointed representative;
- **micro-enterprises** – any person engaged in economic activity, irrespective of legal form, employing fewer than ten persons and having a turnover or balance sheet not exceeding €2 million at the time the complaint is raised;
- **charities** with an annual income of less than £1 million at the time the complaint is raised; and
- **a trustee of a trust** with a net asset value of less than £1 million at the time the complaint is raised.

A further condition for eligibility is that the complaint must arise out of a business relationship with the firm. For example, they are a customer, or they have a beneficial interest in a pension scheme, or they are a policyholder.

Other authorised firms are generally not eligible complainants, although they may be eligible if the complaint is in respect of an activity for which they do not have permission themselves.

Eligible counterparties and professional clients (other than a trustee of a pension scheme) are generally not eligible complainants, but they may be so if the complaint was about an activity other than that for which they are classified.

1.4 Stages and Timings

The FSA sets certain standards which must be observed when a firm receives a complaint. These should be reflected in a firm's internal complaints handling procedures, as follows. On receipt of a complaint, a firm must:

- send the complainant a prompt written acknowledgement that the complaint is being dealt with;
- keep the complainant informed of progress;
- within eight weeks, send a written to response to the complainant. This will either be a **final response** or a holding response.

A **final response** does one of the following:

- accepts the complaint and offers redress or remedial action; or
- offers redress or remedial action without accepting the complaint; or
- rejects the complaint and gives reasons for doing so;

The final response must also:

- inform the complainant that if they are still dissatisfied they may refer the matter to the FOS and they should do this within six months; and
- include a copy of the FOS leaflet.

If the firm is not able to send a final response within eight weeks it must send a written response that:

- explains why the firm is not yet able to make a final response and indicate when this will be provided;
- informs the complainant that they may now refer the matter to FOS;
- includes the FOS leaflet.

1.5 Record-Keeping and Reporting

Records must be kept in relation to complaints, both for FSA monitoring purposes and to enable the firm to co-operate fully with the FOS, if necessary. These should include:

- the name of the complainant;
- the substance of the complaint; and
- the measures taken for the resolution of the complaint.

The records must be retained for a minimum of five years from the date the complaint was received if the complaint relates to MiFID business, and three years for all other complaints.

The FSA requires firms to provide it with twice-yearly reports on the following complaints opened, complaints closed within four or eight weeks, complaints closed after eight weeks; and amounts of redress paid.

Firms receiving 500 or more reportable complaints in a six-month reporting period are obliged to publish specified data. The FSA produces a report based on the firm's published data.

2. The Financial Ombudsman Service (FOS)

Learning Objective 5.1.2

Know the role of the Financial Ombudsman Service (FOS) [DISP Complaints Sourcebook – Dispute Resolution: Complaints: Introduction] and the awards which can be awarded [DISP 3.7.2/4]

2.1 The Role of the FOS

Under the provisions of FSMA, the FSA was given the power to make rules relating to the handling of complaints (outlined in Section 1) and an independent body was established to administer and operate a dispute resolution scheme. The dispute resolution scheme is known as the Financial Ombudsman Service (FOS), and the body that operates it is the Financial Ombudsman Service Ltd (FOS). The FOS is designed to resolve complaints about financial services firms quickly and with minimum formality. Importantly, it is free to complainants, which removes the deterrent effect of anxiety over legal costs. The FOS does not replace the court system, however, and any complainant is entitled to take civil action against a firm regardless of whether or not the complaint has been considered by the FOS.

2.2 Compulsory versus Voluntary Jurisdictions

The FOS comprises two jurisdictions:

1. Its **compulsory jurisdiction** extends to complaints from eligible complainants against FSA-authorised firms in relation to their regulated activities (and any ancillary activities) which the firm is unable to resolve to the satisfaction of the complainant within the timescales outlined above. Authorised firms are automatically subject to the compulsory jurisdiction.

2. Its **voluntary jurisdiction (VJ)** covers complaints which are not within the compulsory jurisdiction. Businesses can opt into the VJ by entering into a contractual arrangement with the FOS. In doing so, they become 'VJ participants'. The FSA has stated that certain complaints which do not fall within the compulsory jurisdiction can be considered under the VJ.

2.3 FOS Awards

The FOS can require the firm to pay over money as a result of a complaint. This monetary award against the firm will be an amount which the FOS considers to be fair compensation; however, the sum cannot exceed £150,000. Where the decision is made to make a monetary award, this can be as compensation for **financial loss, pain and suffering, damage to reputation** and **distress or inconvenience**.

In calculating the maximum amount of award, the FOS excludes interest on the award, costs which were reasonably incurred by the complainant in respect of the complaint, and interest on costs.

When the FOS has adjudicated on complaint they will write to the complainant asking for confirmation of whether the complainant accepts or rejects the decision. If the decision is accepted, it is final and binding on both parties.

3. The Financial Services Compensation Scheme (FSCS)

Learning Objective 5.1.4

Know the circumstances in which the Financial Services Compensation Scheme will pay compensation [COMP 3.2, 4.2.1/2/3] and the compensation payable in respect of protected deposits and protected investment business [COMP 10.2.1/3]

3.1 Purpose

The Financial Services Compensation Scheme (FSCS) has been established to pay compensation to eligible claimants in the event of a default by an authorised person, which is typically the firm's insurance cover becoming exhausted and the firm suffering insolvency. It is essentially an insurance policy that is paid for by all authorised firms and provides protection to valid claims for compensation in the event of a firm collapsing. Eligible claimants are certain persons who have a protected claim against an authorised person who is in default. They include most clients of the defaulting firm, except:

- other authorised firms – but see the note below;
- overseas financial institutions;
- collective investment schemes (CISs), their trustees and operators;
- some pension and retirement funds – but see the note below;
- supranational institutions, governments and central administrative authorities;
- provincial, regional, local and municipal authorities;
- directors and managers of the firm in default and their relatives (unless the firm is a small mutual association and the directors/ managers are not salaried; or unless the firm is a credit union);

- companies in the same group as the firm in default unless that company is also a trustee of certain pension schemes;
- persons holding 5% or more of the defaulting firm's capital, or of any firm in the same group;
- auditors of the firm in default;
- any person who has contributed to the firm's default;
- large companies or large mutual associations;
- large partnerships;
- persons whose claim arises from transactions in connection with which they have been convicted of money laundering;
- persons whose claim arises under the Third Parties (Rights against Insurers) Act 1930.

There are special arrangements for protected insurance claims; generally, all small businesses are eligible claimants. There is an exception, however, for claims arising out of contracts entered into before 30 November 2001, which is that only if the small business is a partnership can they be eligible claimants.

Note: although generally other authorised firms are not eligible, the following types of authorised firms are eligible if the claim arises from an activity for which they don't have permission:

- sole trader firms;
- credit unions;
- trustee or operator of stakeholder or personal pension scheme;
- small businesses – those with an annual turnover of less than £1 million.

Also, although pension funds are generally excluded, trustees of small self-administered schemes or occupational schemes, where the employer is not a large company, large partnership or large mutual association, are also brought back in as eligible claimants.

The protected claims can relate to money on deposit with a bank (protected deposits); or claims on contracts of insurance (protected contracts of insurance); or in connection with protected investment business. (designated investment business); or any claims against the manager or trustee of an authorised unit trust or the authorised corporate director (ACD) or depository of an ICVC, providing that, in each case, the claim is made by the holder of the units.

For the activities to be 'protected investment business', they must be carried on within the UK.

It is important to note that, as operating an unregulated CIS is designated investment business, claims against a UK-authorised unregulated scheme operator carrying on business in the UK are eligible under FSCS. There are similar arrangements under the Investor Compensation Directive to cover claims against a UK MiFID investment firm carrying on investment business via a branch in another EEA state.

In summary, in order to receive compensation, the person making the claim must be an eligible claimant and he must have a protected claim against an authorised firm that is in default. The precise amount of compensation that is payable depends upon the amount of money lost by the claimant and the type of protected claim.

3.2 Compensation Payable

There are limits to the amount of compensation which the FSCS will pay to eligible claimants:

- **For protected deposits** – 100% of the first £85,000 of the claim. This is the sterling equivalent of the €100,000 deposit compensation limit applying to deposit takers within the EEA.
- **For protected investment business** – 100% of the first £50,000 of the claim.

End of Chapter Questions

Think of an answer for each question and refer to the appropriate section for confirmation.

1. How must a firm publicise its complaints-handling procedures?

   Answer Reference: Section 1.2

   ....

   ....

   ....

2. What situations should be included within a firm's complaints-handling arrangements?

   Answer Reference: Section 1.2

   ....

   ....

   ....

3. List the types of eligible complainant.

   Answer Reference: Section 1.3

   ....

   ....

   ....

4. What are the record-keeping requirements in relation to complaints- handling?

   Answer Reference: Section 1.5

   ....

   ....

   ....

5. What is the role of the Financial Ombudsman Service?

   Answer Reference: Section 2.1

   ....

   ....

   ....

6. What is the difference between compulsory jurisdiction and voluntary jurisdiction?

   Answer Reference: Section 2.2

   ....

   ....

   ....

7. In addition to costs, what is the maximum monetary award the Financial Ombudsman can compel a firm to pay to a complainant?

   Answer Reference: Section 2.3

   ....

   ....

   ....

8. What is the role of the Financial Services Compensation Scheme?

   Answer Reference: Section 3.1

   ....

   ....

   ....

9. Who are normally excluded from claiming compensation from the Financial Services Compensation Scheme?

   Answer Reference: Section 3.1

   ....

   ....

   ....

10. What compensation is available under the Financial Services Compensation Scheme for protected deposits?

    Answer Reference: Section 3.2

    ....

    ....

    ....

11. What is the compensation limit for protected investment business?

    Answer Reference: Section 3.2

    ....

    ....

    ....

Glossary

Glossary

Aggregation

Multiple client orders are bulked together and processed as a single order. Customers must be notified of this procedure and its advantages and disadvantages.

Allocation

The division of a single aggregated order between two or more investors' accounts.

Alternative Trading System (ATS)

The term formerly used for a facility provided by authorised firms to allow for multilateral trading, by bringing together buyers and sellers of securities. ATSs were not exchanges. From 1 November 2007, ATSs were authorised as multilateral trading facilities (MTFs), the term used under the **Markets in Financial Instruments Directive (MiFID)**.

American Depositary Receipt (ADR)

A negotiable instrument representing rights to a block of shares in (generally) a non-US company; the **ADR** is an acknowledgement from a bank or trust company that the block of shares is held by it for the account of its client. ADRs are a common means for non-US companies to have their shares traded in the US.

Ancillary Services

Activities, such as giving advice on **MiFID** instruments, which are passportable only if the firm is already passported in relation to a core investment service or activity (such as dealing), and if that firm is providing those services as ancillary services to that activity.

Appointed Representative

Any type of person, ie, an individual or a company. It must be a party to a contract with an authorised person that allows it/him to carry on certain regulated activities – and the authorised person must have accepted responsibility for the conduct of these regulated activities in writing.

Approved Persons

Individuals who are approved by the **Financial Services Authority (FSA)** to undertake controlled functions. These individuals are required to comply with the FSA's Statements of Principle and Code of Practice for **Approved Persons** (APER).

ARROW

ARROW is an **FSA** acronym standing for the Advanced Risk-Responsive Operating frameWork for supervision. It is the primary process and tool through which the **FSA** assesses the risks and compliance requirements appropriate to each firm.

Authorisation

The **Financial Services and Markets Act (FSMA)** requires firms to obtain authorisation prior to conducting investment business. Authorisation is gained by receiving one or more Part IV permissions from the **FSA**.

Bank of England

The UK's central bank which acts as the government's banker and determines interest rates via its **Monetary Policy Committee (MPC)**.

Base Requirement

Part of the financial resources requirement of an authorised firm.

Banking Consolidation Directive (BCD) Credit Institution

A credit institution which has its registered office in a **European Economic Area (EEA)** state, excluding any institution to which the BCD does not apply.

Best Execution

Requires that firms take into account not only price factors, but also such issues as other costs, speed, likelihood of execution and settlement, and all these in the light of the size and nature of the deal, in determining the means of obtaining the best outcome for a client when executing his deal.

Capital Requirements Directive (CRD)

A European Union (EU) directive setting out the financial rules for financial firms, formerly known as the Capital Adequacy Directive (CAD). The aim of the CRD is to ensure that firms hold adequate financial resources and have adequate systems and controls to prudently manage the business and the associated risks.

Chinese Walls

Organisational barriers to the flow of information set up in large firms, to prevent the movement of confidential, sensitive information between departments and to manage any potential conflicts of interest.

Churning

Excessive trading by a broker in order to generate commission, regardless of the interests of the customer.

Client

Individuals or firms that conduct business through an authorised person. Clients are categorised as retail, professional or eligible counterparty.

Client Assets

Securities or other assets held by a firm on behalf of its clients. The assets have to be kept separate from the firm's own assets (segregated).

Code of Practice for Approved Persons

A code established by the **FSA** with regard to the behaviour of approved persons (see above).

Collective Investment Schemes (CIS)

A generic term for open-ended funds such as a unit trust and an **open-ended investment company (OEIC)**, also known as an investment company with variable capital (ICVC).

Compulsory Jurisdiction

The term used to describe that range of activities that fall compulsorily within the jurisdiction of the **Financial Ombudsman Service (FOS)**.

Common Platform Firms

Firms subject to either of the **Capital Requirements Directive (CRD)** or the **Markets in Financial Instruments Directive (MiFID)**.

Conduct of Business (COBS) Rules

Rules made by the **FSA** under the **Financial Services and Markets Act 2000 (FSMA)** dealing mainly with the relationship between an authorised firm and its clients.

Contract for Difference (CFDs)

An investment instrument consisting of a contract under which the parties hope to make a profit (or avoid a loss) by reference to movements in the price of an underlying asset. The underlying asset does not change hands.

Contracts of Insurance

Financial products specified by Part III of the **Regulated Activities Order 2001**, with two subdivisions: general and long-term insurance contracts.

Controlled Functions

Certain roles within authorised firms for which the **FSA** requires the job-holder to be approved (see Approved Persons).

Counterparty Risk Requirement (CRR)

Part of the financial resources requirement for authorised firms, requiring that timely provision is made in case of bad debts/non-deliveries.

CREST

A system that facilitates the clearing and settlement of trades in UK and Irish company shares, particularly in dematerialised form. CREST is operated by **Euroclear UK & Ireland**.

Criminal Justice Act 1993

A substantial Act which includes provisions relating to **insider dealing**, including a definition of that offence.

Customer Function

The **controlled function** conducted by persons who interact with a firm's customers, such as an investment manager or an investment adviser.

Data Protection Act 1998

Legislation governing how personal data should be held and the rights of access to it.

Debt Securities

Securities whereby the issuer acknowledges a loan made to it. The term includes instruments such as bonds, certificates of deposit (CDs) and commercial paper.

Dematerialised

The term used to describe stock which is held in electronic form rather than having ownership evidenced by way of paper certificates.

Depositary Receipts

Bearer instruments evidencing rights over a block of shares which are held with a depositary – usually a bank or trust company. **American Depositary Receipts (ADRs)** are a good example. Depositary receipts are specified investment instruments under the **Financial Services and Markets Act (FSMA)**.

Designated Investment Exchange (DIE)

An overseas exchange designated by the **Financial Services Authority** as meeting certain standards of investor protection in terms of such criteria as market efficiency, transparency and liquidity.

Designated Professional Body (DPB)

Professional bodies whose members are able to carry on limited financial services business without the need for authorisation from the **Financial Services Authority**, providing that the limited financial services offered to clients are incidental to their main business. These are the professional bodies for lawyers, accountants, chartered surveyors, licensed conveyancers and actuaries.

Directors' Model Code

The Model Code for directors of a listed company. This sets out standards of conduct for these people, adherence to which should avoid their falling foul of insider dealing legislation. For example, it stipulates that a company director should not deal in his own company's shares without permission, and may only do so at certain times.

Disclosure and Transparency Rules

Contained in the **Financial Services Authority** DTR Sourcebook. The rules apply to issuers of securities on certain markets and aim to ensure that information is properly handled.

Durable Medium

Paper or any instrument which enables the recipient to store information addressed personally to them in a way accessible for future reference for a period of time adequate for the purposes of the information.

European Union (EU) Directives

Legislation issued by the European Union to its member states requiring them to enact and implement local legislation.

Euroclear UK & Ireland

A recognised clearing house, Euroclear UK & Ireland is the organisation in the UK that operates the **CREST** clearing and settlement system.

European Central Counterparty Ltd (EuroCCP)

EuroCCP is a UK-incorporated **recognised clearing house (RCH)** regulated by the **Financial Services Authority**.

European Economic Area (EEA)

The member states of the European Union, plus Iceland, Liechtenstein and Norway.

Exempt Persons

Firms exempt from the need to be authorised to carry on regulated activities. The term includes bodies such as **recognised investment exchanges** and **recognised clearing houses**.

Financial Conduct Authority (FCA)

Under the government's plans, the UK will move to a new model of regulation. The Financial Conduct Authority will replace the **Financial Services Authority** as the body responsible for regulating conduct in retail and wholesale markets' supervising the trading infrastructure that supports those markets and for the prudential regulation of firms not prudentially regulated by the Prudential Regulation Authority (PRA).

Financial Ombudsman Service (FOS)

The body established to investigate and determine the outcome of complaints made by eligible complainants. The FOS can make awards where appropriate, up to a maximum of £150,000 plus costs.

Financial Resources Requirement (FRR)

The requirements as to the specific financial resources held by an **Financial Services Authority**-authorised firm.

Financial Services and Markets Act 2000 (FSMA)

The legislation that established the **Financial Services Authority**, and empowered it to regulate the financial services industry. The FSA is required to ensure that the industry adheres to its statutory objectives.

Financial Services Authority (FSA)

The agency created by the **Financial Services and Markets Act 2000 (FSMA)** to be the single financial regulator in the UK.

Financial Services Compensation Scheme (FSCS)

The scheme created to provide a safety net for customers in the case of firms which cannot meet their obligations in respect of valid claims.

Fit and Proper

Under the **Financial Services and Markets Act 2000 (FSMA)** every firm conducting investment business must be fit and proper, and ensure that its affairs are conducted soundly and prudently. This is also the minimum standard for becoming and remaining an approved person.

FSA Handbook

The document containing the **Financial Services Authority** rules, guidance and other provisions, with which authorised firms must comply. The Handbook is divided into a number of separate Sourcebooks and Manuals covering different subjects.

Future

A futures contract is a legally binding arrangement by which parties commit to buy/sell a standard quantity and (if applicable) quality of an asset from another party on a specified date in the future, but at a price agreed today. Because the price is agreed at the outset, the seller is protected from a fall in the price of the underlying asset in the intervening time period (and vice versa).

Her Majesty's Revenue & Customs (HMRC)

The government department responsible for the administration and collection of tax in the UK, and the guidance notes on **HM Treasury's** rules for ISAs. HMRC is the result of the merger of two formerly separate departments, HM Customs & Excise and the Inland Revenue.

HM Treasury

The government department that is responsible for formulating and implementing the government's financial and economic policies. Among other things this means that it is responsible for financial services regulation in the UK.

Home State

The term used for the European Union (EU) country where a financial services firm conducting cross-border business is based.

Host State

The term used for an European Union (EU) country in which a financial services firm is doing business from elsewhere.

Inside Information

Information relating to a security, or an issuer, which is not publicly known and which would affect the price of the security if it were made public.

Insider Dealing

One of several offences created under the **Criminal Justice Act 1993** which may be committed by an insider in possession of unpublished price-sensitive information if he attempts to deal in affected securities, encourages others to deal, or passes the information on.

Integration

The third stage of **money laundering**; integration is the stage at which the laundered funds appear to be of legitimate provenance.

Investment Company With Variable Capital (ICVC)

See **open-ended investment company (OEIC)**.

Joint Money Laundering Steering Group (JMLSG)

A group whose membership is made up of trade bodies in the financial services industry. The JMLSG has published guidance notes which set out how firms should interpret and implement the Money Laundering Regulations. This guidance is not binding but, where there is a breach, compliance with the guidance is relevant to an enforcement court.

Know Your Customer (KYC)

The **Money Laundering Regulations 2007** and the FSA Rules requiring firms to undertake sufficient due diligence, before taking on a client, to satisfy themselves of the identity of that client.

Layering

The second stage of **money laundering**, in which money or assets are typically passed through a series of transactions to obscure their origin.

LCH.Clearnet

A **recognised clearing house** serving major international exchanges and platforms.

LIFFE Administration & Management

A **recognised investment exchange** for **futures** and traded **options**, the largest derivatives exchange in the UK.

London Metal Exchange (LME)

Market for trading contracts in base metals and some plastics.

London Stock Exchange (LSE)

The dominant UK market for trading in securities, especially shares and bonds. The LSE is a **recognised investment exchange**.

Market Abuse

A set of offences introduced under the **Financial Services and Markets Act 2000 (FSMA)**, judged on what a regular user would view as a failure to observe required market standards. The offences include abuse of information, misleading the market, and distortion of the market.

Market Maker

A firm which quotes bid and offer prices for a named list of securities in the market. Such a firm is normally under an obligation to make a price in any security for which it is market maker, at all times.

Markets in Financial Instruments Directive (MiFID)

A European Union (EU) directive that took effect in the UK on 1 November 2007. It allows firms authorised in one member state to provide/ offer investment services to customers in another member state, without requiring further authorisation.

Misleading Statement

The term used for false information given about an investment, in order to (or with the effect of) affecting its value – a criminal act under Section 397 of the **Financial Services and Markets Act 2000 (FSMA)** and a potential form of **market abuse**.

Monetary Policy Committee (MPC)

The committee chaired by the Governor of the **Bank of England** which sets sterling interest rates.

Money Laundering

The process whereby criminals attempt to conceal the true origins of the proceeds of their criminal activities, and to give them the appearance of legitimacy by introducing them into the mainstream financial system.

Money Laundering Regulations 2007

The regulations under which authorised firms, and some other businesses, are required to comply with certain administrative obligations in order to prevent **money laundering**. The obligations include record-keeping, identification of clients, appointment of a **nominated officer** to receive suspicion reports, and staff training. Failure to comply may result in a fine and/or imprisonment.

Money Laundering Reporting Officer (MLRO)

A senior employee who is responsible for a firm's arrangements for the prevention of financial crime, for assessing internal suspicion reports, and, where these appear justified, for reporting those suspicions to the **Serious Organised Crime Agency (SOCA)**.

Multilateral Trading Facilities (MTFs)

A system operated by authorised firms which brings together multiple buyers and sellers of securities, but which is not an exchange. Prior to 1 November 2007, when the **Markets in Financial Instruments Directive (MiFID)** provisions came into force, most MTFs were operated as **alternative trading systems (ATSs)**.

Nominated Officer

A term for the officer who is required to receive a firm's internal suspicion reports under the Proceeds of Crime Act (POCA), the Terrorism Act and the **Money Laundering Regulations**; in practice, usually the same individual as the **money laundering reporting officer (MLRO)**.

Nominee

The party which, under a legal arrangement, holds assets in its own name on behalf of the true beneficial owner.

Open-Ended Investment Company (OEIC)

A **collective investment scheme** constituted as an open-ended company. This means that its share capital can expand or contract to meet investor supply and demand. It is also referred to as an **investment company with variable capital (ICVC)**.

Option

Gives the holder the right (but not the obligation) to buy or sell a fixed quantity of an underlying asset on, or before, a specified date in the **future**. There are two basic types of option – puts and calls. The holder of a call option has the right to buy the underlying asset at a given price. The holder of a put option has the right to sell the underlying asset at a given price.

Prudential Regulation Authority (PRA)

Under the government's plans, the UK will move to a new model of regulation. The Prudential Regulatory Authority (PRA), which will be subsidiary of the **Bank of England**, will be responsible for the **prudential regulation** of financial firms, including banks, investment banks, building societies and insurance companies.

Part IV Permission

The term used where persons are granted authorised status by the **Financial Services Authority** under Part IV of the **Financial Services and Markets Act 2000 (FSMA)**.

Passporting

The method by which firms authorised in one European Union (EU) member state are – under **Markets in Financial Instruments Directive (MiFID)** – permitted to carry on regulated financial services activities in another state without the need to become fully authorised in that other state.

Placement

The first stage of **money laundering**, in which money is introduced into the financial system.

PLUS Stock Exchange plc

A **recognised investment exchange** that offers trading and listing facilities for small and mid-cap companies.

Principles for Businesses

Eleven key principles established by the **Financial Services Authority** which must be observed by authorised firms. These Principles are detailed in the **Financial Services Authority's** Handbook.

Proceeds of Crime Act 2002 (POCA)

Legislation which contains, among other things, anti-money laundering provisions.

Prohibition Order

An order which may be exercised by the **Financial Services Authority** under powers given to it under Section 56 of the **Financial Services and Markets Act 2000 (FSMA)**. Such an order prohibits the individual in connection with whom it is granted from carrying out particular **controlled functions** on the grounds that they are not fit and proper.

Prudential Regulation

The aspect of financial services regulation which deals with firms' financial resources and governance. The **Financial Services Authority**, as the financial services industry's main regulatory body, is responsible for ensuring the financial soundness of authorised firms.

Public Interest Disclosure Act 1998

Among other things, provides protection for employees who, in good faith, disclose suspicions of wrongdoing within an organisation.

Recognised Clearing House (RCH)

A term used to denote those clearing houses recognised by the **Financial Services Authority** as providing appropriate standards of protection in the provision of clearing and settlement facilities to certain markets. **LCH. Clearnet** and **Euroclear UK & Ireland** are the two organisations granted this status.

Recognised Investment Exchange (RIE)

A term used to denote those UK exchanges which operate markets in investments, meeting certain standards set by the **Financial Services Authority**.

Recognised Overseas Investment Exchange (ROIE)

An overseas exchange offering membership or providing facilities within the UK, and having been recognised by the **Financial Services Authority** as meeting appropriate standards of investor protection.

Regular User

A hypothetical person regularly using a particular market. It is through the eyes of the regular user that behaviour is assessed for determining whether it meets the standards required under the legacy offences of the **market abuse** regime.

Regulated Activities

Activities for which authorisation from the **Financial Services Authority** (or exemption from the need for that authorisation) is required. Regulated activities are defined in relation both to the activities themselves, and to the investments to which they relate.

Regulated Activities Order 2001 (as amended)

The statutory instrument which defines the range of **regulated activities** and specified investments.

Regulatory Decisions Committee (RDC)

A committee of the **Financial Services Authority** which is responsible for disciplinary decisions.

Serious and Organised Crime Agency (SOCA)

The law enforcement agency to which suspicions of money laundering must be reported by a firm's **money laundering reporting officer (MLRO)**.

Significant Influence Functions

Certain functions carried out by directors and other senior personnel. In the approved persons regime, these comprise the governing functions, the required functions, the systems and control functions and the significant management functions.

Stabilisation

The activity of supporting the price of a new issue of securities or bonds in order to minimise the volatility that can sometimes arise with new issues.

Statements of Principle for Approved Persons

A set of principles established by **Financial Services Authority** with which **approved persons** are required to comply at all times.

Stock Exchange Trading Service (SETS)

The **London Stock Exchange's (LSE's)** electronic order book system for UK blue chip securities.

Tax and Chancery Chamber of the Upper Tribunal (Upper Tribunal)

The Upper Tribunal took over the role of the Financial Services and Markets Tribunal (FSMT) on 6 April 2010. It is independent of the **Financial Services Authority** and is appointed by the Government's Ministry of Justice (formerly the Department of Constitutional Affairs).

Threshold Conditions

The conditions which a firm must meet before the **Financial Services Authority** will authorise it.

Tipping Off

An offence established under various pieces of anti-money laundering and terrorist financing legislation. It involves disclosing the fact that an investigation is, or is likely to be, under way, if that disclosure may imperil any such investigation.

Training and Competence Sourcebook

Sets out **Financial Services Authority's** requirements in connection with all staff, and with additional requirements for some specified activities. The Sourcebook includes rules relating to training and competence, and specifies which qualifications are required for certain activities.

Trustee

A person or organisation who is the legal owner of assets held in trust for someone else. The trustee is responsible for safeguarding the assets, complying with the trust deed and (where the trust is a unit trust) overseeing the activities of the unit trust's manager.

UK Listing Authority (UKLA)

Under European Union (EU) regulations each member state must appoint a competent authority for the purpose of listing securities. The competent authority for listing in the UK is the **Financial Services Authority**; in this capacity, the **Financial Services Authority** is called the UK Listing Authority.

Undertakings for Collective Investment in Transferable Securities (UCITS)

Collective investment schemes established under the UCITS Directives. These directives aim to harmonise European Union (EU) member states' laws so as to allow for the operation and marketing of UCITS schemes across EU borders.

Warrant

An investment instrument giving the holder the right to buy a set number of the underlying equities at a predetermined price on specified dates, or at any time, up to the end of a predetermined time period. Warrants are usually issued by companies or by securities houses.

Whistleblowing

The term used when an individual raises concerns over potential wrongdoing. The **Public Interest Disclosure Act 1998** provides some statutory protections for whistleblowers.

Abbreviations

ABI	Association of British Insurers
ACD	Authorised Corporate Director
ADR	American Depositary Receipt
AIFM	Alternative Investment Fund Manager
AIFMD	Alternative Investment Fund Managers Directive
AML	Anti-Money Laundering
APER	Statements of Principle and Code of Practice for Approved Persons
ARROW	Advanced Risk-Responsive Operating frameWork
ASX	Australian Stock Exchange
ATS	Alternative Trading System
AUT	Authorised Unit Trust
BBA	British Bankers' Association
BCBS	Basel Committee on Banking Supervision
BCD	Banking Consolidation Directive
BIPRU	Banks, building societies and Investment firms PRUdential handbook
BOE	Bank Of England
CAD	Capital Adequacy Directive
CASS	Client Assets Sourcebook
CBOT	Chicago Board Of Trade
CDD	Customer Due Diligence
CEO	Chief Executive Officer
CF	Controlled Function
CFA	Chartered Financial Analyst
CFD	Contract for Difference
CFEB	Consumer Financial Education Body
CII	Chartered Insurance Institute
CIOBS	Chartered Institute Of Banking in Scotland
CIS	Collective Investment Scheme
CISI	Chartered Institute for Securities & Investment
CISX	Channel Islands Stock Exchange
CJA	Criminal Justice Act
CMAR	Client Money and Assets Return
CMBU	Consumer and Markets Business Unit
CML	Council of Mortgage Lenders
COBS	Conduct of Business Sourcebook
COMP	Compensation Sourcebook
COND	Threshold Conditions
CPD	Continuing Professional Development
CRD	Capital Requirements Directive
CRR	Capital Requirements Regulation
CTA	Counter-Terrorism Act
CTF	Child Trust Fund
DEPP	Decisions Procedure and Penalties Manual
DIE	Designated Investment Exchange
DIR	Disclosure and Transparency Risks
DISP	Dispute Resolution: Complaints
DMD	Distance Marketing Directive
DPA	Data Protection Act
DPB	Designated Professional Body
DTCC	Depository Trust & Clearing Corporation
DTI	Department of Trade and Industry
DvP	Delivery versus Payment
EBA	European Banking Authority
EC	European Community
ECB	European Central Bank
ECO	Electronic Commerce Directive Sourcebook
ECP	Eligible Counterparty
EEA	European Economic Area

EG	Enforcement Guide
EIB	European Investment Bank
ESA	European Supervisory Authority
ESRB	European Systemic Risk Board
EU	European Union
EVA	Economic Value Added
FATF	Financial Action Task Force
FCA	Financial Conduct Authority
FIT	Fit and Proper Test for Approved Persons
FOS	Financial Ombudsman Service
FPO	Financial Promotion Order
FSA	Financial Services Authority
FSCS	Financial Services Compensation Scheme
FSMA	Financial Services and Markets Act (2000)
FSP	Financial Skills Partnership
FX	Foreign eXchange
GABRIEL	GAthering Better Regulation Information ELectronically
GDR	Global Depositary Receipt
GENPRU	The General Prudential Sourcebook
HMRC	Her Majesty's Revenue & Customs
ICAEW	Institute of Chartered Accountants in England and Wales
ICE	InterContinental Exchange
ICO	Information COmmissioner
ICOBS	Insurance: Conduct of Business Sourcebook
ICVC	Investment Company with Variable Capital
IFA	Independent Financial Adviser
IFP	Institute of Financial Planning
ILAA	Individual Liquidity Adequacy Assessment
ILAS	Individual Liquidity Adequacy Standards
IMF	International Monetary Fund
IPRU	Interim Prudential Sourcebooks
ISA	Individual Savings Account
ISD	Investment Services Directive
IT	Information Technology
ITC	Investment Trust Company
JISA	Junior Individual Savings Account
JMLSG	Joint Money Laundering Steering Group
KFD	Key Features Document
KFI	Key Features Illustration
KIID	Key Investor Information Document
KYC	Know Your Customer
LCH	London Clearing House
LIFFE	London International Financial Futures and Options Exchange
LLP	Limited Liability Partnership
LME	London Metal Exchange
LSE	London Stock Exchange
MAD	Market Abuse Directive
MAR	Market Conduct Sourcebook
MCOB	Mortgages and Home Finance Conduct of Business Sourcebook
MiFID	Markets in Financial Instruments Directive
ML	Money Laundering
MLRO	Money Laundering Reporting Officer
MOU	Memorandum Of Understanding
MPC	Monetary Policy Committee
MTF	Multilateral Trading Facility
NASDAQ	National Association of Securities Dealers Automated Quotations
NED	Non-Executive Director
NOS	National Occupation Standards
NS&I	National Savings and Investments
NURS	Non-UCITS Retail Scheme
NYMEX	New York Mercantile EXchange
NYSE	New York Stock Exchange
OEIC	Open-Ended Investment Company

OFT	Office of Fair Trading
OPS	Occupational Pension Scheme
OTC	Over-the-Counter
OTF	Organised Trading Facility
PBU	Prudential Business Unit
PEP	Politically Exposed Person
PERG	Perimeter Guidance Manual
PIDA	Public Interest Disclosure Act (1998)
PLC	Public Limited Company
PMI	Pensions Management Institute
POCA	Proceeds of Crime Act (2002)
PRA	Prudential Regulation Authority
PRIN	Principles for Businesses
PS	Policy Statement
QIS	Qualified Investor Scheme
RAO	Regulated Activities Order
RCH	Recognised Clearing House
RDC	Regulatory Decisions Committee
RDR	Retail Distribution Review
RIE	Recognised Investment Exchange
RIS	Regulated Information Service
RMAR	Retail Mediation Activities Return
RNS	Regulated News Service
ROIE	Recognised Overseas Investment Exchange
SETS	Stock Exchange Electronic Trading Service
SIF	Significant Influence Function
SIPP	Self-Invested Personal Pension
SOCA	Serious and Organised Crime Agency
SOCPA	Serious and Organised Crime Police Act 2005
SPS	Statement of Professional Standing
SRO	Self-Regulatory Organisation
SUP	Supervision Manual
SYSC	Senior Management Arrangements, Systems and Controls Sourcebook
TC	Training and Competence Sourcebook
TCF	Treating Customers Fairly
UCITS	Undertakings for Collective Investment in Transferable Securities
UKLA	United Kingdom Listing Authority
VJ	Voluntary Jurisdiction

Multiple Choice Questions

Multiple Choice Questions – Part 1

The following questions have been compiled to reflect as closely as possible the standard you will experience in your examination. Please note, however, they are not the CISI examination questions themselves.

Tick one answer for each question. When you have completed all the questions, refer to the end of this section for the answers.

1. Why does the Money Laundering Reporting Officer have responsibility for the training of staff in relation to identifying money laundering activity?

   A. Compliance officers require MLROs to undertake this function

   B. It is required by the Joint Money Laundering Steering Group

   C. It is required by the Financial Services Authority

   D. It is required by the Proceeds of Crime Act

2. Which of the following does NOT summarise any of the CISI Principles?

   A. To act honestly and fairly at all times when dealing with clients

   B. To ensure that staff for whom you are responsible maintain relevant standards of competence

   C. To observe standards of market integrity

   D. To identify and manage conflicts of interest to the best of your ability

3. When a firm gives permission to an employee to undertake a personal account transaction it must:

   A. Promptly notify the FSA

   B. Promptly notify the employee

   C. Receive prompt notification that the transaction has been conducted

   D. Obtain permission from the FSA

4. For how long must MiFID firms retain copies of confirmations of transactions carried out for retail clients?

   A. Indefinitely

   B. Three years

   C. Five years

   D. Six years

5. Who might deal with unresolved disputes between an authorised firm and complainants?

   A. Financial Ombudsman Service

   B. Tax and Chancery Chamber of the Upper Tribunal

   C. Financial Services Compensation Scheme

   D. FSA's Regulatory Decisions Committee

6. The Proceeds of Crime Act 2002 includes provisions relating to which ONE of the following?

   A. The offence of market abuse
   B. The offence of making false and misleading statements
   C. The protection of persons who inform authorities of their concerns
   D. The requirement to disclose suspicious money laundering transactions

7. Dealing on the basis of inside information on which of the following investments constitutes an offence under the Criminal Justice Act?

   A. Commodity futures
   B. Energy futures
   C. Options on gold
   D. Options on shares

8. When must a firm normally send a written confirmation after carrying out an order for a retail client?

   A. The same business day
   B. The next business day
   C. Within three business days
   D. Within five business days

9. Which of the following bodies is established to provide a safety net for customers of financial services firms that become insolvent?

   A. Financial Services Compensation Scheme
   B. Financial Services Authority
   C. Financial Ombudsman Service
   D. Tax and Chancery Chamber of the Upper Tribunal

10. Which type of statutory notice can be issued by the FSA only with the consent of the recipient?

   A. Final Decision Notice
   B. Further Decision Notice
   C. Notice of Discontinuance
   D. Supervisory Notice

11. With whom must the firm register a data controller under the Data Protection Act?

   A. UK Department for Business, Innovation and Skills
   B. The FSA
   C. The Information Commissioner
   D. The Treasury

12. In relation to the FSA's complaints-handling requirements, which of the following is TRUE?

   A. The complaint must be dealt with at the firm by an individual involved in the original matter
   B. Firms are not obliged to advise the complainant of their rights to take the complaint to the FOS
   C. Firms' procedures for the receiving of eligible complaints apply to complaints received by both oral and written notification
   D. Firms must maintain a document on its internal procedures for dealing with complaints, however it is only required to provide this to clients/complainants when requested to do so

13. Financial Services Compensation Scheme can make awards to:

   A. Eligible complainants
   B. Eligible counterparties
   C. Eligible claimants
   D. Approved persons

14. Which of the following is TRUE in connection with a MiFID firm communicating with retail clients?

   A. The firm's name must be included in the communication
   B. The information can highlight benefits without having to highlight risks
   C. Financial promotions must name the FSA as the firm's regulator
   D. Where comparisons are made, the source of the information does not have to be identified

15. In normal market conditions, which of the following criteria is most important when a firm achieves best execution for a client?

   A. The size and nature of the client order
   B. The likelihood of settlement
   C. Total consideration, including costs relating to execution
   D. How the client is categorised

16. Which of the following is an exempt person in the conduct of regulated activity?

   A. A member of the Society of Lloyds
   B. A firm dealing as principal
   C. The London Stock Exchange
   D. An appointed representatives

17. ADRs are included in which category of specified investment?

    A. Certificates representing securities
    B. Contracts for difference
    C. Lloyd's investments
    D. Warrants

18. Overseas persons are excluded from the need for authorisation when conducting business after a legitimate approach from a UK client for which ONE of the following activities?

    A. Accepting deposits
    B. Carrying out insurance contracts
    C. Dealing in investments as principal
    D. Establishing stakeholder pension schemes

19. Best execution requires a firm to:

    A. Achieve the fastest result for the order
    B. Execute orders on the most favourable terms for the client
    C. Obtain consistent rules by using the same venue for the majority of orders
    D. Select venues based on commissions receivable

20. A firm is permitted to deal for itself prior to the publication of a research recommendation under which of the following circumstances?

    A. It anticipates customer demand
    B. It is a market maker acting in good faith
    C. The market price is likely to be unaffected by publication
    D. The firm's documentation states it may deal ahead of publication

21. In relation to an eligible complaint that reaches the Financial Ombudsman, which of the following is true?

    A. It is resolved between the firm and the complainant under supervision
    B. It is resolved by the Ombudsman
    C. It is resolved by an FSA inspector
    D. It is funded by the Ombudsman and considered in a court of law

22. Which of the following is a regulated activity?

    A. Discussing term assurance generally
    B. Explaining different types of investments
    C. Advising on shares
    D. Advising on bank deposit accounts

23. Which of the following types of client is entitled to the most protection?

    A. Professional
    B. Institutional
    C. Eligible counterparty
    D. Retail

25. Which of the following are a type of MiFID financial instruments?

    A. Bank deposit accounts
    B. Financial contracts for difference
    C. Residential mortgages
    D. Contracts of insurance

Answers to Multiple Choice Questions – Part 1

Answer		Reference
1.	C	Chapter 3, Section 3.5
2.	B	Chapter 1, Section 5
3.	C	Chapter 4, Section 6.8
4.	C	Chapter 4, Section 7.1
5.	A	Chapter 5, Section 2.1
6.	D	Chapter 3, Section 3.1
7.	D	Chapter 3, Section 1.4
8.	B	Chapter 4, Section 7.1
9.	A	Chapter 1, Section 7.2
10.	B	Chapter 2, Section 8.2
11.	C	Chapter 3, Section 6
12.	C	Chapter 5, Section 1.2
13.	C	Chapter 5, Section 3.1
14.	A	Chapter 4, Section 3.5
15.	C	Chapter 4, Section 6.4.1
16.	D	Chapter 2, Section 2
17.	A	Chapter 2, Section 1.2.1
18.	C	Chapter 2, Section 1.3.5
19.	B	Chapter 4, Sections 6.4
20.	B	Chapter 4, Section 6.2.3
21.	B	Chapter 5, Section 2.1
22.	C	Chapter 2, Section 1.2.2
23.	D	Chapter 4, Section 2.1.3
24.	B	Chapter 3, Section 8.1.3
25.	B	Chapter 3, Section 8.1.3

Multiple Choice Questions – Part 2

The following additional questions have been compiled to reflect as closely as possible the examination standard you will experience in your examination. Please note, however, they are not the CISI examination questions themselves.

1. Which ONE of the following is one of the FSA's statutory objectives?

   A. To ensure retail clients are not over charged for financial products
   B. To prevent authorised firms from going into default
   C. To secure the appropriate degree of protection for consumers
   D. To ensure authorised firms have adequate financial resources

2. Appeals against FSA disciplinary decisions are normally considered by which body?

   A. Advisory, Conciliation and Arbitration Service
   B. Financial Ombudsman Service
   C. Office of Fair Trading
   D. Tax and Chancery Chamber of the Upper Tribunal

3. Which ONE of the following statements is TRUE concerning a Designated Investment Exchange?

   A. It is an overseas exchange that does not conduct regulated activity in the UK
   B. It must apply to the FSA for authorisation
   C. Firms must apply to the FSA for approval to use a designated investment exchange
   D. A designated investment exchange is not obliged to offer consumer protection

4. The 'management and control' Principle for Businesses requires firms to have adequate systems in place specifically relating to:

   A. Customer fairness
   B. Cash flow resources
   C. Risk management
   D. Staff training

5. Which of the following is a statutory consequence of contravening the general prohibition?

   A. Approved persons lose their approved status
   B. A firm may not conduct any business within the UK
   C. Civil proceedings may commence
   D. Financial services agreements are likely to be unenforceable

6. Which of the following must be directly authorised under the FSMA to carry on regulated activities?

   A. Recognised investment exchange
   B. Hedge fund manager
   C. Recognised clearing house
   D. Appointed representative

7. Which of the following is an excluded activity and, hence, does not require authorisation under FSMA?

   A. Safeguarding and administering investments
   B. Dealing on an agency basis
   C. Dealing as principal in connection with an employee share scheme
   D. Accepting deposits

8. Which of the following types of investment is a specified investment under the Regulated Activities Order?

   A. NS&I certificates
   B. Building society bank accounts
   C. Commodity futures for commercial purposes
   D. OEIC shares

9. Which of the following may conduct a limited range of regulated activity under the Part XX regime, without the need for authorisation?

   A. Accountants
   B. Independent Financial Advisers
   C. Market makers dealing in principal
   D. Home finance advisers

10. In order to satisfy the suitability threshold conditions for authorisation, firms are specifically required to:

    A. Commission an external assessment
    B. Appoint a standards officer
    C. Prove that they are fit and proper
    D. Provide an acceptability declaration

11. A director of a firm, who is responsible for compliance, must apply for which of the following controlled functions?

    A. Director function
    B. Non-executive director function
    C. Customer function
    D. Director function and compliance oversight function

12. What is the FSA's general approach to the supervision of authorised firms?

    A. Precedent-based
    B. Advisory-based
    C. Risk-based
    D. Experience-based

13. Which of the following types of statutory notice is published by the FSA on its website?

    A. Warning notices
    B. Final notices
    C. Notices of discontinuance
    D. Decision notices

14. If someone deposits criminally obtained banknotes in a building society account, what stage of the money laundering process is this normally known as?

    A. Integration
    B. Layering
    C. Phasing
    D. Placement

15. What action should a Money Laundering Reporting Officer take if a member of staff has identified a suspicious transaction?

    A. Make a notification to HM Treasury
    B. Make a notification to the Financial Services Authority
    C. Contact the Serious Fraud Office for advice
    D. Make a report to the Serious Organised Crime Agency

16. Which ONE of the following instruments are caught under the insider dealing legislation?

    A. Corporate debentures
    B. Commodities
    C. Foreign exchange
    D. Open-ended investment companies

17. Which of the following would be an inside deal?

    A. An investment manager buys shares in his brother's company that is about to be taken over
    B. An investment manager sells units in a collective investment scheme held jointly with his wife
    C. A director encourages an employee to purchase units in a collective investment scheme
    D. A director makes a loan to his own company

18. Which ONE of the following is a 'special' defence against the charge of insider dealing under the Criminal Justice Act?

    A. An individual is providing information in the role of a journalist
    B. An individual is acting on behalf of a friend or relative
    C. A market maker is acting in good faith in the course of his business as a market maker
    D. A market maker is providing data purely for information purposes

19. An individual has acquired inside information and has encouraged a friend to deal in the affected securities. Which one of the following statements is TRUE?

    A. This is a perfectly legitimate action
    B. The individual is likely to have committed an offence
    C. Only the friend will be guilty of an offence
    D. Any deal will be automatically void

20. To satisfy the definition of 'market abuse', an individual's behaviour must:

    A. Be based on generally available information
    B. Be likely to distort the market
    C. Constitute a breach of the Criminal Justice Act 1993
    D. Constitute a breach of the Money Laundering Regulations 2007

21. The guidance provided by the Joint Money Laundering Steering Group:

    A. has been approved by the FSA and forms part of the FSA's Handbook
    B. is mandatory for all investment firms
    C. has been approved by the EU Commission and derives from the Money Laundering Directive
    D. highlights best practice and has been approved by the Treasury

22. Which ONE of the following is a safe harbour against a charge of market abuse under FSMA?

    A. Adherence with the Conflicts of Interest rules
    B. Price support activities carried out in accordance with the price stabilisation rules
    C. Transactions carried out on a recognised investment exchange with an FSA-authorised and approved firm
    D. Information is available on a subscription service and thought to be widely available

23. Which ONE of the following is TRUE of the market abuse regime under FSMA?

    A. The offence is considered a criminal act
    B. The FSA is not permitted to impose a fine on offenders
    C. The FSA can withdraw approval and authorisation of anyone found guilty of this offence
    D. Offenders can be fined up to a maximum of £100,000

24. Which ONE of the following is a MiFID financial instrument?

    A. Bank account
    B. Contracts for differences on sporting events
    C. Foreign exchange
    D. Credit derivatives

25. If a firm is carrying on activity on an eligible counterparty basis, which of the following rules applies to them?

    A. Provision of information about the firm
    B. Client order handling
    C. Conflicts of interest
    D. Use of dealing commission

26. Under the COBS rules, which financial promotions communicated by their appointed representatives are firms responsible for?

    A. Only those promoting MiFID financial instruments
    B. Those which are openly published in the consumer press
    C. Those which relate to high-risk investments
    D. All of them

27. Why is a commodity derivatives dealer classified as a per se professional client?

    A. Commodity derivatives are MiFID financial instruments
    B. The activity is conducted by way of business
    C. The dealer is an investment firm
    D. The dealer is unable to qualify as a retail client

28. In relation to non-MiFID business, which of the following retail clients may be suitable for reclassification as an elective professional client?

    A. A newly-appointed trustee of a trust exceeding €500,000
    B. A client to whom the firm regularly sends financial promotions for non-mainstream investment opportunities
    C. A client who has recently inherited a sizeable portfolio
    D. The spouse of one of the firm's investment managers

29. Which of the following is a retail investment product?

    A. Home income plan
    B. Occupational pension scheme
    C. Unregulated collective investment scheme
    D. Commodity derivative

30. Which of the following statement is TRUE about a client that is an eligible counterparty for executing orders?

    A. If the client requires investment advice they would be classified as a per se professional client for that service
    B. The eligible counterparty status provides the client with regulatory protection for the execution of orders
    C. The firm must conduct both qualitative and quantitative assessments on the client before executing orders
    D. The firm is only required to conduct a qualitative assessment on the client before executing orders

31. Which ONE of the following is TRUE of the client categorisation requirements in the FSA handbook?

    A. Customers are classed as either retail clients or private clients
    B. Retail clients cannot be opted up to be professional clients
    C. Professional clients can be either elective or per se professional clients
    D. The client classification rules do not apply to non-MiFID business

32. Firms carrying on MiFID business must provide clients with appropriate information on which ONE of the following?

    A. Compliance officer's name
    B. The firm's major shareholders
    C. Where the firm's shares are listed
    D. Costs and associated charges

33. Client agreements must be provided for designated investment business carried out for:

    A. Eligible counterparties (in respect of non-MiFID business)
    B. Professional clients (in respect of non-MiFID business)
    C. Professional clients (in respect of MiFID business)
    D. Eligible counterparties (in respect of MiFID business)

34. Which ONE of the following is TRUE in relation to the rules on disclosure of costs and associated charges?

    A. Applies to retail and professional clients
    B. Commissions do not have to be shown separately
    C. All fees, commissions and charges must be disclosed by the firm
    D. A firm does not have to disclose any taxes payable via the firm

35. Unless a retail client has agreed otherwise with the firm, what is the frequency that an investment manager must send a periodic statement?

A. Weekly
B. Quarterly
C. Six-monthly
D. Annually

36. In which ONE of the following circumstances does a firm have to send a suitability report?

A. If the recommendation is to increase a regular premium to an existing life insurance contract
B. If the recommendation is for a client to undertake a pension transfer
C. If the firm is acting as an investment manager for a retail client and recommends a regulated collective investment scheme
D. If the recommendation is to make a further investment into an existing packaged product

37. In which If of the following circumstances do the rules on appropriateness apply?

A. Personal recommendation to a retail client to purchase a UK-authorised collective investment scheme
B. Retail client responding to a direct offer financial promotion to deal in warrants
C. Discretionary portfolio management for a retail client
D. Personal recommendation to a professional client to invest in a hedge fund

38. In which ONE of the following circumstances is a suitability assessment NOT required ?

A. Portfolio manager making a discretionary decision to deal
B. Financial adviser who advises a client to invest in an UK-authorised collective investment scheme
C. Private wealth manager who advises a professional client to invest in a hedge fund
D. A firm transmitting an execution-only order in a security admitted to trading on a recognised investment exchange

39. Why must a suitability report be issued within 14 days of concluding a personal pension scheme?

A. To allow the client the opportunity to consider the recommendations before the end of the 14 days cancellation period
B. To allow the pension scheme provider to establish the scheme
C. To enable the client to compare the costs of the scheme with others
D. Because this is a MiFID requirement

40. The three categories of products for which key features documents must be provided to clients are packaged products, cash-based ISAs and:

    A. Deposit accounts
    B. Cash-based child trust funds
    C. Conventional annuities
    D. Wrap accounts

41. Which ONE of the following is exempt from the financial promotion rules?

    A. A promotion to a professional client
    B. The promotion of non-MiFID business to a retail client
    C. The promotion of packaged products to a UK-domiciled retail client
    D. One-off promotions of non-MiFID business that are not cold calls

42. The rules requiring charges to be included in a direct offer promotion to retail clients can be waived if:

    A. The product is considered to be low-risk
    B. The product has previously been promoted
    C. The charges are included in another document that the client needs to refer to in order to respond to the offer
    D. The charges are below a threshold level which is assessed each year in line with the retail price index

43. What action might a firm take to ensure investment research staff do not pass price sensitive information to other departments?

    A. Make this a condition of employment for all staff
    B. Establish a Chinese wall policy
    C. Conduct appropriate supervision
    D. Establish a training and competence scheme

44. MiFID firms may accept payments or non-monetary benefits from a third party only if:

    A. The client is a professional client
    B. The amount is below that specified in the firm's conflicts of interest policy
    C. The payment is recorded and details provided to the client on request
    D. The payment enhances the quality of service and is disclosed to the client

45. Which ONE of the following is permitted to be paid from client dealing commissions?

A. Order and execution management systems
B. Research that involves analysis or data manipulation to reach meaningful conclusions
C. Subscription for publications and journals which directly or indirectly relate to the services provided
D. Seminar and conference fees

46. The FSA's best execution rules apply:

A. When a firm owes contractual or agency obligations
B. To eligible counterparty business
C. To prevent the firm from using client money for its own purposes
D. To professional clients unless they choose to opt out

47. What is the main purpose of the client money rules?

A. To compensate clients if an authorised firm becomes insolvent
B. To ensure client money benefits from the best possible rate of returns
C. To segregate client money from a firm's own money
D. To prevent clients from encashing client money before the due date

48. How often must a firm internally reconcile client assets?

A. Every day
B. Monthly
C. As often as is necessary
D. At whatever frequency is requested by the client

49. A firm must hold client money accounts in trust with a bank to ensure that:

A. The firm cannot use client money to repay its own creditors
B. The bank is able to maintain its regulatory status as designated trustee
C. No loss will be borne by the client money accounts should the bank become insolvent
D. The bank is able to retain the client money should the firm become insolvent.

50. What is the MAXIMUM amount of monetary award against an authorised firm that the Financial Ombudsman Service can make?

A. £35,000
B. £50,000
C. £100,000
D. £150,000

Answers to Multiple Choice Questions – Part 2

Q1. Answer: C Ref: Chapter 1, Section 2.1

The FSA does not operate a 'no-fail' regime for authorised firms, therefore option 'B' is incorrect. The FSA is not a price regulator and does not specify the cost/charges that authorised firms can charge on financial products, therefore option 'A' is incorrect. The FSA does specify the amount of financial resource firms must have, but this is not one their statutory objectives, therefore option 'D' is incorrect.

The correct answer is option 'C'. One of the FSA's statutory objectives is to ensure that there is appropriate protection for consumers; one example of this is the client money rules where cash managed/held by a firm is held in client money bank accounts and not in the name of the firm.

Q2. Answer: D Ref: Chapter 1, Section 7.6

The Tax and Chancery Chamber of the Upper Tribunal operates the appeals procedure for FSA disciplinary decisions.

Q3. Answer: A Ref: Chapter 1, Section 1.5

Designated investment exchanges are overseas exchanges that do not conduct regulated activity in the UK. They may apply to the FSA for designated status; the FSA considers consumer protection as part of the process. Once designated status is granted, firms may treat transactions on the exchange in the same way as they would treat transactions on recognised exchanges.

Q4. Answer: C Ref: Chapter 1, Section 3.1

The third principle requires firms to have adequate risk management systems.

Q5. Answer: D Ref: Chapter 1, Section 1.1

Option D is a statutory consequence; other statutory consequences are imprisonment and/or an unlimited fine.

Q6. Answer: B Ref: Chapter 2, Section 2

A hedge fund manager needs to be authorised when it undertakes the activity of portfolio management. The others are exempt from the FSMA when carrying on specific regulated activities. For instance, an appointed representative will have a contract with an authorised firm, which allows them to carry on regulated activities, with the authorised firm accepting responsibility for the appointed representative's conduct in respect of the regulated activities undertaken.

Q7. Answer: C Ref: Chapter 2, Section 1.3.1

Dealing as principal in connection with an employee share scheme is an excluded activity and so does not require authorisation.

Q8. Answer: D Ref: Chapter 2, Section 1.2.1

Commodity futures for commercial purposes, NS&I products and building society bank accounts are specifically excluded from the RAO, whereas OEIC shares are included.

Q9. Answer: A Ref: Chapter 2, Section 2.3.2

The correct answer is 'A' – accountants do not need authorisation under FSMA when they carry on a limited range of regulated activity which is incidental to their main business. In addition they must operate within a set of rules laid down by the Institute of Chartered Accountants in England and Wales, which is their designated professional body. In these circumstances, the accountant is operating within FSMA Part XX regime.

Q10. Answer: C Ref: Chapter 2, Section 3.3

The suitability condition requires firms to prove themselves fit and proper to be granted Part IV permission, namely that their affairs will be conducted soundly and prudently.

Q11. Answer: D Ref: Chapter 2, Section 5.3

Compliance oversight function is a required function; the person performing this function has to be separately approved to do so, even if they are also approved for a governing function such as director function.

Q12. Answer: C Ref: Chapter 2, Section 4

The FSA adopts a risk-based approach to supervision. This means that it focuses its resources on mitigating those risks which pose a threat to the achievement of its statutory objectives and that it has regard to the efficient and economic use of its resources.

Q13. Answer: B Ref: Chapter 2, Section 8.2

The FSA publishes final notices on its website; it does not publish warning or decision notices and notices of discontinuance.

Q14. Answer: D Ref: Chapter 3, Section 3.2

The placement stage of the money laundering process is the first stage and involves placing criminally obtained cash with a financial institution.

Q15. Answer: D Ref: Chapter 3, Section 3.5

A firm's MLRO must report suspicious activity to SOCA.

Q16. Answer: A Ref: Chapter 3, Section 1.4

Debt securities are caught under the insider dealing legislation; however, the other three options are not.

Q17. Answer: A Ref: Chapter 3, Section 1.2

Units in collective investment schemes and loans are not 'securities' for the purpose of insider dealing legislation.

Q18. Answer: C Ref: Chapter 3, Section 1.6

One of the special defences is where a market maker acts in good faith carrying out its roles as a market maker. The other three options are all general defences under the CJA.

Q19. Answer: B Ref: Chapter 3, Section 1.3

Someone commits the offence of insider dealing if they encourage someone else to deal in price-affected securities when in possession of inside information.

Q20. Answer: B Ref: Chapter 3, Section 2.1

The definition of market abuse behaviour includes the requirement that it must be likely to distort the market in the investment.

Q21. Answer: D Ref: Chapter 3, Sections 3.1, 3.4.2

Option 'D' is correct. Guidance provided by the JMLSG is not approved by the FSA, nor has it been approved by the EU Commission nor forms part of the Money Laundering Directives. The JMLSG guidance is not mandatory; it is industry guidance provided on best practices within the financial services industry.

Q22. Answer: B Ref: Chapter 3, Section 2.6

Option 'B' is correct. Compliance with the conflicts of interest rules is not specified as a safe harbour. Likewise for Option 'C'. in respect of widely available information, again this does not amount to a safe harbour.

Q23. Answer: C Ref: Chapter 3, Sections 2.1, 2.5

Option 'C' is correct. The offence of market abuse is civil rather than criminal, unlike insider dealing which is a criminal offence. The FSA is permitted to impose an unlimited fine (there is no maximum) as well as withdrawing approval/authorisation of anyone found guilty of market abuse.

Q24. Answer: D Ref: Chapter 3, Section 8.1.3

The correct option is 'D', as credit derivatives are a MiFID instrument. Both bank accounts ('A') and foreign exchange ('C') are not classed as MiFID instruments. Contracts for difference (CFD) on non-financial instruments (ie, sporting events) are not a MiFID instrument, but a CFD on a financial instrument, such as a security is a MiFID financial instrument.

Q25. Answer: C Ref: Chapter 4, Section 1.3

Options 'A', 'B' and 'D' are disapplied for eligible counterparties (COBS 1 – Annex 1) business. The conflicts of interest rules (SYSC 10) are applicable to all authorised/regulated firms.

Q26. Answer: D Ref: Chapter 4, Section 1.4

Firms are responsible for ensuring that appointed representatives comply with the COBS 4 rules when communicating all types of financial promotions.

Q27. Answer: C Ref: Chapter 4, Section 2.1.3

Clients that are investment firms are, by default, classified as per se professional clients. The dealer does not have to 'qualify' for re-classification to retail client, they could request this in order to obtain greater regulatory protection.

Q28. Answer: B Ref: Chapter 4, Section 2.1.5

For non-MiFID business, clients for whom the firm assesses as capable of making their own investment decisions could be reclassified as elective professional clients. If a firm considers a client sophisticated to the extent that the firm is able to promote non-mainstream investments, that client would be likely to satisfy the qualitative assessment for elective professional client. The other examples do not give any indication of investment expertise.

Q29. Answer: C Ref: Chapter 4, Section 2.5

A unit in any type of collective investment scheme, whether or not the scheme is regulated, is classed as a retail investment product.

Q30. Answer: A Ref: Chapter 4, Section 2.1.1

An eligible counterparty only has that classification in relation to eligible counterparty business, such as the execution of orders. If the client requires another service such as investment advice, they would be classified as a per se professional client for that service. Eligible counterparties have little or no protection under the regulatory system. Options C and D are only relevant for retail client reclassification.

Q31. Answer: C Ref: Chapter 4, Section 2.1.3

The term 'customers' applies to either retail clients or professional clients (not private clients). Retail clients can be opted up to professional client status providing that they meet certain criteria. The client classification requirements apply to both MiFID and non-MiFID firms and business.

Q32. Answer: D Ref: Chapter 4, Section 2.3.1

Firms carrying on MiFID must provide their clients with appropriate information, in a comprehensible form, about themselves and their service, the investments and strategies to be used, the execution venues on which these may be dealt and any costs and associated charges.

Q33. Answer: C Ref: Chapter 4, Section 2.2

Client agreements are required for business carried out for retail clients and (for MiFID business) professional clients.

Q34. Answer: C Ref: Chapter 4, Section 2.4

The disclosure of costs and charges only has to be disclosed to retail clients. Commission charges/ costs must be itemised separately. A firm has to disclose all related fees, commissions, charges and expenses and any taxes payable via the firm.

Q35. Answer: C Ref: Chapter 4, Section 7.1.2

Option 'C' is correct. For retail clients the firm must send a statement to them on at least a six-monthly basis, although the retail client can request a quarterly statement from the firm. For leveraged portfolios, the firm must send monthly statements to the client.

Q36. Answer: B Ref: Chapter 4, Section 4.2.2

Option 'B' is correct; the other options are all exempt from the requirement to send a suitability report.

Q37. Answer: B Ref: Chapter 4, Section 4.3

The rules on non-advised sales (appropriateness) apply to a range of MiFID and non-MiFID investment services which do not involve advice or discretionary portfolio management.

Therefore options 'A', 'C' and 'D' are covered by the suitability rules, therefore they are incorrect. Option 'B' is correct.

Q38. Answer: D Ref: Chapter 4, Section 4

A suitability assessment is not required if the firm is acting on specific instructions from the client.

Q39. Answer: A Ref: Chapter 4, Section 4.2.2

The 14-day rule for the issue of suitability reports applies to personal and stakeholder pension schemes, because here the cancellation rules apply.

Q40. Answer: B Ref: Chapter 4, Section 5.1

KFDs are required for packaged products, cash ISAs and cash CTFs.

Q41. Answer: D Ref: Chapter 4, Section 3.2

The financial promotions rules are disapplied in certain cases, notably excluded communications. One such rule is a one-off promotion that is not a cold call, if related to non-MiFID business.

All the other options are covered by the financial promotion rules.

Q42. Answer: C Ref: Chapter 4, Section 3.7

The mandatory data need not be included if the client has to refer to another document containing that information in order to respond to the offer.

Q43. Answer: B Ref: Chapter 4, Section 6.2

The Chinese walls approach prevents information from one part of the firm flowing to another, as part of a firm's arrangements to mitigate against conflicts of interest.

Q44. Answer: D Ref: Chapter 4, Section 6.3.1

The inducements rules apply to both retail and professional clients, and apply regardless of a firm's conflicts of interest policy.

For a third-party payment to be acceptable it must satisfy all of the following criteria:

- Disclosed to the client prior to the provision of the service.
- Enhances the quality of the service that the firm is providing to the client.
- Does not impair compliance with the firm's duty to act in the best interest of the client.

Q45. Answer: B Ref: Chapter 4, Section 6.3.2

Options 'A', 'C' and 'D' are incorrect because they do not fall into the criteria for permitted payments – execution or research, as defined in COBS 11.6.

Q46. Answer: A Ref: Chapter 4, Section 6.4

Option 'B' is incorrect as the rules are disapplied for eligible counterparty business.

Option 'C' is covered by the client money rules not the best execution rules.

Retail and professional clients cannot opt out of the best execution rules.

Q47. Answer: C Ref: Chapter 4, Section 8.1

The purpose of the client money rules is to protect the client money by requiring segregation away from the firm's own money.

Q48. Answer: C Ref: Chapter 4, Section 8.2

It is up to a firm to decide the necessary frequency of completing reconciliations of MiFID client money accounts.

Q49. Answer: A Ref: Chapter 4, Section 8.1

The purpose of holding the client money in trust is to protect the client money against the firm using it for its own needs, such as repaying creditors.

Q50. Answer: D Ref: Chapter 5, Section 2.3

The maximum monetary amount that the FOS can award against a firm is £150,000.

Syllabus Learning Map

CISI
CHARTERED INSTITUTE FOR SECURITIES & INVESTMENT

Syllabus Unit/ Element		Chapter/ Section
ELEMENT 1	**THE REGULATORY ENVIRONMENT**	Chapter 1
1.1	**The Role of the Financial Services Authority (FSA)**	
	On completion, the candidate should:	
1.1.1	know FSA's statutory objectives and rule making powers in respect of authorisation, supervision, enforcement, sanctions and disciplinary action [FSMA]	Sections 1 and 2
1.1.2	understand the Principles for Businesses [PRIN 1.1.2, 1.1.7, 2.1.1] and the requirement to act honestly, fairly and professionally and to treat customers fairly [COBS 2.1]	Section 3
1.1.3	know the Statements of Principle 1 to 4 and Code of Practice for approved persons for all approved persons functions [APER 1.1.1, 1.2.3, 2.1.2, 3.1.1, 4.1, 4.2, 4.3.1, 4.4.1/3/4/9]	Section 4
1.1.4	know the Statements of Principle 5 to 7 and Code of Practice for approved persons in respect of significant influence functions [APER 4.5.1/12/13/14 + 4.6.1/2/3/5/6/8 + 4.7.1/2/12/13]	Section 4.3
1.1.5	know the Chartered Institute for Securities & Investment's Code of Conduct	Section 5
1.1.6	understand the FSA's rules regarding Senior Management Arrangements, Systems and Controls for both common platform firms and Non-MiFID firms (SYSC 1.2.1, 3.1.1, 4.1.1/2 + 19.2.1)	Section 6
1.1.7	know the FSA's supervisory approach to more 'outcomes-focused and more intrusive' regulation [FSA Discussion Paper DP 09/2 pp 183-196 and Turner report pp 86-104]	Section 2
1.2	**The Regulatory Infrastructure**	
	On completion, the candidate should:	
1.2.1	know the regulatory infrastructure generated by the FSMA 2000 and the status of and relationship between the Treasury, the Office of Fair Trading, the Financial Skills Partnership and the FSA and also the relationship between FSA and the RIEs, ROIEs, DIEs, RCH, MTFs and DPBs	Section 7
1.2.2	know the role of the Tax and Chancery Chamber of the Upper Tribunal	Section 7.6
1.2.3	know HM Revenue and Custom's responsibility for issuing guidance on Treasury regulation for ISAs	Section 7.7
1.2.4	know the six types of provisions used by the FSA in its Handbook and the status of FSA's approved industry guidance	Section 8.8

ELEMENT 2	**THE FINANCIAL SERVICES AND MARKETS ACT 2000**	
2.1	**Regulated and Prohibited Activities**	
	On completion, the candidate should:	
2.1.1	know the regulated and prohibited activities [Part II/III of FSMA 2000, Regulated Activities Order 2001 and the under-noted guidance in the FSA's Perimeter Guidance Manual (PERG)]:	Sections 1 and 2
	• authorised persons [PERG 2.2.3]	

Syllabus Unit/ Element		Chapter/ Section
	• exempt persons [PERG 2.10] and FSMA [Exemption Order 2001 (SI 2001/1201)]	
	• offences under the Act [PERG 2.2.1/2]	
	• enforceability of agreements entered into with an unauthorised business [PERG 2.2.2]	
	• defences available under the Act [PERG 2.2.1]	
2.1.2	understand the FSA's actions in respect of prohibition orders and actions for damages and how private clients can sue for damages when a firm is declared in breach [FSMA 2000 s.56, 59, 71, 150]	Section 1.1.1
2.2	**Performance of Regulated Activities**	
	On completion, the candidate should:	
2.2.1	know the role of the FSA's enforcement division, the power of the FSA to make decisions by executive procedures and the role, scope and consequences of the Regulatory Decisions Committee's responsibility for decision making [DEPP 3.1–3.4, 4.1]	Section 8
2.2.2	know the outcomes of the FSA's statutory notices (DEPP 1.2), the regulatory enforcement processes: warning, decision, supervisory and final notices (DEPP 2.2 + 2.3) and the firm's right to refer to the tribunal [DEPP 2.3.2/3]	Sections 8.2–8.4
2.3	**Information Gathering and Investigations**	
	On completion, the candidate should:	
2.3.1	know the FSA's power to require information and to appoint persons to carry out investigations [FSMA 2000 s.165/7/8]	Section 9
2.4	**Regulated Activities**	
	On completion, the candidate should:	
2.4.1	know the activities specified in Part II of the Regulated Activities Order	Section 1.2.2
2.4.2	know the main exclusions from the need for authorisation under the FSMA 2000 [Regulated Activities Order]	Section 1.3
	• dealing as principal [PERG 2.8.4]	
	• advice in newspapers [PERG 2.8.12 & 7.1.2]	
	• trustees, nominees and personal representatives [PERG 2.9.3]	
	• employee share schemes [PERG 2.9.13]	
	• overseas persons [PERG 2.9.15]	
2.4.3	know the investments specified in Part III of the Regulated Activities Order	Section 1.2.1
2.4.4	know the authorisation procedures for firms:	Section 3
	• the need for authorisation [FSMA s.19. PERG 2.3, Annex 1 & 2, 2.10.9 - 16]	
	• the threshold conditions for authorisation [FSMA Sch 6. COND 2]	
2.4.5	know the supervisory process:	Section 4
	• purpose of FSA's supervision arrangements [SUP 1.1.2/3]	
	• focus on a firm's senior management [SUP 1.1.4, SYSC 1.2.1(1)/4.2.1/4.3.1]	
	• FSA's risk based approach to regulation – ARROW II [SUP 1.3.1/2/3/4/5/8]	

Syllabus Unit/ Element		Chapter/ Section
	• FSA's tools for supervision [SUP 1.4.1/2/4/5]	
	• FSA's transaction reporting regime [SUP 17.1.4]	
2.4.6	• know the approval processes for Approved Persons:	Section 5
	• the application process [SUP 10.12.1/2/3]	
	• the criteria for approval as an Approved Person [FIT 1.3, 2.1, 2.2, 2.3]	
2.4.7	understand FSA's controlled functions: the five functional areas, the required functions, the four areas of significant influence functions, the requirement for FSA approval prior to performing the function [SUP 10.5.1, 10.6.1, 10.7.1, 10.8.1, 10.9.1/2, 10.10.1/3 and the types of functions listed under Table 10.4.5. FSMA s.59]	Section 5.3
2.4.8	know the Training and Competence regime:	Section 6
	• the application of the systems and control responsibilities in relation to the competence of employees [SYSC 3.2.13/14/5.1.1]	
	• the application of T&C for retail activities [TC 1.1.1/3]	
	• assessing and maintaining competence [TC 2.1.1(1), 2.1.2], the examination requirements before starting activities [TC 2.1.6/7(1)], firms must assess at the outset and at regular intervals the training needs of its employees [TC 2.1.11], maintaining competence [TC 2.1.12/13]	
	• activities to which the T&C rules apply [TC Appendix 1]	
2.4.9	know the legal and regulatory basis for whistle blowing [SYSC 18.1.2, 18.2.3]	Section 7
2.5	**Miscellaneous Offences under FSMA 2000**	
	On completion, the candidate should:	
2.5.1	know the purpose, provisions, offences and defences of FSMA s.397 (1)(2)(3)(4)(5) – misleading statements and practices	Section 10

ELEMENT 3	ASSOCIATED LEGISLATION AND REGULATION	
3.1	**Insider Dealing**	
	On completion, the candidate should:	
3.1.1	understand the meaning of 'inside information' and 'insider'; the offences and the instruments covered by the legislation [CJA 1993 s.52/56/57/58 + Schedule 2]	Sections 1.2–1.4
3.1.2	know the general defences available with regard to insider dealing [CJA 1993 s.53]	Section 1.5
3.1.3	know the special defences: market makers acting in good faith, market information and price stabilisation [CJA 1993 s. 53 and Schedule 1 paras 1–5]	Section 1.6
3.1.4	know the FSA's powers to prosecute insider dealing [FSMA s.402, EG 12.7-10]	Section 1.7
3.2	**Market Abuse**	
	On completion, the candidate should:	
3.2.1	understand the statutory offence of market abuse [FSMA 2000 s.118(1-8)]	Section 2.1

Syllabus Unit/ Element		Chapter/ Section
3.2.2	know the status of the FSA's Code of Market Conduct [FSMA 2000 s.119(1) – (3)]; the territorial scope of the legislation and regulation [FSMA 2000 s.118]	Section 2.2
3.2.3	know the offences outlined in the Code of Market Conduct [MAR 1.2.2/7, 1.3.1, 1.4.1, 1.5.1, 1.6.1, 1.7.1, 1.8.1, 1.9.1, 1.2.22]	Section 2.2
3.2.4	know the concept of effect rather than intention [MAR 1.2.3]; the concept of a reasonable regular user [MAR 1.2.20/21] and accepted market practices (MAR 1 Annex 2)	Section 2.3
3.2.5	understand the enforcement regime for market abuse [MAR 1.1.4/5/6] and a firm' s duty to report suspicious transactions (SUP 15.10.2)	Sections 2.4–2.5
3.2.6	know the statutory exceptions (safe harbours) to market abuse [MAR 1.10.1-4 (excl. table1.10.5)]	Section 2.6
3.2.7	understand the distinction between offences under market abuse, insider dealing [CJA] and under FSMA 2000 s.397	Section 2.7
3.3	**Money Laundering**	
	On completion, the candidate should:	
3.3.1	understand the terms 'money laundering', 'criminal conduct' and 'criminal property' and the application of money laundering to all crimes [Proceeds of Crime Act 2002 s.340] and the power of the Secretary of State to determine what is 'relevant criminal conduct'	Section 3
3.3.2	understand that the UK legislation on money laundering is found in the Proceeds of Crime Act 2002 [POCA], as amended by the Serious Organised Crime and Police Act 2005 [SOCPA], the Money Laundering Regulations 2007, the FSA Senior Management Arrangements, Systems and Controls Sourcebook [SYSC] and that guidance to these provisions is found in the Joint Money Laundering Steering Group Guidance and understand the interaction between them	Section 3
3.3.3	understand the main offence set out in the Money Laundering Regulations (internal controls), which includes obligations on firms for adequate training of individuals on money laundering	Section 3.3.1
3.3.4	understand the three stages of money laundering	Section 3.2
3.3.5	understand the main offences set out in POCA Part 7 Sections 327, 328, 329, 330, 333A, 342 [Assistance ie, concealing, arrangements, acquisition use and possession; failure to disclose; tipping off in the regulated sector] and the implications of Part 7 regarding the objective test in relation to reporting suspicious transactions; that appropriate disclosure [internal for staff and to the Serious Organised Crime Agency (SOCA) for the firm] is a defence	Section 3.3.5
3.3.6	understand the approach adopted by the FSA as covered by the Senior Management Arrangements, Systems and Controls Sourcebook [SYSC], in particular, the systems and controls that the FSA expects firms to have adopted, the role of the Money Laundering Reporting Officer, Nominated Officer and the compliance function [SYSC 3.2.6, 3.2.6 (A)-(J), 3.2.7, 3.2.8, SYSC 6.3]	Sections 3.4.1 and 3.5

Syllabus Unit/ Element		Chapter/ Section
3.3.7	understand the standards expected by the JMLSG Guidance particularly in relation to:	Section 3.4.2
	• Risk-based approach	
	• Requirements for directors and senior managers to be responsible for money laundering precautions	
	• Need for risk assessment	
	• Need for enhanced due diligence in relation to politically exposed persons [JMLSG 5.5.1 – 5.5.29]	
	• Need for high level policy statement	
	• Detailed procedures implementing the firm's risk based approach [JMLSG 1.20, 1.27, 1.40 – 1.43, 4.17 – 4.18]	
	• Financial Sanctions regime [JMLSG Part III 4.1 – 4.10]	
3.3.8	understand the money laundering aspects of know your customer (Joint Money Laundering Steering Groups' Guidance for the Financial Sector [Para 5.1.1 - 5.1.14]	Section 3.4.3
3.3.9	understand the importance of ongoing monitoring of business relationships and being able to recognise a suspicious transaction and the requirement for staff to report to the MLRO and for the firm to report to the Serious Organised Crime Agency [SOCA]	Section 3.5
3.3.10	know what activities are regarded as 'terrorism' in the UK [Terrorism Act 2000 Part 1], the obligations on regulated firms under the Counter-Terrorism Act 2008 [money laundering of terrorist funds] [part 5 section 62 and s.7 part 1-7] and the Anti-Terrorism Crime & Security Act 2001 Schedule 2 Part 3 [Disclosure of Information] and where to find the sanction list for terrorist activities	Section 3.6
3.3.11	understand the importance of preventative measures in respect of terrorist financing and the essential differences between laundering the proceeds of crime and the financing of terrorist acts [JMLSG Guidance 2007 paras 1.38 – 1.39, Preface 9 as amended December 2011] and the interaction between the rules of FSA, the Terrorism Act 2000 and the JMLSG Guidance regarding terrorism [JMLSG Guidance 2007 Preface 27, 28, 29 as amended December 2011]	Section 3.6.1
3.4	**Model Code**	
	On completion, the candidate should:	
3.4.1	know the main purpose and provisions of the FSA's Model Code on share dealing by directors and other persons discharging managerial responsibilities, including:	Section 4
	• close periods	
	• undisclosed inside information	
	• chairman's approval	
	• dealings by the chairman	
	• short-term dealing	
	• exceptional circumstances	
	• application and record keeping	

Syllabus Unit/ Element		Chapter/ Section
3.5	**Disclosure and Transparency Rules**	
	On completion, the candidate should:	
3.5.1	know the purpose of the Disclosure and Transparency Rules and the control of information [DTR 2.1.3, 2.6.1]	Section 5
3.6	**Data Protection Act 1998**	
	On completion, the candidate should:	
3.6.1	know the eight Data Protection Principles; the need for notification of data controllers with the Information Commissioner; the record-keeping requirements of FSA regulated firms [DPA Schedule 1, Part 1 & COBS Schedule 1 – record keeping requirements and SYSC 3 & 9]	Section 6
3.7	**Relevant European Regulation**	
	On completion, the candidate should:	
3.7.1	know the relevant European Union Directives and the impact on the UK financial services industry in respect of:	Section 8
	• Passporting within the EEA (MiFID)	
	• Home vs host state regulation (MiFID)	
	• Selling cross-border collective investment schemes (UCITS)	
	• Selling securities cross border (Prospectus Directive)	
3.8	**Prudential Standards**	
	On completion, the candidate should:	
3.8.1	know the purpose of the FSA's Capital Adequacy Requirements [GENPRU 1.2.12/13]	Section 7
3.8.2	know the purpose, scope and application of the FSA's liquidity framework requirements and how they apply to regulated firms (BIPRU 12.1.1, 12.2.1/2/4/5/7 + 12.3.4/5)	Section 7.3

ELEMENT 4	THE FSA CONDUCT OF BUSINESS SOURCEBOOK / CLIENT ASSETS	
4.1	**The Application and General Provisions of the FSA Conduct of Business Sourcebook**	
	On completion, the candidate should:	
	The Firms Subject to the Conduct of Business Sourcebook COBS 1	
4.1.1	know the firms subject to the FSA Conduct of Business Sourcebook [COBS 1.1.1-1.1.3, COBS 1 Annex 1 Part 3, section 3]	Section 1.2
	Activities Subject to the Conduct of Business Sourcebook COBS 1	
4.1.2	know the activities which are subject to the FSA Conduct of Business Sourcebook including Eligible Counterparty Business and transactions between regulated market participants [COBS 1.1.1–1.1.3, Annex 1, Part 1(1) & (4)]	Section 1.3
	Impact of Location COBS 1	
4.1.3	know the impact of location on firms/activities of the application of the FSA Conduct of Business Sourcebook: permanent place of business in UK [COBS 1.1.1-1.1.3 & Annex 1, Part 2 & Part 3 (1–3)]	Section 1.2

Syllabus Unit/ Element		Chapter/ Section
	Appointed Representatives COBS 1	
4.1.4	know how the application of the FSA Conduct of Business Sourcebook applies to appointed representatives [COBS 1.1.1] including financial promotions and firm's responsibilities for appointed representatives [COBS 4.1]	Section 1.4
	Electronic Media	
4.1.5	know the provisions of the FSA Conduct of Business Sourcebook regarding electronic media [glossary definitions of 'durable medium' and 'website conditions']	Section 1.5
	Telephone & Electronic Communications COBS 11.8	
4.1.6	know the recording of voice conversations and electronic communications requirements [COBS 11.8]	Section 1.6
4.2	**Accepting Clients**	
	On completion, the candidate should:	
	Client Categorisation COBS 3	
4.2.1	understand client status [PRIN 1.2.1/2/3, Glossary, COBS 3]:	Section 2.1
	• the application of the rules on client categorisation [COBS 3.1]	
	• definition of client [COBS 3.2]	
	• retail client [COBS 3.4]; professional client [COBS 3.5] and eligible counterparty [COBS 3.6]	
4.2.2	understand client status [PRIN 1.2.1/2/3, Glossary, COBS 3]:	Section 2.1
	• when a person is acting as agent for another person [COBS 2.4.1–3]	
	• the rule on categorising elective professional clients [COBS 3.5.3–9]	
	• the rule on elective eligible counterparties [COBS 3.6.4 - 6]	
	• providing clients with a higher level of protection [COBS 3.7]	
	• the requirement to provide notifications of client categorisation [COBS 3.3]	
	Client Agreements and Information Provision COBS 2, 6, 7, 8 & 14	
4.2.3	know the requirement for firms to provide client agreements, when a client agreement is required to be signed and when it is acceptable to be provided to clients [COBS 8.1.1 - 8.1.3]	Section 2.2
4.2.4	know the requirement to provide information to clients prior to providing services to clients including information relating to the nature and risk of the services and designated investments being offered [COBS 2.2, 6.1.1–4 & 14.3.1–10]	Section 2.3
4.2.5	know the rules on the provision of information in connection with the service of managing investments [COBS 6.1.6]	Section 2.3
4.2.6	know the rules on the provision of information concerning safeguarding of designated investments belonging to clients and client money [COBS 6.1.7]	Section 2.3
4.2.7	know the rules on disclosure of costs and associated charges, timing of disclosure; medium of disclosure, changes to information provided to the client and compensation information [COBS 6.1.9–6.1.16]	Section 2.4

Syllabus Unit/ Element		Chapter/ Section
4.2.8	know the rules on disclosure of information regarding packaged products [COBS 6.2.1/2/3/6/11, 6.3.1/2/3/7/8/14/17]	Section 2.5
	Reliance on Others COBS 2.4	
4.2.9	know the rules, guidance and evidential provisions regarding reliance on others [COBS 2.4.4/6/7]	Section 2.6
4.3	**Communicating with Clients, Including Financial Promotions**	
	On completion, the candidate should:	
	Application of the Rules on Communication with Clients, including Financial Promotions COBS 4.1	
4.3.1	know the application of the rules on communication to clients and on fair, clear and not misleading communications and financial promotions [COBS 4.1, 4.2.1–4]	Section 3.1
	The Rule on Fair, Clear and Not Misleading Communications and Identifying Financial Promotions As Such COBS 4.1, 4.2 & 4.3	
4.3.2	know the purpose and application of the financial promotion rules and the relationship with Principles for Businesses 6 and 7 [COBS 4.1]	Section 3.1
4.3.3	know the rule on identifying promotions as such [COBS 4.3]	Section 3.1
	The Main Exceptions (Financial Promotions Order ('FPO'), COBS 4.1 & 4.8 and Glossary Definition of 'Excluded Communications')	
4.3.4	know the main exceptions to the financial promotion rules in COBS [COBS 4.1, 4.8], the limitations in connection to MiFID business and the existence of the FPO	Section 3.2
	Types of Communication COBS 4	
4.3.5	know the types and methods of communication addressed by COBS 4	Section 3.3
4.3.6	know the rules on prospectus advertisements [PR 3.3]	Section 3.4
	Communicating with Retail Clients COBS 4.5	
4.3.7	know the general rule in connection with communicating with retail clients [COBS 4.5]	Section 3.5
	Past, Simulated Past and Future Performance COBS 4.6	
4.3.8	know the rules on past, simulated past and future performance [COBS 4.6 excluding 4.6.4–4.6.4B]	Section 3.6
	Financial Promotions Containing Offers or Invitations COBS 4.7	
4.3.9	know the rule on financial promotions containing offers or invitations [COBS 4.7.1 - 4]	Section 3.7
	Cold Calls and Other Promotions that are Not in Writing COBS 4.8 & 4.9	
4.3.10	know the rules on unwritten promotions [COBS 4.8.3] and the restriction on cold calling [COBS 4.8.2]	Section 3.8
4.3.11	know the rule on financial promotions for overseas persons [COBS 4.9.3]	Section 3.9

Syllabus Unit/ Element		Chapter/ Section
	Systems and Controls and Approving and Communicating Financial Promotions COBS 4.10 and SYSC 3 & 4	
4.3.12	know the requirement for approving financial promotions and the circumstances of relying on an another firm's confirmation of compliance [COB 4.10, SYSC 3 & 4]	Section 3.10
4.4	**Suitability**	
	On completion, the candidate should:	
	Suitability (including basic advice) COBS 9.1	
4.4.1	understand the application of the rules on identifying client needs and advising [COBS 9.1.1-9.1.4] and the rules on churning and switching [COBS 9.3.2]	Section 4.1
	Assessing Suitability COBS 9.2, 9.3 & 9.4	
4.4.2	understand the purpose of the suitability rules and the requirement for assessing suitability [COBS 9.2.1 - 3]	Section 4.2.1
4.4.3	understand the information which a firm must obtain from a client in order to make a suitability assessment [COBS 9.2.1–7); and the guidance on assessing suitability [COBS 9.3.1]	Section 4.2.3
4.4.4	know the application of the assessing suitability rules for professional clients [COBS 9.2.8]	Section 4.2.4
4.4.5	understand the obligation to provide a retail client with a suitability report [COBS 9.4.1–3]	Section 4.2.2
4.4.6	know the timing and contents of a suitability report [COBS 9.4]	Section 4.2.2
	Advising on Packaged Products COBS 6.2	
4.4.7	know the application and purpose of the rules on advising on packaged products, including the scope and range of advising [COBS 6.2.1 - 6, 6.2.8 - 11]	Section 2.5
	Appropriateness (Non-Advised Services) COBS 10	
4.4.8	understand the application and purpose of the rules on non-advised sales [COBS 10.1]	Section 4.3
4.4.9	understand the obligations for assessing appropriateness [COBS 10.2]	Section 4.3
4.4.10	know the circumstances in which it is not necessary to assess appropriateness [COBS 10.4–10.6]	Section 4.3
4.5	**Product Disclosure and the Client's Right to Cancel**	
	On completion, the candidate should:	
	Product disclosure COBS 13, 14 & 15	
4.5.1	know the purpose of the rules on the sale of packaged products to retail clients, the rules requiring the provision of key features to retail clients and the main features to be explained in the key features [COBS 13.1.1/3/4, 13.2.1/2/4, 13.3.1/2 (excluding Annex 1R) & 14.1.1, 14.3.1/2]	Section 5.1
4.5.2	know the purpose and requirements of the cancellation and withdrawal rights [COBS 15.1.1, 15.2.1, 15.2.3, 15.2.5, 15.3.1, 15.3.2]	Section 5.2
4.6	**Dealing and Managing**	
	On completion, the candidate should:	

Syllabus Unit/ Element		Chapter/ Section
	Application of the Rules on Dealing and Managing COBS 11.1	
4.6.1	know the application of the rules on dealing and managing [COBS 11.1]	Section 6.1
	Conflicts of Interest COBS 12, SYSC 10 and PRIN 2.1	
4.6.2	understand the application and purpose of the principles and rules on Conflict of Interest; the rules on identifying conflicts and types of conflicts; the rules on recording and disclosure of conflicts [PRIN 2.1.1 Principle 8, SYSC 10.1.1–6 + 10.1.8/9]	Section 6.2.1
4.6.3	know the rule requiring a conflicts policy and the contents of the policy [SYSC 10.1.10–10.1.15]	Section 6.2.2
4.6.4	understand the rule on managing conflicts of interest (SYSC 10.1.7) and how to manage conflicts of interest to ensure the fair treatment of clients (SYSC 10.2) including; information barriers such as 'Chinese walls'; reporting lines; remuneration structures; segregation of duties; policy of independence	Section 6.2.1
4.6.5	know the rules on managing conflict in connection with investment research and research recommendations [COBS 12.2.1/3/5/10, 12.3.2/3/4, 12.4.1/4/5/6/7/9/10/15/16/17]	Section 6.2.3
	Inducements and Use of Dealing Commission COBS 2.3 & 12.6	
4.6.6	know the application of the inducements rules [COBS 2.3.1–2 & 2.3.10–16] and the use of dealing commission, including what benefits can be supplied/obtained under such agreements [COBS 11.6]	Section 6.3
	Best Execution COBS 11	
4.6.7	understand the requirements of providing best execution [COBS 11.2.1–13]	Section 6.4.1
4.6.8	understand the requirements for an order execution policy, its disclosure, the requirements for consent and review [COBS 11.2.14–18, 11.2.22-26 & 11.2.28]	Section 6.4.2
4.6.9	understand the rules on following specific instructions from a client [COBS 11.2.19–21]	Section 6.4.3
4.6.10	understand the rules on monitoring the effectiveness of execution arrangements and policy; demonstrating compliance with the execution policy; and the duties of portfolio managers and receivers and transmitters to act in a clients' best interest [COBS 11.2.27, 11.2.29–34]	Section 6.4.2
	Client Order Handling COBS 11.3	
4.6.11	understand the rule on client order handling [COBS 11.3.1] and the conditions to be satisfied when carrying out client orders [COBS 11.3.2–6]	Section 6.5
	Aggregation and Allocation COBS 11.3	
4.6.12	understand the rules on aggregation and allocation of orders [COBS 11.3.7-8] and the rules on aggregation and allocation of transactions for own account [COBS 11.3.9-13]	Section 6.6
	Client Limit Orders COBS 11.4	

Syllabus Unit/ Element		Chapter/ Section
4.6.13	know the rules on client limit orders - the obligation to make unexecuted client limit orders public [COBS 11.4]	Section 6.7
	Personal Account Dealing COBS 11.7	
4.6.14	understand the purpose and application of the personal account dealing rule and the restrictions on personal account dealing [COBS 11.7.1–3]	Section 6.8
4.6.15	know the arrangements required to comply with the personal account dealing rules including the notification requirements; and exceptions regarding personal account dealing [COBS 11.7.4–7]	Section 6.8
4.7	**Reporting to Clients**	
	On completion, the candidate should:	
	Confirmation of Transactions and Periodic Statements COBS 16.1, 16.2, 16.3	
4.7.1	know the general client reporting and occasional reporting requirements [COBS 16.1–16.2]	Section 7.1
4.7.2	know the rules on periodic reporting to retail and professional clients, the exceptions to the requirements and the record keeping requirements (COBS 16.3)	Section 7.1
4.8	**Client Assets**	
	On completion, the candidate should:	
4.8.1	understand the purpose of the client money and custody rules in CASS including the requirement for segregation and that it is held in trust [CASS 6.2.1-3, 7.3.1-2, 7.4.11, 7.7.1-2]	Section 8.1
4.8.2	know the requirements for reconciling client assets and client money including the timing and identification of discrepancies [CASS 6.5.4-13, 7.6.9-16, 7.7.1]	Section 8.2
4.8.3	know the exemptions from the requirements of the CASS rules [CASS 1.2.3-4, 6.1.1-6, 7.1.1-12]	Section 8.3

ELEMENT 5	COMPLAINTS AND REDRESS	
5.1	**Customer Complaints**	
	On completion, the candidate should:	
5.1.1	know the procedures a firm must implement and follow to handle customer complaints [DISP 1.2.1/3, 1.3.3, 1.4.1, 1.6.1/2/5, 1.9.1, 1.10.1]	Sections 1.2–1.3
5.1.2	know the role of the Financial Ombudsman Service (FOS) [DISP Complaints Sourcebook – Dispute Resolution: Complaints: Introduction] and the awards which can be awarded [DISP 3.7.2/4]	Section 2
5.1.3	know the criteria for a complainant to be eligible to lodge a complaint [DISP 2.2]	Section 1.3
5.1.4	know the circumstances in which the Financial Services Compensation Scheme will pay compensation [COMP 3.2, 4.2.1/2/3] and the compensation payable in respect of protected deposits and protected investment business [COMP 10.2.1/3]	Section 3

Examination Specification

Each examination paper is constructed from a specification that determines the weightings that will be given to each element. The specification is given below.

It is important to note that the numbers quoted may vary slightly from examination to examination as there is some flexibility to ensure that each examination has a consistent level of difficulty. However, the number of questions tested in each element should not change by more than plus or minus 2.

Element Number	Element	Questions
1	The Regulatory Environment	5
2	The Financial Services and Markets Act 2000	7
3	Associated Legislation and Regulation	12
4	The FSA Conduct of Business Sourcebook/Client Assets	24
5	Complaints and Redress	2
	Total	**50**

CISI Membership

Studying for a CISI qualification is hard work and we're sure you're putting in plenty of hours, but don't lose sight of your goal! This is just the first step in your career, there is much more to achieve!

The securities and investments industry attracts ambitious and driven individuals. You're probably one yourself and that's great, but on the other hand you're almost certainly surrounded by lots of other people with similar ambitions. So how can you stay one step ahead during these uncertain times?

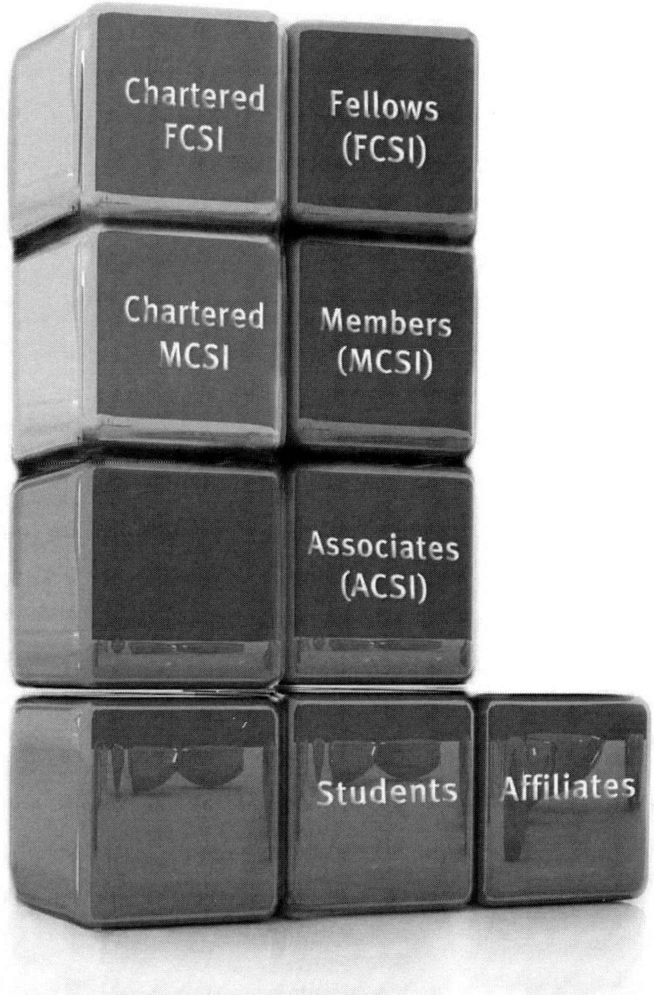

Entry Criteria:	Pass in either: • Investment Operations Certificate (IOC, formerly known as IAQ), IFQ, ICFA, CISI Certificates in, eg, Securities, Derivatives or Investment Management, Advanced Certificates • one or two CISI Diploma/Masters papers
Joining Fee:	£25 or free if applying via prefilled application form
Annual Subscription (pro rata):	£115
International Annual Subscription:	£86.25

Using your new CISI qualification* to become an Associate (ACSI) member of the Chartered Institute for Securities & Investment could well be the next important career move you make this year, and help you maintain your competence.

Join our global network of over 40,000 financial services professionals and start enjoying both the professional and personal benefits that CISI membership offers. Once you become a member you can use the prestigious ACSI designation after your name and even work towards becoming personally chartered.

* ie, Investment Operations Certificate (IOC, formerly known as IAQ), IFQ, CISI Certificate Programme

Turn over to find out more about CISI membership

CISI

CHARTERED INSTITUTE FOR SECURITIES & INVESTMENT

Feedback to CISI

Have you found this workbook to be a valuable aid to your studies? We would like your views, so please email us (learningresources@cisi.org) with any thoughts, ideas or comments.

Accredited Training Providers

Support for examination students studying for the Chartered Institute for Securities & Investment (CISI) Qualifications is provided by several Accredited Training Providers (ATPs), including 7City Learning and BPP. The CISI's ATPs offer a range of face-to-face training courses, distance learning programmes, their own learning resources and study packs which have been accredited by the CISI. The CISI works in close collaboration with its accredited training providers to ensure they are kept informed of changes to CISI examinations so they can build them into their own courses and study packs.

CISI Workbook Specialists Wanted

Workbook Authors

Experienced freelance authors with finance experience, and who have published work in their area of specialism, are sought. Responsibilities include:

* Updating workbooks in line with new syllabuses and any industry developments
* Ensuring that the syllabus is fully covered

Workbook Reviewers

Individuals with a high-level knowledge of the subject area are sought. Responsibilities include:

* Highlighting any inconsistencies against the syllabus
* Assessing the author's interpretation of the workbook

Workbook Technical Reviewers

Technical reviewers provide a detailed review of the workbook and bring the review comments to the panel. Responsibilities include:

* Cross-checking the workbook against the syllabus
* Ensuring sufficient coverage of each learning objective

Workbook Proofreaders

Proofreaders are needed to proof workbooks both grammatically and also in terms of the format and layout. Responsibilities include:

* Checking for spelling and grammar mistakes
* Checking for formatting inconsistencies

Notes

Notes

Notes